Emerging Perspectives in Japanese Human Resource Management

Wirtschaftspsychologie

Herausgegeben von Detlev Liepmann

Band 15

PETER LANG
Frankfurt am Main · Berlin · Bern · Bruxelles · New York · Oxford · Wien

Sierk A. Horn (ed.)

Emerging Perspectives in Japanese Human Resource Management

PETER LANG
Internationaler Verlag der Wissenschaften

Bibliographic Information published by the Deutsche Nationalbibliothek
The Deutsche Nationalbibliothek lists this publication in the Deutsche Nationalbibliografie; detailed bibliographic data is available in the internet at http://dnb.d-nb.de.

ISSN 0945-182X
ISBN 978-3-631-62098-4

www.peterlang.de

Preface

In the wake of the steady economic gravity shift towards East Asia, and the continuing enthusiasm surrounding the rapid rise of emerging Asian economies (most notably China and most lately India), it is sometimes tempting to feel as if interest in Japanese-style management has taken a back seat to concerns elsewhere. Despite these trends, research into Japanese managerial approaches has for some decades been a source of worldwide inspiration and curiosity, and this was particularly the case during the heyday of the learn from Japan movement in the 1980s. At that time Japanese firms were widely perceived as being more efficient than their Western counterparts, and academics and practitioners alike were enthused by the perceived idiosyncratic but cutting edge nature of Japanese personnel management principles. Kaizen (continuous improvement), Quality Circles (QC), and Total Quality Management (TQM), are just three of the many contributions that Japanese firms have made to world knowledge and practice in the management of business organizations.

Nevertheless, and as various studies have indicated, the transfer and adaptation of these superior techniques to different cultural settings has not been unproblematic, or uniformly welcomed. In challenging conventional management approaches, many Western firms have attempted to implement Japanese practises, and failed. Explanations for this lack of success soon focussed on the possible untranslatability of assumed culturally specific concepts to overseas contexts. Accompanying the appearance of these globalization-localization contradictions, the economic slowdown that followed the collapse of Japan's 1980s asset price Bubble then contributed to a decline in interest in Japanese management among overseas managers, scholars, and students.

Yet, Japanese-style human resource management continues to offer a success story to the rest of the world. It is widely acknowledged, for example, that the persistence of Japanese firms' competitive advantages substantially derives from their organizational abilities, information processing capabilities, group cohesion, and rapidity of decision implementation. In this sense, Japanese and American-style management paradigms have served as juxtaposing poles along a dimension of contrasting national capitalisms, being described respectively as being rooted in Japanese consensus-based cultural and social orientations, or an Anglo-Saxon neo-liberal market economy. It comes as no surprise that these competing approaches also continue to dominate academic analysis of the international transferability and internationalization of management techniques; with this being due in no small part to Japanese management practices continuing to contribute to the global competitiveness of Japanese firms. Even though it is currently outside the immediate limelight and just now in the descent phase of a fashion life-cycle, the Japanese firm's international role model function persists into the 21st century.

While understanding of Japanese management is now relatively advanced, it would be a mistake to assume a standstill in its key drivers as portrayed in some of the extant literature. After all, the burst of the bubble economy, the concurrent prolonged recession with intermittent deflation, and the rapidly evolving international market environment have inevitably triggered major adjustments in the Japanese economic system. More recently, the global financial crises of the outgoing decade are likely to be regarded as a caesura for Japanese firms and will certainly accelerate transitions already underway. Companies unresponsive to incremental changes may also be left with few alternatives but to remodel traditional success factors. How a firm responds to being caught between inertia and pro-active successful adaptation will certainly contribute to determining corporate performance in the coming years. Rigorous attention to possible reconfigurations of Japanese firm responses in general, and Japanese human resource management in particular, is still uncommon. Yet, the recalibration of organizational structures and management systems has, however, irreversibly changed Japan's corporate landscape. Cornerstones of the working environment, including the employment system, recruiting and compartmentalised career tracks, and ambiguous job demarcation and remuneration processes are in flux. Even though new contours are as yet unclear, the once monolithic model of Japanese human resource management is giving way to more diverse constituents of the so-called 'J-firm'.

The dominant model of consensus-based, collective, long-term oriented development of employees in Japan (epitomised in lifelong employment, seniority based promotion and corporate unionism) has over the last 20 years become increasingly permeable and allows for more pluralistic employment practices. This redesign process is gradual and ongoing. Moving away from once cherished practices, 'new' Japanese-style management (*shin-nihonteki keiei*) is likely to result in amalgamated approaches nestled between old-style Japanese management and Western thinking. This hybridity is however not new and is inherent in Japan's corporate structures and cultures. The internalization of Western thinking and the ability to fuse this with indigenous strengths is one of the foundational myths of modern Japan. Japanese firms have often demonstrated their capability to redefine and change their *modus operandi*. Despite the brevity of discourses on management fads it would be premature to underestimate or even discard Japanese answers to present-day changes in the global business environment. As modifications to Japanese-style management are taking shape, key drivers of a renewed competitiveness need charting. It is plausible to argue that the re-emergence of globally successful Japanese companies – despite or because of prolonged economic malaise in their home market (increasingly being dubbed the 'Two Lost Decades' or *ushinawareta nijūnen*) – showcases one of the most salient symptoms of Japanese management today: resilience, persistence and adaptability. Is Japanese management evolving? The short answer must be 'yes'. The long answer as to how is explored in the contributions in this special issue on Japanese workplace scenarios.

This volume collects selected papers charting developments in the most significant areas of people management in Japanese organizations: lifelong employment, remuneration, personnel selection, assessment, and female career tracks. It also reflects on how these processes affect subsidiary management of foreign firms operating in Japan. By bringing together leading experts who are all interculturally and linguistically competent with contemporary Japanese HRM this anthology provides unique, contemporary and realistic insights into how and with what consequences Japanese firms are managing change. It is the gap created all too often by Euro- or better Anglo-centric descriptions of Japanese management that this anthology is attempting to bridge. Situated at the juncture of area and organization studies it hopes to overcome abridged, over-simplified and possibly myopic perceptions of the Japanese employment system. It challenges preconceived understandings influenced by research that traditionally concentrates on Japanese corporate icons. In so doing, it becomes evident that characterisations derived from predominantly large and globally operating firms fall short of accurately capturing the workplace complexities at the *genba*, or Japanese shop floor.

Let us not forget that the terminology of 'lifelong employment' (*shūshin koyō*) and the 'seniority principle' (*nenkō joretsu*) were first introduced by James Abegglen in his seminal work *The Japanese Factory* in 1958. These not only became synonymous with Japanese management, but this 'brand' took on a life of its own that continues to influence scholarly thinking of the inner working of the Japanese firm – even though at no point in post-war history did it reflect the full diversity of employment mechanisms existent in Japan. Management in small or medium sized enterprises has often followed a very different trajectory. Practices and fringe benefits such as non-specialisation, automatic promotion or progressive remuneration have for the most part been restricted to employees in larger organizations. Quality circles (*QC undō*), consensus decision-making (*ringi-seido*) or automation (*jidōka*) are not consistently practised across the full range of Japanese firms. Even the quintessentially 'Japanese' just-in-time (JIT) production system is largely interdependent with varying industrial design systems. In fact, it has been argued that Ohno Taiichi's innovation may have been driven by a pragmatic response to industrial policy laid down by the Ministry of Trade and Industry (MITI) (E. Anderson, Australian Catholic University) and not, as commonly understood, by a domestication and acculturation of the Western Human Relations ideal.

In short, Japanese management has often served as a formidable projection of anything 'Non-American' (i.e. high effectiveness, flexibility of human resources), sometimes resulting in mythologization at the expense of an accurate portrayal. Analogies such as 'worker bee' and 'corporate warrior' emphasise the particularity of this alternative model and conceivably superimposed similarities. If this over-generalisation prevented access to the pluralist realities of Japanese practises, then the ongoing fragmentation as a result of reform to Japanese management mechanisms inevitably necessitates a fresh approach, not driven by singular explanations but by consistency in diversity. The contributions presented in this book embrace this framework and offer cross-sectional and contemporary perspectives on the organization and structure of Japanese management. Collating country-specific expertise for a wider specialist audience is an important and simultaneously challenging endeavour. With Japanese employment management constantly developing, the volume sends out a call for further interdisciplinary investigation into the managerial responses to the emerging environment of globalization. Here, not only managerial challenges in one of the world's largest economies but also their impact and consequences for the redesign of globally operating Japanese firms, certainly deserve our future attention.

It would be impossible to list by name all who have assisted in bringing this volume to life. Nevertheless I would like to extend my gratitude to my wife, Katrin Horn, for all her support. I would also like to thank the School of Modern Languages of the University of Leeds, Great Britain Sasakawa Foundation, Canon Foundation and the British Academy for the generous financial support. Last but not least I am indebted to Detlev Liepmann of Freie Universitaet Berlin for generously facilitating a volume that cuts across disciplines.

University of Leeds, August 2011

Sierk Horn

Contents

Preface 5

Lifetime Employment in 21st Century Japan: Stability and Resilience Under Pressure in the Japanese Management System 15

Peter Matanle and Kenji Matsui

1. Introduction 15
2. Fifty Years of Research on Lifetime Employment 17
3. Job Tenure in Post-Bubble Japan 22
4. Organizational and Employee Perspectives 30
   4.1 Organizational Perspectives 30
   4.2 Employee Perspectives 34
5. Summary and Conclusions 37
6. References 40

The Introduction of Competency Pay in Japan 'Performance in Appraisal and Remuneration' 45

Arjan B. Keizer

1. Introduction 45
2. Performance-related Pay and Its Challenges 47
3. Japanese Employment Practices and Performance-related Pay 51
4. The Introduction of a Competency System 55
5. Discussion 62
6. Implications and Lessons 65
7. References 68

Faceted Intelligence Concept in Japan 73

Sierk Horn, André Beauducel and Detlev Liepmann

1. Introduction 73
2. Methodology 78
   2.1 Introduction to the Facet Model of Fluid and Crystallized Intelligence 79
   2.2 Introduction to the Research Instrument 80
   2.3 Participants 84
3. Empirical Evidence 85
4. Discussion 92
5. Outlook 95
6. References 97

Applied Perspectives on Recruiting and Work Assessment in Japan 101

Sierk Horn, Detlev Liepmann and André Beauducel

1. Introduction 101
2. Rationale: Changes in Japanese Recruiting Practises 103
3. Conceptual Framework 105
4. Research Hypotheses 108
5. Methodology 110
   5.1 Introduction to the Research Instrument 110
   5.2 Sample(s) 112
6. Empirical Findings 113
7. Discussion and Implications 119
8. References 124

Changes in Japanese Companies' Personnel Management Practices Relating to Female Employees: From the Early 1980s to the Early 2000s 129

Kuniko Ishiguro

1. Introduction 129
2. Women and Work in Japan 131
3. Case Studies 136
4. Analysis 155
5. Conclusion 158
6. References 160

The "Lost Decade" and Changes in the Japanese Business Environment: Consequences for Foreign Direct Investment and Human Resource Management in Foreign Subsidiaries in Japan 165

Harald Dolles and Yoshiaki Takahashi

1. Barriers to Japanese Market Entry in the 1980s 165
2. The Conceptual Framework of Local Adaptation and Global Standardisation 167
3. Methodology and Research Samples 168
4. Subsidiary Management in Japan in the 1980s 169
5. Subsidiary Management in Japan Today 175
6. Conclusion 185
7. References 187

Biography 191

Lifetime Employment in 21st Century Japan: Stability and Resilience Under Pressure in the Japanese Management System

Peter Matanle and Kenji Matsui

1. Introduction

Despite repeated predictions of its demise, lifetime employment remains the core institution of the Japanese management system, and regular employment in a large and prestigious organization continues to be the aspiration of the majority of Japanese younger people. Although organizations have continuously adapted their systems to developments in the domestic and international political economies, prompting debates as to the nature and significance of such change, assertions that lifetime employment is disappearing, or has even collapsed, have thus far proven incorrect.

In this chapter we root our analysis in the social constructionist assumption that all employment relationships are produced and reproduced as a continuously negotiated settlement between the past, current, and anticipated requirements of employers and employees. Thus, the persistence of lifetime employment depends upon both the willingness of employers to offer it to current and prospective employees, and the extent to which current and prospective employees wish to accept that offer. However, we also assume that all meetings of employers' and employees' needs are to some degree context dependent, and it is therefore necessary to frame our analysis within an understanding of the environment within which lifetime employment rests.

After reviewing the key literature, we will pull together statistical data since the late 1980s to analyse job tenure in the post-Bubble era, as well as provide a summary of qualitative research from the same period, to argue that the institution of lifetime employment shows little sign of weakening; that from the employer's perspective the rationale for maintaining it continues, and that it still provides the best means available within Japan for the satisfaction of employees' needs over the course of their working lives. We base much of our discussions around analysis of labour throughput mechanisms, including legal constraints on organizational flexibility, and we end with the conclusion that lifetime employment remains stable, despite the pressures that Japanese organizations have encountered in recent decades. In this way, the Japanese management system demonstrates its fundamental strength and resilience throughout the long period of Japan's postwar expansion, and its subsequent globalization and post-industrial transformations.

But first we need to define lifetime employment and provide an estimate of its prevalence. In his research Ono (2010: 4-5) presented ten previously published definitions which differed according to factors such as gender, organization size, and whether the workplace is unionized. To some extent changes in social attitudes and behaviours as well as continuous organizational adaptation to the external environment are at the root of these definitional differences, which makes providing a lasting unambiguous definition difficult, and some definitions include mathematical constraints that do not always reflect the real circumstances of some groups of employees. For example, Ono (2010) notes that there is no theoretical or methodological justification for segmentation at 500 employees. Moreover, it shows researcher bias in the 21st century to be excluding all female university graduates employed on the regular career track. However, the real reason for such difficulty in providing a definition of lifetime employment is that the practise has no formal basis in Japanese employment law, being as it is an implicit mutual commitment.

Nevertheless, and drawing from Araki (2002), since non-regular workers by definition cannot be lifetime employees, as an initial foundation we include all employees considered by their employing organization as regular workers under the terms of both the Labour Standards Law and the body of case law on abusive dismissal. This is the broadest possible *de jure* interpretation of the meaning of 'lifetime employment', including within it 65.6 per cent of non-executive employees (Statistics Bureau, 2011b); meaning that these workers can remain employed in their organizations until mandatory retirement unless they either voluntarily resign, are deemed unable to work, commit acts worthy of dismissal, or their employer can reasonably claim that, without dismissal, the organization would cease operating.

However, we recognize that not all *de jure* regular workers are *de facto* lifetime employees. Some lack effective recourse to legal challenge and, for various reasons, may feel compelled to resign by employers that are not facing bankruptcy. Others on joining may have the future intention, with the understanding of their employer, to resign midway through their employment for reasons such as marriage and childbirth – though some of these may later change their minds. Also, some regular workers who were recruited mid- or late-career and did not experience the organization's training system cannot reasonably be considered lifetime employees; though we might consider 'lifetime' to include permanent transfers between keiretsu affiliates (*tenseki*) (Sako, 2006) or transfers of senior managers between the public sector and affiliated semi-governmental or private sector organizations (*amakudari*) (Blumenthal, 1985). In addition, we consider it arbitrary to exclude all regular employees of small companies, as the collapse of Yamaichi Securities in 1998, among other spectacular corporate bankruptcies, showed that there is also no cast-iron guarantee of permanent employment in large organizations. Accordingly, and considering all of the above, we estimate that roughly 30-40 per cent of current employees (15-20 million workers) in Japan can reasonably be considered as being both *de jure* regular workers and *de facto* lifetime employees.

2. Fifty Years of Research on Lifetime Employment

The concept of an implicit and reciprocal lifetime commitment between an employee and his company in Japan was first introduced to the English speaking world in 1958 by James Abegglen in *The Japanese Factory: Aspects of its Social Organization.* He described a system in which:

> ... the worker commits himself on entrance to the company for the remainder of his working career. The company will not discharge him even temporarily except in the most extreme circumstances. He will not quit the company for industrial employment elsewhere. He is a member of the company in ways resembling that in which persons are members of families, fraternal organizations, and other intimate and personal groups in the United States (1958: 11).

At that time, Abegglen assumed that the culture of welfare paternalism that had developed within the Japanese firm had to a large extent evolved organically out of Japan's pre-industrial values. Although he also recognized the rational appeal to management of maintaining it, Abegglen concluded that economic justifications for the existence of lifetime employment 'might be seen more accurately as a rationalization of a system rather than as an explanation of a real cause of a system of job relations' (1958: 16). Moreover, Abegglen envisaged that, though the corporate system itself was consistent with the structure of the emerging postwar economy, there was potential for incompatibility between it and changes that might derive from further macro-economic expansion and technological development, and that risked steering the Japanese firm towards a convergence with the American model.

Later, Abegglen updated his thesis to argue that the pattern of long-term employment at a single organization produced and reinforced an emotional identification between employer and employee that leads to personal, family, and corporate success being 'inextricably enmeshed' in what he called a 'partnership of fate' (Abegglen, 1973; Abegglen and Stalk, 1985). Abegglen argued that though the suggestion that Japan's employment situation is changing is a recurring one and that 'some change has occurred at the margins of the system .. it is not changing in any basic or extensive way' (1973: 47-8). Nevertheless, again he suggested that in the future patterns of employment could be transformed as basic social relations and value preferences changed with the growing internationalization and affluence that Japanese people were experiencing (Abegglen, 1973: 49).

Coming at the peak of Japan's industrial ascendancy, Abegglen produced his insider's guide to competing against the Japanese challenge, *Kaisha: The Japanese Corporation* (Abegglen and Stalk, 1985). He repeated the argument that comparative advantages lay in the Japanese firm's high levels of social integration around lifetime employment. Indeed, in its resolution of the needs and values of both employer and employee the system was proving to be more durable than perhaps even Abegglen had anticipated. He described lifetime employment as a trade-off between opportunities for high reward and long-term security, and in this case Japanese salarymen appeared to prefer the latter. Though he speculated about younger people's greater propensity to take risks, Abegglen forecast that, 'dramatic changes in the internal structure of the kaisha appear unlikely' (Abegglen and Stalk, 1985: 286). He explained that any change in consciousness might, instead, lead to a gradual abandonment of seniority-based pay and promotion but the core principle of lifetime employment would remain in place. Later still, and almost fifty years after publishing his first book, in *21st Century Japanese Management: New Systems, Lasting Values* (2006) Abegglen again stressed the importance to management and employees of a shared commitment to the firm as a corporate community, despite the increase in management's use of peripheral workers as a method for securing long-term stability.

Abegglen identified lifetime employment as the defining institutional characteristic of the Japanese corporation as a distinctive bureaucratic capitalist organizational type. It is worth reviewing his work here because within it are encapsulated the key discussions concerning the structure and nature of the Japanese firm that have taken place through the years of Japan's economic expansion and globalization. It was Abegglen who set down the initial framework and direction of those discussions and who moved these along at strategically important moments. Indeed, it was he who had, inadvertently, initially coined the expression 'lifetime employment' when his 1958 description of a 'lifetime commitment' was incorrectly translated back from Japanese into English.

Alongside Abegglen's research, other scholars have offered their perspectives on lifetime employment amid the ongoing globalization of the Japanese economy and internationalization of society, the achievement of mass affluence and mass consumption and, more recently, the ascendancy of the United States in a unipolar global political economy. Early works by Robert E. Cole (1971), Rodney Clark (1979), and Ronald Dore (1973) made their contributions, with the latter initiating the global Japanization literature (See: Elger and Smith, 1994; Oliver and Wilkinson, 1988) by suggesting that Japan's late development had enabled it to leap ahead of the Anglo-American system, which would henceforth converge on the Japanese organizational model.

Since then, a consistent theme in the literature has been the suggestion that lifetime employment is changing such that in the future it would no longer resemble in its forms and functions the system which became entrenched in the post-war years. The reasons put forward for the system's reform were various, but may be classified into two broad streams. The first viewed change being forced on the system from without, with the pressures associated with globalization being the major cause and differing degrees of socio-economic convergence the predicted result (Lincoln, 1993; Lincoln and Nakata, 1997; Nara, 1997; Rowley and Benson, 2002). The second saw change as coming from within as a consequence of Japan's endogenous development, citing a variety of causes and anticipated consequences (Ahmadjian and Robinson, 2001;

Berggren, 1995; Beck and Beck, 1994; Benson, 1998; Inoue, 1997; Sato, 2001; and Takahashi, 1997).

Mirroring these trends, through the 1990s and early 2000s a large number of press reports, television programmes and popular books appeared which argued that lifetime employment was disappearing under the weight of the long stagnation, or 'Lost Decade', that accompanied the collapse of the 1980s 'Bubble Economy'. Populist books came with eye-catching titles such as *Sarariiman hōkai* ('Fall of the Salaryman'; Utsumi, 2000) and *Denai kui wa suterareru* ('Nails that do not stick out are thrown away'; Terao, 1998), while others cautioned salarymen to develop marketable generic skills since, so they claimed, a new relationship of mutual independence between employer and employee was developing whereby the Japanese employment system would resolve to a global standard of employment mobility and corporate downsizing (Ishige, 1998; Shibata, 1999; Udagawa, 1997).

More recently, in the light of evidence that very long-term employment of regular workers persists in large Japanese organizations even as companies expand their recruitment of peripheral workers, a third stream of literature is emerging that emphasizes the continued resilience of lifetime employment (Baba, 2004; Inagami, 2004; Kato, 2001; Matanle, 2003; 2006a; 2006b; Ono, 2010; Saito and Vuszkun, 2010; Shimizutani and Yokoyama, 2009). Scholars of organizational change describe adaptive modifications to a basically stable Japanese management system, such as the intensification of workplace pressures, emphasis on results-based performance evaluations, ageing-related reforms to the pay and pensions systems, and increasing reliance on peripheral workers to bolster regular employment (Conrad, 2008; Keizer, 2010; Hassard, McCann and Morris, 2009; Meyer-Ohle, 2009), while others see the Japanese system as being embedded within its socio-economic context (Pudelko, 2006), adjusting incrementally to externally evolving factors such as the ageing of society (Conrad and Heindorf, 2008), or even intensifying as its regime of accumulation encounters pressures for reform (Wolff, 2008).

Lastly, among studies that analyse the persistence of lifetime employment, Ono (2010) has produced the most comprehensive recent numerical measurement of its prevalence. Using government data up to 2005, he adopts a narrow interpretation of the meaning of lifetime employment, either segmenting at 500 employees and excluding women and executives (*ex-ante* method), or adopting a survival analysis of the proportion of so-called 'inbred' (*haenuki*) workers who have worked for 30 years or more at the same organization since completing education (*ex-post*). Although Ono notes some of the weaknesses associated with these interpretations, for reasons of precise calculation he estimates that just 19.2 per cent (*ex-ante*) or 20 per cent (*ex-post*) of Japanese workers are lifetime employees.

Since lifetime employment has no formal basis in Japanese employment law, and because we know that lifetime employees are a sub-classification of regular workers, the most suitable methods for discovering whether and how it is changing are, first, to examine data on job tenure and job classification and, second, to find out if there have been any changes to legal requirements regarding the employment of regular workers. Beyond these, it is also useful to investigate industrial and organizational arrangements, as well as employers' and employees' attitudes to regular and lifetime employment.

In the next section, therefore, we present numerical data on employment tenure across the Japanese labour force in the post-Bubble era, demonstrating the persistence of very long-term regular employment in Japan alongside an increase in the number and proportion of non-regular workers. We also look at the legal requirements governing regular employment and find that although these remain in place, organizations are being required to raise their retirement ages for regular workers in order to keep pace with the ageing of the labour force, thereby presenting management with difficult labour throughput pressures. We then present research on industrial and organizational arrangements, as well as employee perceptions of lifetime employment, and lay out reasons why the system appears stable and resilient amid so much apparent pressure for change.

Statistical data is taken from government sources and we also make use of case study and interview data collected from fifteen years of qualitative investigations into the phenomenon of Japan's lifetime employment system. This includes research among salarymen and management within large Japanese companies (1996-2003) and among university students and graduates (2004-present).

3. Job Tenure in Post-Bubble Japan

Table 1: Average job tenure by gender in years, and job tenure indices in selected countries (1991, 1998 and 2008).

	Male Job Tenure 1991	Male Job Tenure 1998	Male Job Tenure 2008	Male Tenure Gap with Japan 1991	Male Tenure Gap with Japan 1998	Male Tenure Gap with Japan 2008	Female Job Tenure 1991	Female Job Tenure 1998	Female Job Tenure 2008	Female Tenure Gap with Japan 1991	Female Tenure Gap with Japan 1998	Female Tenure Gap with Japan 2008	Gender Tenure Gap 1991	Gender Tenure Gap 1998	Gender Tenure Gap 2008	% Change in Gender Gap (1998-2008)	% Change in Gender Gap (1991-2008)
Japan	12.5	13.1	13.1	100	100	100	7.3	8.2	8.6	100	100	100	58	63	66	4.8	13.8
France	10.6	11.7	11.6	85	89	89	9.6	10.8	11.5	132	132	134	91	92	99	7.6	8.8
Germany	*12.1*	11.3	11.5	*97*	86	88	*8.0*	9.2	10.1	*110*	121	117	*66*	81	88	8.6	*33.3*
S. Korea	ND	ND	6.7	ND	ND	51	ND	ND	4.0	ND	ND	47	ND	ND	60	ND	ND
Sweden	ND	12.0	9.9	ND	92	76	ND	11.8	10.7	ND	144	124	ND	98	108	10.2	ND
UK	9.2	9.2	8.7	74	70	66	6.3	7.1	7.9	86	87	92	68	77	90	16.9	32.3
USA	7.5	7.1	4.2	60	54	32	5.9	6.1	3.9	81	74	45	79	86	93	8.1	17.7

Sources: Auer and Cazes (2000); JILPT (2010); NRKK (2000).
Note: Tenure gaps with Japan and percentage change in gender gaps are authors' calculations. Tenure Gap with Japan: Japan=100. Gender Tenure Gap: Males=100. *Italics*=1990. ND=No Data.

Table 1 presents a comparison of job tenure by gender in seven countries for 1990/91, 1998 and 2008, showing that male average job tenure in Japan increased in the 1990s and remained steady in the 2000s, that Japan has consistently had the highest average tenure for men among the countries presented, and that the male tenure gap between Japan and other countries is widening in the post-Bubble era. Japan, France and Germany showed an increased average tenure among men, while tenure fell in the UK, Sweden and the USA. Male average employment tenure differs by around 10-20 per cent between Japan, and Germany and France; however by 2008 differences in male tenure between Japan and Sweden, the UK and USA had widened, to 312 per cent in the case of the USA. Although male tenure in Japan is the longest among the seven countries, female tenure in Japan is exceeded by Germany, France, and Sweden.

Where data is available, in all the countries stated the gender tenure gap has narrowed. However, given that France had already achieved a 91 per cent female to male tenure gap by 1990, Japan shows the least progress in closing its gap, with only a 4.8 per cent improvement between 1998 and 2008 and 13.8 per cent over the 1990-2008 period; while Germany, Sweden, the UK and USA all show more substantial progress in narrowing their gender gaps. Japan currently exhibits the second widest gender-based tenure gap among the countries listed after South Korea, while Sweden is the only country where women have a longer average job tenure than men. France shows both high levels of job tenure and the greatest degree of gender equality among the seven countries, while the USA shows very high levels of job mobility among both men and women. Presenting data from 16 countries in 1998, Auer and Cazes (2000: 390-1) found that only Greece (13.8 years) exhibited longer employment tenure among males than Japan, while the USA (7.1 years) showed the shortest tenure; and 10 countries showed longer tenures than Japan among women.

Covering the period from just before the collapse of the 'Bubble Economy', through the 'Lost Decade' and on into the 2000s, Table 2 presents amalgamated data from the Ministry of Health, Labour and Welfare's annual *Basic Survey on Wage Structure* (MHLW, Various Years) to show employment tenure across the Japanese labour force by age, gender and organization size (10 employees and above) over the 18 year period between 1989 and 2007. Overall, the table shows that job tenure remains almost identical for both men and women and across all company sizes until about age 30, from where male tenure increases more rapidly than for females, and where tenure has a tendency to increase with firm size. The former phenomenon reflects the continued propensity among some women to leave regular employment on marriage or childbirth and to re-enter the labour force as part-time and temporary workers once the early years of child-rearing are complete (See Table 4). This is reflected in the persistent M-shaped employment curve for women (Macnaughtan, 2006: 33), which is steadily smoothing out, and moving upwards and to the right, as women increasingly either delay or forego marriage and childbirth, have fewer children, or continue in employment while raising children (JILPT, 2007: 17). The latter phenomenon of job tenure rising with organization size reflects a number of factors, not all of which are inconsistent with the principle of lifetime employment in smaller organizations. These include, a lower than average company survivability ratio among smaller enterprises, a greater propensity for small business employees to voluntarily leave employment to start new ventures or return to managing family (*ie*) holdings, and a lower than average rate of public sector employment, a higher rate of female employment, and a lower union density in smaller organizations.

Table 2 also shows that both the male and female workforces have aged throughout the period, with men ageing by 2.7 years, and women ageing overall by 3.5 years and by 5.3 years in large organizations. The more rapid ageing of females can be partially explained by rising rates of female labour force participation since the 1970s, as well as the impacts of an increase in the number of women in regular employment, which rose from 11.09 to 18.17 million persons between 1980 and 2009 (Statistics Bureau, 2011a). Alongside the ageing of the labour force, average job tenure increased for both men and women and across all firm sizes through to 2002, after which tenure fell among most age groups. However, within these overall trends, job tenure has increased among older age groups, with the greatest increases coming between 1989 and 2002. In addition to being a consequence of the ageing of the workforce, the increase in tenure among older workers can be attributed to organizations recouping their long-term investments in human capital formation (Conrad, 2008), and managerial compliance with government pressure after 1990 to gradually raise organizational mandatory retirement ages from age 55/60 to 60/65 under successive amendments to the Older Workers Law (Ota, 2008).

Table 3 shows that between 1989 and 1997 a large proportion of organizations raised their retirement age to 60, while the 2002-09 period saw further rises to 65. Correspondingly, Table 2 shows that the biggest gains in male employment tenure were achieved in the 1989-97 period among employees aged 50-59, and among employees aged 60-64 between 1997 and 2007. Related to this, employment tenure among younger and middle-aged employees saw some declines in the 1997-2002 period and broader decreases after 2002.

From an organizational perspective, increases in tenure among older workers and decreases among younger and middle-aged workers are inter-dependent in terms of managing the stability of labour throughput. Under an unstable and slower growth macro-economic environment, being constrained by the 'doctrine of abusive dismissal' from shedding regular workers mid-career (Kambayashi, 2010), and simultaneously under pressure from the government to increase the age of retirement of the existing workforce, in order to retain investments in human capital, control costs, and maintain stable labour through-

Table 2: Job tenure in Japan in years by age, gender, and organization size (Selected years: 1989-2007).

Gender and Age		All Organizations					1,000+ Employees					100-999 Employees					10-99 Employees				
		1989	1992	1997	2002	2007	1989	1992	1997	2002	2007	1989	1992	1997	2002	2007	1989	1992	1997	2002	2007
Men	Ave. Age	39.2	39.7	40.5	41.1	41.9	38.7	38.5	39.8	40.5	41.1	38.6	38.9	39.9	40.6	41.4	40.6	41.8	41.8	42.1	43.2
	Ave. Tenure	12.4	12.5	13.3	13.5	13.3	15.9	15.5	16.8	16.7	16.2	11.8	11.8	12.9	13.1	12.7	9.7	10.4	10.6	10.9	10.9
	18-19	1.0	1.0	1.0	1.0	0.9	0.9	1.0	1.0	1.0	0.9	1.0	1.0	1.0	1.0	0.9	1.1	1.1	1.1	1.1	0.9
	20-24	2.7	2.5	2.7	2.6	2.2	2.8	2.4	3.2	2.7	2.1	2.7	2.5	2.7	2.5	2.1	2.5	2.6	2.4	2.6	2.3
	25-29	5.2	5.0	5.2	5.2	4.4	5.8	5.4	5.7	5.7	4.5	5.2	5.0	5.3	5.3	4.5	4.6	4.6	4.5	4.7	4.3
	30-34	8.8	8.4	8.6	8.6	7.9	10.7	9.7	10.1	9.9	8.8	8.7	8.2	8.6	8.7	7.9	7.1	7.2	7.0	7.0	6.8
	35-39	12.8	12.3	12.0	12.1	11.3	16.1	15.2	14.3	14.3	13.4	12.6	12.0	12.0	11.9	11.4	9.5	9.5	9.6	9.4	8.8
	40-44	16.0	16.2	15.8	15.4	14.9	20.2	20.2	19.9	18.6	18.0	15.9	16.0	15.6	15.3	14.7	11.7	12.1	12.0	12.0	11.1
	45-49	19.2	19.5	19.5	19.0	18.3	24.3	24.9	24.7	23.9	22.4	19.0	19.1	19.4	18.9	17.8	13.8	14.1	14.3	14.2	13.7
	50-54	20.5	21.5	22.5	21.9	21.4	26.8	27.9	29.3	28.1	27.5	20.2	21.1	22.3	21.9	20.6	15.3	16.0	16.1	16.0	15.8
	55-59	18.4	20.0	22.6	22.8	22.8	27.1	27.6	30.5	30.2	30.3	17.8	19.7	22.4	22.4	22.0	14.1	16.0	17.0	17.4	17.1
	60-64	11.2	12.1	13.5	14.9	15.5	12.3	14.2	14.1	15.5	16.0	10.5	11.1	12.9	13.8	15.0	11.4	12.3	13.8	15.5	15.6
Women	Ave. Age	35.7	36.0	37.3	37.9	39.2	32.3	32.2	34.8	35.6	37.6	34.6	35.1	36.3	37.2	38.8	38.8	39.6	39.9	40.2	41.0
	Ave. Tenure	7.2	7.4	8.4	8.8	8.7	7.8	7.5	9.5	10.0	9.7	6.9	7.1	7.9	8.4	8.2	7.2	7.6	8.0	8.5	8.3
	18-19	1.0	1.0	0.9	0.9	0.9	1.0	1.0	1.0	1.0	0.9	1.0	1.0	0.9	0.9	0.9	1.0	0.9	0.9	0.9	0.9
	20-24	2.7	2.5	2.7	2.4	2.0	2.9	2.5	3.0	2.4	1.8	2.7	2.6	2.7	2.4	2.0	2.4	2.4	2.3	2.3	2.1
	25-29	5.4	5.2	5.4	5.0	4.3	6.4	6.0	6.0	5.5	4.3	5.3	5.1	5.5	5.0	4.3	4.4	4.3	4.7	4.5	4.1
	30-34	7.7	7.5	7.9	8.0	6.9	9.7	9.0	9.5	9.3	7.7	7.8	7.5	7.9	8.0	6.9	6.1	6.1	6.5	6.5	6.2
	35-39	8.8	9.1	9.4	9.7	9.1	11.5	11.8	12.0	12.3	10.7	8.7	9.3	9.4	9.6	9.0	7.2	7.2	7.5	7.6	7.4
	40-44	9.3	10.0	10.8	10.9	10.3	12.0	13.1	15.0	14.9	12.8	9.4	10.1	10.7	10.6	10.2	8.0	8.3	8.5	8.7	8.3
	45-49	10.7	11.0	11.9	12.5	11.4	14.0	14.3	15.8	17.3	14.8	10.7	11.0	12.0	12.3	10.8	9.5	9.6	10.1	10.4	9.7
	50-54	12.3	12.5	13.3	14.1	13.2	16.0	15.7	17.4	18.3	16.8	12.3	12.5	13.0	13.7	12.2	11.1	11.5	11.9	12.7	12.1
	55-59	13.2	13.7	15.0	15.8	15.5	17.6	16.9	19.0	20.4	19.4	13.0	13.7	14.6	14.9	15.0	12.1	12.9	13.9	14.9	14.1
	60-64	12.9	12.9	13.9	14.1	13.9	16.2	15.3	14.8	15.5	15.7	11.2	11.3	12.8	12.2	13.4	12.8	13.2	14.3	15.0	13.7

Source: MHLW (Various Years).

Table 3: Mandatory retirement age by age of employee and size of organization (Selected years – 1989-2009).

Year	Size of Organization (No. of Employees)	% of Organizations	Up to Age >55	Age 55	Age 56-59	Age 60	Age 61-64	Age 65	Age 66≤
1989	All		0.5	20.7	17.0	57.6	1.1	2.9	0.3
	30-99		0.7	21.8	16.3	56.4	1.1	3.4	0.3
	100-299		0.2	20.0	18.5	57.9	1.0	2.2	0.2
	300-999		-	15.6	19.0	62.8	1.8	0.8	-
	1,000-4,999		-	10.4	14.5	74.0	0.7	0.4	-
	5,000+		-	4.9	8.7	86.4	-	-	-
1992	All		0.2	11.5	11.7	71.4	1.7	3.4	0.1
1997	All		-	4.6	5.2	82.0	1.5	6.6	0.1
	30-99		-	5.7	6.6	78.4	0.9	8.3	0.1
	100-299		-	2.7	2.5	88.1	2.9	3.8	0.1
	300-999		-	1.9	2.3	91.9	2.0	1.9	-
	1,000-4,999		-	0.1	0.4	96.8	1.7	1.0	-
	5,000+		-	-	-	98.0	0.7	1.3	-
2002	All		-	-	0.6	90.3	2.3	6.6	0.2
	30-99		-	-	0.8	89.1	2.0	7.8	0.3
	100-299		-	-	0.2	92.3	3.0	4.5	-
	300-999		-	-	0.3	93.3	2.8	3.6	0.1
	1,000-4,999		-	-	0.2	96.7	1.9	1.0	0.2
	5,000+		-	-	-	98.2	1.2	0.6	-
2004	All		-	-	0.7	90.5	2.4	6.1	0.4
2009	All	98.5	-	-	-	82.4	4.1	12.7	0.7
	30-99	98.2	-	-	-	79.3	4.4	15.5	0.8
	100-299	99.4	-	-	-	88.0	3.8	7.5	0.6
	300-999	98.8	-	-	-	91.9	3.5	4.6	0.1
	1,000+	97.7	-	-	-	94.3	3.3	2.3	-

Sources: Statistics Bureau (2011a). Statistics Bureau (Various Years).

put, the rational managerial response would be to reduce the inflow of new graduates into the organization while waiting for current employees to reach the new retirement age and begin to exit in larger numbers.

In addition, the current group of older workers is particularly numerous, being the so-called 'baby boomer' generation, and the combination of their larger numbers and rising retirement ages has presented organizations with an unusual confluence of labour throughput management challenges which are at present working their way through the system. This analysis is consistent with research that describes the employment 'ice-age' among younger people from the 1990s and on into the 2000s (Ohta, Genda and Kondo, 2008). In this respect, Ono (2010: 23) uses the analogy of maintaining the level of water in a bathtub by regulating the inflow according to the rate of outflow. Significantly, Ono's summary data on separations indicates that companies have been steadily managing downward their labour throughput of regular workers by a factor of around 0.8-1.5 per cent per year through the 1990s and early 2000s, which would be consistent with his 'bathtub hypothesis'.

Table 2 also shows that average job tenure among males aged 50 to 59 in large organizations is currently between 27 and 30+ years of continuous service, meaning that the average age of accession for employees is around age 25. It needs to be borne in mind that many employees will have been in full-time education till at least age 21, that voluntary separations by employees, while not the norm, are not uncommon, and that some job-changing activity can be observed among regular employees within the first three years after graduation, as younger people search out their most suitable employer (Ministry of Labour, 2000). Ono (2010), for example, shows that approximately three quarters of all separations are voluntary and that Japan has the lowest rate of involuntary separations in the OECD. In addition, Ariga *et al.* (2000) found that firms actively hire mid-career employees with full-time work experience in order to fill important skills gaps, thus raising the average age of entry, but that this does not invalidate the principle of permanent employment. With this in mind, it appears that the principle of lifetime employment continues to hold among nearly all male regular workers at large organizations; with some male regular workers at smaller and medium sized organizations, and some female regular workers at organizations of all sizes not being *de facto* lifetime employees.

Alongside the data on employment tenure, other data shows that there has part-time and temporary employment contracts, with this being to a great extent been a steady increase in the proportion of women being employed on

Figure 1: Employees by type of employment, in per cent and actual figures (10,000 persons), plotted against the total size of the Japanese labour force (right hand scale, in millions) (1985-2010).

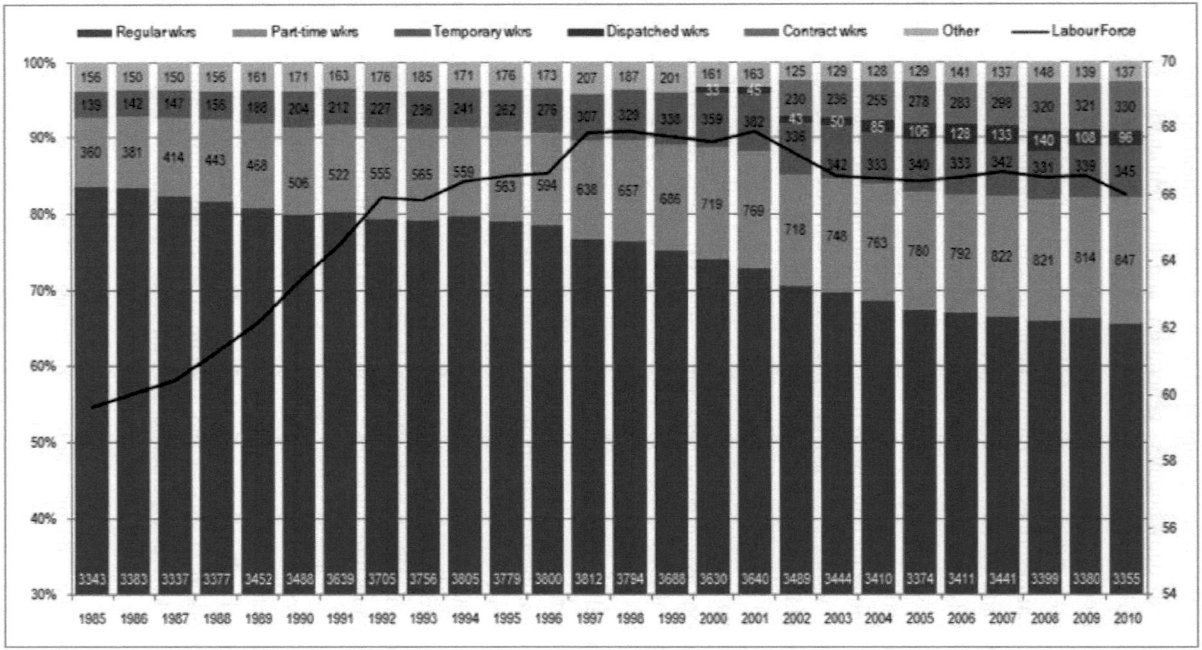

Source: Statistics Bureau (2011b).

Note: Time series changed in 2000 (see Labour Force Survey for details). Left hand axis begins at 30%. Right hand axis begins at 54 million.

Figure 2: Proportion of employees by type of employment and gender (2008).

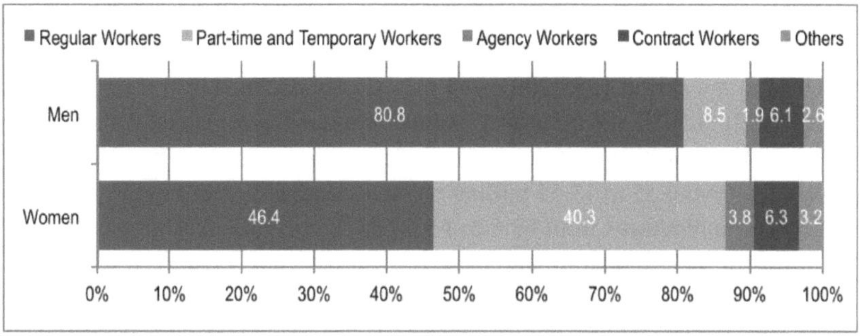

Source: JILPT (2010b: 48).

Table 4: Proportion of employees who are non-regular workers by age and gender (Selected years, 1985-2008).

		1985	1995	2005	2008
Men	15-24	4.7	9.2	17.5	28.6
	25-34	3.2	2.9	5.7	14.2
	35-44	3.1	2.3	1.8	8.2
	45-54	5	2.9	2.5	8
	55-64	19.2	17.4	9.8	27.6
	65+	34.7	48.3	33.3	67.9
Women	15-24	8.3	16.3	26.2	35.4
	25-34	24.3	26.6	25.5	41.2
	35-44	44.4	48.9	43.5	55
	45-54	37.4	46.8	47.8	57.5
	55-64	38.1	43.6	50.8	64
	65+	45.8	48.6	51.7	70.1

Source: JILPT (2010b: 37).

due to the reduced availability of regular employment to both new graduates and post-child-rearing labour force re-entrants.

However, some scholars argue that long term structural changes to society and the economy are also responsible for this trend, with the steady increase in female labour force participation, and the long-term shift to a post-industrial service based economy being significant factors (Baba, 2004; Inagami, 2004; Keizer, 2008). While the mandatory retirement age for regular employees has risen, as has job tenure among older male workers, part-time, temporary, agency, and contract employment as a proportion of total employment have all expanded steadily over the past 25 years, as has the number and proportion of women in these jobs (Figures 1 and 2; Table 4). The fact that this was occurring prior to the 1990s suggests that changes in the size and structure of the labour force are at least partly responsible for the expansion of non-regular employment. Nevertheless, while the labour force expanded by 8.27 million persons (13.9%) in the period 1985-2001, and then slowly declined by 1.89 million persons (2.8%) to 2010, the number of regular workers has remained comparatively stable at 33-38 million, and the number of non-regular workers has dramatically expanded, from 6.55 to 17.55 million workers; leading to a fall in the proportion in regular employment from 83.6 to 65.6 per cent of non-executive employees, and a rise in non-regular employment to 34.3 per cent (Figure 1). Of the total increase in non-regular employment of 11 million persons between 1985 and 2010, we calculate that roughly 5.8 million is due to organizations responding to external pressures, with 5.2 million being due simply to labour force expansion.

Accordingly, the phenomenon of a dual labour market that has been a striking feature of postwar Japanese society, between mostly male regular employees on the one hand, and mostly female non-regular workers on the other, not only continues to persist, but it appears to be widening and becoming more deeply entrenched in the 21st century. This tendency is particularly notable because it has come during a period in which the government has introduced measures aimed specifically at closing gender-based employment gaps, such as the Equal Employment Opportunities Law (1985) and its revisions (1999 and 2006), and the Child Care [and Family Care] Leave Law (1991) and its revisions (1995, 2001, 2004, and 2009). Indeed, it appears that the Japanese management system requires the existence of a dual labour structure in order to be able to maintain lifetime employment – that regular workers enjoy their status in society as a consequence of the existence of a sharply demarcated non-regular workforce (Keizer, 2010).

4. Organizational and Employee Perspectives

4.1 Organizational Perspectives

Table 5 presents an index of job tenure by age, gender, and industry of employment in 2007 using data from the MHLW's *Basic Survey on Wage Structure*. Displaying wide variations between industries as well as by age and gender, the table reflects the impacts on employment tenure of established patterns of human capital formation such as managerial requirements for fixing high value human capital to the organization, structural constraints on managerial flexibility, and the availability of opportunities among employees to change employer at different stages in their working lives.

Sectors with a high average index of job tenure for employees are, in general, where large organizations feature, such as in utility supply, finance and insurance, and compound services (e.g. government services), and/or are where functional constraints on the willingness to shed labour operate, such as the requirement for recouping high value organization-specific human capital formation in manufacturing. In large organizations in these sectors human resource development takes place after graduation from school or university via long-term in-company vocational, or On-the-Job (OJT), experience-based training (Koike, 1996). Training of this type often requires complex coordination by personnel management departments and may last up to 15 years, by the end of which employees are expected to have experienced a broad range of operations. During this time employees must absorb and refine the organization's stock of formal and tacit knowledge, develop specific skills and abilities, and form bonds of camaraderie within their entry cohorts as well as with their seniors and juniors, or *sempai* and *kōhai* (See: Koike, 1996; Nonaka and Takeuchi, 1995). Being organizationally specific, knowledge and human relations of this kind mean that, the longer that an employee remains within the organization, the more difficult it becomes to transfer his or her attributes to another employer.

Furthermore, under a long-term OJT system, apart from helping to raise overall productivity (Kato and Morishima, 2002), high value human capital formation takes place with the intention, on both the employer's and employee's sides, of reducing free-riding on knowledge and skill acquisition by fixing the employee to the company. Ownership of human capital becomes shared and the employer can be confident that employees will not easily free-ride on the organization's long-term investment by switching employer. It is also usually the case that, the larger the organization, the greater the investment in human capital formation through more complex and longer OJT systems; meaning that the higher the value of human capital accumulated, the more that the employer will try to retain its investment. The consequence is a long-term system of steadily increasing financial and status rewards which culminates in a large lump-sum retirement pension, and within which voluntary mid-career resignations incur unbearably high transaction costs for workers.

By the same token, the law discourages employers from free-riding on employees' efforts to acquire high value human capital by preventing the shedding of labour except in circumstances of imminent bankruptcy (Kambayashi, 2010), since employees with organization-specific capital are vulnerable if forced to trade themselves in the external labour market. Japanese courts have developed a body of case law called the 'Doctrine of Abusive Dismissal' (*kaikoken ranyō hōri*), which has been tested in the Supreme Court and written into the 2004 revisions to the Labour Standards Law, whereby organizations should demonstrate that dismissals are objectively and socially reasonable (Kambayashi, 2010). Kambayashi quotes a key 1979 Tokyo High Court judgment which specifies four criteria for reasonable dismissal, where the second states that 'the dismissal must be the last resort to adjust labor input', with 'last resort' subsequently being clarified to mean 'whether or not the firm would go bankrupt' and when other methods of labour adjustment are not available (2010: 11-2).

Conversely, industries with a lower than average index of employment tenure exhibit characteristics which either do not inhibit labour mobility or may facilitate it. Real estate, hospitality, and other service industries have a high proportion of smaller enterprises where average company survivability is lower, or where there is less of a requirement to fix firm-specific human capital because some job tasks do not require the development of high-value employee attributes, such as in eating and drinking establishments, hotels, or various clerical tasks.

Training in education and medical and welfare services is largely generic, taking place via government supervised advanced education programmes in colleges and universities. Here, job mobility is comparatively high, for example among teachers in cram schools and vocational colleges, among professors and researchers in higher education, or among doctors and nurses who begin their employment in large public hospitals, moving later to private clinics after building sufficient experience and financial independence. Recently, there has been substantial growth in employment in nursing care for the elderly in Japan's ageing society, particularly in regional areas. Here again, job mobility is high due to workers attending programmes in vocational training colleges, and the high proportion of low wage part-time employment of predominantly female care workers.

Table 5: Index of job tenure in Japan by age, gender, and industry of employment (2007) (Japan all industries= 100).

	Ave. Tenure	All Inds. (Years)	All Inds. (Index)	Mining	Construction	Manufacturing	Utility Supply	Information and Comms.	Transport	Wholesale and Retail	Finance and Insurance	Real Estate	Hospitality	Medical and Welfare	Education and Training	Compound Services	Other Services
Men	Ave. Tenure	13.3	100	109	104	114	145	94	92	98	123	70	65	62	105	130	74
	18-19	0.9	100	111	111	100	122	100	100	111	111	111	111	100	78	100	100
	20-24	2.2	100	109	114	118	118	68	105	86	55	64	105	77	77	95	86
	25-29	4.4	100	127	123	111	161	91	100	100	89	77	95	86	70	107	82
	30-34	7.9	100	105	110	111	158	91	89	101	111	77	86	68	70	124	82
	35-39	11.3	100	93	103	112	150	106	81	101	119	80	81	65	78	128	85
	40-44	14.9	100	87	94	112	149	109	80	102	117	85	77	68	85	126	83
	45-49	18.3	100	85	93	110	148	111	83	103	123	82	70	70	88	127	84
	50-54	21.4	100	84	96	114	146	117	77	101	126	74	64	74	95	128	78
	55-59	22.8	100	90	93	120	135	127	81	105	113	67	60	72	104	119	69
	60-64	15.5	100	116	109	119	72	124	86	124	80	48	73	82	134	62	65
Women	Ave. Tenure	8.7	100	146	122	125	163	89	102	94	122	77	75	87	106	139	74
	18-19	0.9	100	167	100	100	100	100	89	100	100	111	111	100	89	100	89
	20-24	2.0	100	120	105	125	120	85	95	100	80	70	105	95	95	130	90
	25-29	4.3	100	142	105	119	158	88	112	98	112	81	93	95	93	128	79
	30-34	6.9	100	110	112	123	171	96	104	103	117	87	88	91	93	139	72
	35-39	9.1	100	103	107	120	168	104	97	101	119	95	76	86	102	144	74
	40-44	10.3	100	91	105	112	190	123	96	105	123	95	73	87	117	135	72
	45-49	11.4	100	129	122	109	213	104	103	94	134	85	74	88	125	143	79
	50-54	13.2	100	113	128	110	189	145	104	91	130	94	64	89	134	148	79
	55-59	15.5	100	110	115	109	154	142	110	94	123	81	63	88	143	139	83
	60-64	13.9	100	144	119	112	48	117	99	91	143	64	77	90	145	108	76

Source: MHLW (Various Years).

In addition, where training for work tasks need not be extensive, or where re-employing organizations wish to develop and maintain ties with affiliated or government organizations, employment take-up of workers who for various reasons have become unemployed mid-career is common, with companies sometimes receiving public subsidies for doing so (Ota, 2008). This is common in cases of older government workers, who may be re-employed in regional companies and semi-governmental organizations involved in transportation, communications, or construction via *amakudari*, or descent from heaven, or between keiretsu affiliates (Ota, 2008). In these cases, although employment transfers between organizations will act to bring down the employment index expressed in Table 5, the intention of both the sending and receiving organization is to protect the principle of continuous regular employment until retirement.

Lastly, industries in Japan with high levels of job tenure may display structural factors which inhibit job changing but which also favour the accumulation of organization specific human capital. For example, utility supply (e.g. electricity generation and distribution), compound services organizations (e.g. prefectural and municipal governments), and financial services companies (e.g. retail banking) are either fully or partially territorially arranged and knowledge in these sectors may be geographically specific, with job effectiveness depending upon tacit knowledge of local contexts, as well as the development over the long term of a deep familiarity and close rapport with suppliers and customers.

Indeed, it is in sectors where organization-specific human capital formation takes place via long-term OJT within territorially arranged organizational contexts that we should expect to see the longest average job tenure rates; and the figures in Table 5 bear out this analysis, with utility supply and compound services having the highest rates of job tenure among men and women.

4.2 Employee Perspectives

Among the younger people that we interviewed, few are ready or willing to predict where they will be and what they will be doing when they reach middle age or are approaching their retirement. Few therefore express a specific wish to be employed at a single organization for the duration of their working lives. Some have not even heard of the term 'lifetime employment' (*shūshin koyō*), and some have only vague notions as to what it entails, while others express qualified opinions; voicing an unwillingness to be tied down while young and single, but expressing positive appreciation towards employment security and income stability when they decide to marry and raise a family.

Indeed, although they acknowledge and even may support its *de facto* existence, neither the government nor employers are able to officially endorse lifetime employment as a formal structure, because it has no basis in law beyond that of regular employment. Nevertheless, many younger people come to know through conversations with their parents and friends, their teachers and professors, and their careers officers, and through their job hunting research and experience, that regular employment at a reputable employer carries an implicit guarantee of security and stability through to retirement, and steadily rising levels of challenge, responsibility, and status; and that the alternative of non-regular employment potentially bears a lifetime of instability, low earnings, and, for men especially, low status in the marriage market (See: Cook, 2010). Thus, while some students may express antipathy for a system that appears rigid and confining, they are simultaneously working assiduously throughout their third and fourth years to secure regular employment and avoid freeterdom.

Ultimately, however, most younger people come to understand the full implications of regular employment only after they have joined their organizations; that, first, if the organization continues to exist and they do not encounter a situation where they might wish/have to change jobs, then there is a good chance that they will remain with their employer until the mandatory retirement age; second, that the employment system sets up a lifetime of competitive cooperation with the other members of one's entry cohort for promotion, status, and higher earnings; and, third, that security and stability involve a compromise on the part of the employee that hands to management unilateral responsibility for worker redeployment and work intensification (Mouer and Kawanishi, 2005). One senior executive explained how he came to understand lifetime employment.

> I have never seen a contract or a promise from the company saying that they will employ someone for the next 30 or 35 years. But at that time when I was in my twenties, those salarymen who were in their fifties had for the most part spent 30 or so years in the company and there were quite a lot of them around. So, I thought that if I worked diligently then that would probably happen to me. But I didn't expect it.

Starting with this basic understanding, through the course of their working lives regular workers work intensively and for long hours, establish competitive friendships with their colleagues, and experience levels of frustration and satisfaction that encourage the development of a steadily deepening affective relationship with the organization, as their changing needs are, generally speaking, matched by rising rewards. This reality in the majority of employees' lived experience forms the basis of the concepts of a living wage and loyalty to a corporate community (Inagami and Whittaker, 2005); though the term 'loyalty' here is many-faceted and needs to be understood also in the context of mechanisms to discourage free-riding. Moreover, career structures in regular employment need to be understood differently from terms such as a 'job for life' as expressed elsewhere. In Japan, career formation entails employees experiencing a variety of job tasks and environments over the course of their working lives within a single organization, what Storey *et al.* (1997). refer to as single-company career chimneys, and many experience satisfaction from the steadily rising levels of challenge and responsibility that they encounter. Similar processes of upward progression can be experienced in Anglo-American work contexts, except here it is more often achieved via a multi-organization career chimney. It is notable in this respect that job changing patterns for elite workers in Japan and western countries appear strikingly different. It is usually the case for male university graduates in Japan that, the higher the level of earnings and employment status gained, the fewer the number of job changes experienced, with most corporate executives and senior public sector managers only having worked for a single organization; whereas in most western economies corporate executives normally change employer more frequently than the labour force average for their country (NKSSK, 1995).

It also needs to be appreciated that approximately half of total employment in Japan is outside of the Tokyo, Osaka and Nagoya regions, where economic activity is often regionally based and more deeply enmeshed with enduring cultural practices. In this respect, territorially arranged organizational contexts are attractive for those employees who do not wish to periodically uproot their households or be posted on extended sojourns in distant or overseas locations because, in the case of eldest (or only) sons or daughters, they may expect to take care of elderly parents(-in-law) and inherit, live in, and farm the familial land and home. For those that remain in the family property there also comes the duty to uphold wider community responsibilities and values, such as contributing to school, home-help, and cooperative groups in the case of women, and local agricultural, political, and religious functions in the case of men. These duties have a tendency to fix workers and their families to specific locales, and maintaining stable employment in a visible and respected institution, such as the prefectural or city government or with the regional electricity supplier, becomes more attractive to employees as they marry, have children, and move into middle-age.

It is noteworthy that the rate of divergence in job tenure from the national norm for utility supply and compound services in Table 5 increases for men and, especially, women as they move into middle age, when they would be expected to be most involved in community maintenance tasks. From the perspective of many employees in regional areas, very long-term regular employment at a single organization can be as much about fulfilling semi-ascribed familial and social roles as a '*shakaijin*', or a responsible mature adult, as it is related to realizing individual occupational preferences and abilities.

Finally, among factors that help to explain the persistence of the dual labour structure, many jobs that are comparatively unattractive or tedious for workers to maintain as career options may attract some workers for reasons other than long-term career building, such as married women working part-time to supplement family incomes, aspiring artists and musicians needing time and space for personal development, or keeping oneself in education (JILPT, 2007). There are also a small number who engage in non-regular employment because they reject the social system and living arrangements that come with regular employment in a standard organization (Honda, 2005). Nevertheless, while it is true that some non-regular workers do so out of personal choice and preference, the majority unwillingly take up non-regular employment for want of entry opportunities into regular employment; and this is especially the case with younger people engaged in temporary, agency, and contract/entrusted employment (Honda, 2005; Ishiguro, 2008; Kosugi, 2003). Once engaged in such employment, the likelihood of being recruited into regular employment decreases dramatically, particularly for women.

5. Summary and Conclusions

In this chapter we have described the phenomenon of lifetime employment in Japan by combining numerical analysis of job tenure and type of employment since the 1980s with discussions of legal restrictions on employment flexibility and qualitative examinations of attitudes to lifetime employment in Japanese companies and among Japanese executives, employees, and university students.

Despite the pressures bearing on Japanese organizations from a long period of economic instability and slower growth, the number of regular workers employed at Japanese organizations has remained stable throughout the economic dislocations of the post-Bubble years, with the tenure gap between Japan and other countries widening. While the number of regular workers in 1985 was 33.43 million persons, after rising to 38 million in 1996/7, by 2010 that figure had returned to almost exactly its 1985 level, standing at 33.55 million workers. Moreover, overall job tenure rates have barely changed, with increases among older workers since the late-1980s, and decreases among younger and middle-aged workers. Underlying this there have been other related developments. The labour force continued its steady expansion through to 1998, with this being due in some measure to an increase in female labour force participation, and since 2001 it has been gradually shrinking. In 2009-10 the labour force shrank by 570,000 workers, with larger annual decreases expected in future, as the baby boomer cohorts reach retirement and Japan's population continues to age and shrink.

Coterminous with this, the Japanese government requested employers to gradually raise their mandatory retirement ages by approximately 10 years, from age 55/60 to 60/65, in the space of about 20 years (1990-2010), thereby keeping the baby boomer generation in employment; while throughout this time the external economic environment has not been conducive to a continuous expansion in regular employment that would compensate for the resulting slowdown in labour throughput. In addition, the doctrine of abusive dismissal has remained in place, preventing employers from shedding labour except in cases where the only alternative is bankruptcy. In our analysis, it is this confluence of demographic, socioeconomic, and regulatory factors that has been a major cause of the large increase in the number of non-regular workers since the early 1990s. There are also various functional, structural and socio-cultural factors which persist and which favour the continuation of lifetime employment, especially at large organizations. Lastly, for those unlucky enough to have been born in the 1970s and 1980s, and to be at the receiving end of the slowdown in recruitment into regular employment over the last 20 years, the consequence of Japan's sharply demarcated dual labour force has seen serious and lasting negative impacts on personal well-being and life chances; with downward pressure on lifetime earnings, especially for those who are in non-regular employment, as well as restricted opportunities for personal development, forging relationships, and building families.

From the perspective of Japan having experienced two decades of slower growth, as well as encountered continuing instability in the international economy, it would be tempting to conclude that secure and stable lifetime employment is indeed disappearing and giving way to more precarious forms of employment, as those that are already in regular employment experience its benefits for as long as possible, leaving those that, for various reasons, are not already regular employees to face steadily greater barriers to entry. To a great extent this is the correct interpretation of the situation that Japanese working people face in 2011. However, in view of the recent slowdown in labour throughput in organizations and the coming reductions in the size of the labour force, it is our view that the current very tight labour throughput conditions may unwind somewhat in the future, resulting in comparatively less restricted entry into regular employment; though this will probably not help those younger people and women who are presently non-regular workers. In addition, there is a possibility that the government will raise the retirement age still further, or the retirement age may be abolished altogether to encourage older people to remain in work as long as they are able and willing. The government may also decide to change the law on abusive dismissal in favour of organizations being able to shed regular employees more easily. However, as yet there are no immediate signs of these things occurring.

Although Figure 1 above shows that the proportion of regular employees in the Japanese labour force has steadily declined since 1985, the actual number has remained stable. Moreover, the rate of decline has slowed since 2005, and the rate of increase in non-regular employment has also slowed since 2007. It is possible that this is the first evidence of the unwinding of the slowdown in labour throughput as organizations complete the required raising of their retirement ages, and the baby boomer generation commences its exit from the labour force. Undoubtedly, the current direction of change will not be smooth, but if the Japanese economy continues to expand then we may see a trend towards greater stability in employment appearing, as the rate of labour force shrinkage increases in the coming years. In view of this, therefore, we believe that the prospects are good for the future stability and resilience of lifetime employment in 21st century Japan.

6. References

Abegglen, J. C. (1958). *The Japanese Factory: Aspects of its Social Organization*. Glencoe, IL: The Free Press.

Abegglen, J. C. (1973). *Management and Worker: The Japanese Solution.* Tokyo: Kodansha International.

Abegglen, J. C. (2006). *21st Century Japanese Management: New Systems, Lasting Values*. Basingstoke: PalgraveMacmillan.

Abegglen, J. C. & Stalk, G. Jr. (1985). *Kaisha: The Japanese Corporation.* New York: Basic Books.

Ahmadjian, C. & Robinson, P. (2001). Safety in Numbers: Downsizing and the Deinstitutionalization of Permanent Employment in Japan. *Administrative Science Quarterly, 46(4),* 622-654.

Araki, T. (2002). *Labor and Employment Law in Japan.* Tokyo: Japan Institute of Labor.

Ariga, K., Brunello, G. & Ohkusa, Y. (2000). *Internal Labor Markets in Japan.* Cambridge: Cambridge University Press.

Auer, P. & Cazes, S. (2000). The Resilience of the Long-Term Employment Relationship: Evidence from the Industrialized Countries. *International Labour Review, 139(4),* 379-408.

Baba, S. (2004). Remodelling Employment for Competitive Advantage: What will follow Japan's 'Lifetime employment'? *Asian Business and Management, 3(2),* 221-240.

Beck, J. C. & Beck, M. N. (1994). *The Change of a Lifetime: Employment Patterns Among Japan's Managerial Elite.* Honolulu: University of Hawaii Press.

Benson, J. (1998). Labour Management During Recessions: Japanese Manufacturing Enterprises in the 1990s. *Industrial Relations Journal, 29(3),* 207-219.

Berggren, C. (1995). Japan as Number Two: Competitive Problems and the Future of Alliance Capitalism after the Burst of the Bubble Boom. *Work, Employment & Society, 19(1),* 53-95.

Blumenthal, T. (1985). The Practice of *Amakudari* within the Japanese Employment System. *Asian Survey, 25(3),* 310-321.

Clark, R. (1979). *The Japanese Company.* New Haven: Yale University Press.

Cole, R. E. (1971). *Japanese Blue Collar: The Changing Tradition.* Berkeley: University of California Press.

Conrad, H. (2008). Human Resource Management Practices and the Ageing Workforce. In F. Coulmas, H. Conrad, A. Schad-Seifert, & G. Vogt (Eds.), *The Demographic Challenge: A Handbook About Japan.* Leiden: Brill.

Conrad, H. & Heindorf, V. (2008). *Human Resource Management in Ageing Societies: Perspectives from Japan and Germany.* Basingstoke: PalgraveMacmillan.

Cook, E. (2010). Marry a Freeter?! Perceptions of Marriage and Stability Among Japanese Women. Paper Presented at British Association for Japanese Studies Annual Conference 2010, School of Oriental and African Studies, 9-10 September.

Dore, R. (1973). *British Factory Japanese Factory: The Origins of National Diversity in Industrial Relations*. London: George Allen and Unwin.

Elger, T. & Smith, C. (1994). *Global Japanization? The Transnational Transformation of the Labour Process.* London: Routledge.

Hassard, J., McCann, L. & Morris, J. (2009). *Managing in the Modern Corporation: The Intensification of Managerial Work in the USA, UK and Japan.* Cambridge: Cambridge University Press.

Honda, Y. (2005). 'Freeters': Young Atypical Workers in Japan. *Japan Labor Review, 2(3),* 5-25.

Inagami, T. (2004). Changes in the Employment System and Future Labour Policies. *Japan Labor Review, 1(1),* 39-51.

Inagami, T. & Whittaker, D. H. (2005). *The New Community Firm: Employment, Governance and Management Reform in Japan.* Cambridge: Cambridge University Press.

Inoue, S. (1997). Changing Employment in Japan. *Japan Forum, 9(2)*, 160-164.

Ishige, A. (1998). *Shin jidai no kyaria kaihatsu* (Career development in the new era). Tokyo: Shakai Keizai Seisansei Honbu.

Ishiguro, K. (2008). Japanese Employment in Transformation: The Growing Number of Non-regular Workers, *electronic journal of contemporary japanese studies.* Available at: http://www.japanesestudies.org.uk/articles/2008/Ishiguro.html, accessed: January 2011.

JILPT (Japan Institute of Labour Policy and Training, 2007). Labor Situation in Japan and Analysis 2006/2007, JILPT Website. Available at: http://www.jil.go.jp/english/lsj.html, accessed: January 2011.

JILPT (Japan Institute of Labour Policy and Training, 2010). Databook of International Labour Statistics, JILPT Website. Available at: http://www.jil.go.jp/english/estatis/databook/index.htm, accessed: January 2011.

JILPT (Japan Institute of Labour Policy and Training, 2010b). Labor Situation in Japan and Analysis 2009/2010, JILPT Website. Available at: http://www.jil.go.jp/english/lsj.html, accessed: January 2011.

Kambayashi, R. (2010). Dismissal Regulation in Japan, Discussion Paper 119, Research Unit for Statistical and Empirical Analysis in Social Sciences (Hi-Stat). Institute of Economic Research, Hitotsubashi University. Available at: http://hermes-ir.lib.hit-u.ac.jp/rs/bitstream/10086/18321/1/gd09-119.pdf, accessed: January 2011.

Kato, T. (2001). The End of Lifetime Employment? Evidence from National Surveys and Field Research. *Journal of the Japanese and International Economies, 15(4),* 489-514.

Kato, T. & Morishima, M. (2002). The Productivity Effects of Participatory

Employment Practices: Evidence from New Japanese Panel Data. *Industrial Relations, 41(4),* 487-520.

Keizer, A. (2008). Non-Regular Employment in Japan: Continued and Renewed Dualities. *Work, Employment and Society, 22(2),* 407-422.

Keizer, A. (2010). *Changes in Japanese Employment Practices: Beyond the Japanese Model.* London: Routledge.

Koike, K. (1996). *The Economics of Work in Japan.* Tokyo: LTCB International Library Foundation.

Kosugi, R. (2003). *Furiitaa to iu ikikata* (The way of life of freeters). Tokyo: Keiso Shobō.

Lincoln, J. R. (1993). Work Organization in Japan and the US. In B. Kogut (Ed.), *Country Competitiveness: Technology and the Organization of Work* . Oxford: Oxford University Press.

Lincoln, J. R. & Nakata, Y. (1997). The Transformation of the Japanese Employment System: Nature, Depth and Origins. *Work and Occupations, 24(1),* 33-55.

Macnaughtan, H. (2006). From 'Post-War' to 'Post-Bubble': Contemporary Issues for Japanese Working Women. In P. Matanle, & W. Lunsing (Eds.), *Perspectives on Work, Employment and Society in Japan.* Basingstoke: PalgraveMacmillan.

Matanle, P. (2003). *Japanese Capitalism and Modernity in a Global Era: Refabricating Lifetime Employment Relations.* London: RoutledgeCurzon.

Matanle, P. (2006a). The Habit of a Lifetime? Japanese and British University Students' Attitudes to Permanent Employment. *Japan Forum, 18(2),* 229-254.

Matanle, P. (2006b). Beyond Lifetime Employment? Re-fabricating Japan's Employment Culture. In P. Matanle, & W. Lunsing (Eds.), *Perspectives on Work, Employment and Society in Japan.* Basingstoke: PalgraveMacmillan.

MHLW (Ministry of Health, Labour and Welfare, Various Years). Chingin kōzō kihon tōkei chōsa (Basic Survey on Wage Structure), MHLW Website. Available at: http://www.mhlw.go.jp/toukei/list/52-19-2.html, accessed: January 2011.

Ministry of Labour (2000). *Rōdō Hakusho* (White Paper on Labour). Tokyo: Ministry of Labour.

Mouer, R. & Kawanishi, H. (2005). *A Sociology of Work in Japan.* Cambridge: Cambridge University Press.

Nara, K. (1997). Sekai junka de kuzureru nihon no shūshin koyōsei (The Collapse of Lifetime Employment into the World Standard). *Kokusai Shōgyō, 30(352),* 12-15.

NKSKK (Nihongata Koyō Shisutemu Kenkyū Kai – Japanese-Style Employment System Research Group, 1995). *Hōkokusho* (Report). Tokyo: Nihongata Koyō Shisutemu Kenkyū Kai.

Nonaka, I. & Takeuchi, H. (1995). *The Knowledge Creating Company: How Japanese Companies Create the Dynamics of Innovation*. New York: Oxford University Press.

NRKK (Nihon Rōdō Kenkyū Kiko – Japan Institute of Labour, 2000). *Deetabukku Kokusai Rōdō Hikaku 2000* (International Labour Comparison Databook). Tokyo: NRKK.

Ohta, S., Genda, Y. & Kondo, A. (2008). The Endless Ice-Age: A Review of the Cohort Effect in Japan. *Japanese Economy, 35(3),* 55-86.

Oliver, N. & Wilkinson, B. (1988). *The Japanization of British Industry*. Oxford: Blackwell.

Ono, H. (2010). Lifetime Employment in Japan: Concepts and Measurements. *Journal of the Japanese and International Economies, 24(1),* 1-27.

Ota, M. (2008). Japan: Towards Employment Extension for Older Workers. In P. Taylor (Ed.), *Ageing Labour Forces: Promises and Prospects*. Cheltenham: Edward Elgar.

Pudelko, M. (2006). A Comparison of HRM Systems in the USA, Japan and Germany in their Socio-economic Context. *Human Resource Management Journal, 16(2),* 123-153.

Rowley, C. & Benson, J. (2002). Convergence and Divergence in Asian Human Resource Management Systems. *California Management Review, 44(2),* 90-109.

Saito, T. & Vuszkun, B. (2010). What is the Lifetime of the 'Lifetime Employment'? Empirical Research from Japan. *Journal of Asia Pacific Studies, 1(3),* 591-614.

Sako, M. (2006). *Shifting Boundaries of the Firm: Japanese Company – Japanese Labour*. Oxford: Oxford University Press.

Sato, H. (2001). Atypical Employment: A Source of Flexible Work Opportunities? *Social Science Japan Journal, 4(2),* 161-181.

Shibata, M. (1999). *Nantoka kaisha wo kaete yarō* (Somehow let's change the company). Tokyo: Nihon Keizai Shinbunsha.

Shimizutani, S. & Yokoyama, I. (2009). Has Japan's Long-Term Employment Practice Survived? Evidence from the 1990s. *Industrial and Labor Relations Review, 62(3),* 313-26.

Statistics Bureau (2011a). Japan Statistical Yearbook 2011, Ministry of Internal Affairs and Communications Statistics Bureau Website. Available at: http://www.stat.go.jp/english/data/nenkan/index.htm, accessed: January 2011.

Statistics Bureau (2011b). Labour Force Survey (Historical Data), Ministry of Internal Affairs and Communications Statistics Bureau Website. Available at: http://www.stat.go.jp/english/data/roudou/lngindex.htm, accessed: February 2011.

Statistics Bureau (Various Years). Historical Statistics of Japan, Ministry of Internal Affairs and Communications Statistics Bureau Website. Available at:

http://www.stat.go.jp/english/data/chouki/index.htm, accessed: January 2011.

Storey, J., Sisson, K. & Edwards, P. (1997). *Managers in the Making: Careers, Development and Control in Corporate Britain and Japan*. London: Sage.

Takahashi, Y. (1997). The Labor Market and Lifetime Employment in Japan. *Economic and Industrial Democracy, 18(1),* 55-66.

Terao, M. (1998). *Denai kui wa suterareru* (Nails that do not stick out are thrown away). Tokyo: Fusosha.

Udagawa, S. (1997). *Jiritsugata shain wo tsukuru senryaku* (A strategy for creating independent-minded employees). Tokyo: Doyukan.

Utsumi, S. (2000). *Sarariiman hōkai* (Fall of the salaryman). Tokyo: Mikkasa Shobō.

Wolff, L. (2008). The Death of Lifelong Employment in Japan? In L. Nottage, L. Wolff, & K. Anderson (Eds.), *Corporate Governance in the 21st Century: Japan's Gradual Transformation.* Cheltenham: Edward Elgar.

The Introduction of Competency Pay in Japan 'Performance in Appraisal and Remuneration'

Arjan B. Keizer

1. Introduction

Over two decades ago Lawler (1990) introduced the concept of 'New Pay' to indicate a new type of reward and performance management which stresses the need to align pay systems to organisational design and, in particular, the organisation's strategy. It fitted the rising importance of strategic human resource management, and the alignment with strategy has informed many developments in performance and reward management since (Bach 2005; Gilman 2009; Redman 2009). Performance appraisal has become widespread and has been extended to new types of organisations, occupational groups, and lower levels of organisational hierarchies. Performance-related pay has seen a similar strong rise in popularity. Moreover, support to business goals has been 'by far the most common objective' for organisations with a reward strategy and the 'need for a link between business objectives and rewards has continued as something of an orthodoxy in leading textbooks on reward' (Kessler 2005: 325). However, the rising popularity has come with a greater awareness of its complications and limitations and the management of performance and rewards remains a major challenge for firms. As pointed out by Price (2004: 529), 'there has been considerable dissatisfaction with the management of pay on both sides of the employment relationship'.

This rise in performance appraisal and performance-related pay has extended to non-Western countries (Redman 2009). However, the latter was long considered problematical within the Japanese context. Koike (1997) argued that 'pay-by-result' plans, just like 'pay-for-job' plans, cannot be effective within Japanese organisations because they do not provide a fair assessment of the skill development so fundamental to their functioning. Employees rewarded for specific results or a particular job position would no longer be motivated to engage with training through job rotation and on-the-job learning as this would negatively affect pay. Similar concerns were expressed by Itoh (1994) and Dore (1998).

Koike instead argued for 'pay-for-skill' plans, a solution that corresponds to the actual employment practices in Japanese firms. They define an internal labour market that rewards employees according to the skills they have acquired as assessed through an ability qualification system (*shokunō shikaku seido*). Elaborate processes for appraisal, known as *satei*, exist but they do not immediately translate into pay and promotion. Instead, employees are motivated through efficiency wages and career concerns. However, in spite of these practices and concerns, performance-related pay, known in Japan as *seikashugi*, can be considered the dominant innovation for the management of regular employees in the last decade (Keizer 2009; Rebick 2005). It raises the question whether performance-related pay can be successfully integrated into the personnel management in Japanese firms.

This chapter aims to answer this question by discussing the introduction of a competency system with performance-related pay at a major electronics firm. The choice for a single case study allows sufficient detail for an in-depth analysis of the implications of change and this case is particularly interesting as it suggests a fundamental transformation. Most firms have introduced performance-related pay by adding management-by-objectives to their existing ability qualification system (Keizer 2009). They therefore continue to allocate pay according to the skills that a person has acquired, albeit in a new combination with performance-related pay. However, the competency system at the case study firm ascribes competencies to specific jobs and this suggests an evolution towards a job-based evaluation. This chapter discusses the extent of these changes and argues that they have not disrupted the firm's personnel management. It illustrates that earlier concerns about the introduction of performance-related and job-related pay in Japan have underestimated the flexibility of Japanese employment practices. Moreover, the insights extend beyond the Japanese situation and may inform the further improvement of appraisal and reward systems. First, the study confirms the need to distinguish the various contingencies of pay – person, job, and performance – as all three can play an important role in a well-balanced personnel system. Secondly, it underlines that strategy is only one – and not necessarily the dominant – factor in developing personnel systems. Other objectives like the ambition to reduce labour cost may provide alternative motivation. Moreover, the firm's institutional context will have a major impact on the 'strategic space' available. This aspect is core to comparative research but often ignored in human resource management studies with their dominant focus on 'strategy'. The chapter argues that this weakens the insights that the latter perspective provides. The structure of this chapter is as follows. The next section discusses the literature on performance appraisal, performance-related pay, and the challenges and problems involved. The subsequent sections focus on Japan by discussing respectively the dominant employment practices, the trend of performance-related pay, and the case study. The remainder will discuss the findings, their implications, and the lessons they may provide.

2. Performance-related Pay and Its Challenges

Both performance appraisal and performance-related pay must be considered a major element of strategic human resource management as they offer a means to relate organisational goals to individual performance (Gilman 2009; Kessler and Purcell 1992). However, this importance has not translated into a straightforward implementation. A first issue concerns the wide range of objectives that may motivate performance appraisal. Redman (2009) lists how it can be used for clarifying and defining performance expectations, identifying training and development needs, providing career counselling, succession planning, improving performance, facilitating communications and involvement, allocating financial rewards, determining promotion, motivating and controlling employees, and achieving cultural change. This is particularly relevant as the objectives are often conflicting. The direction and extent of developments has also been a source of debate. Redman (2009) observes a rise in 'hard' result-oriented types of performance appraisal at the expense of 'softer' developmental approaches. Kessler (2008), on the other hand, describes a 'backlash' in the mid-1990s against the emergence of individual performance-related pay because it is considered rigid, too much focused on specific objectives, and at the expense of inter-personal relations. Bach (2005: 291) also recognises a shift in the 1990s 'from an almost exclusive emphasis on reward driven systems, based on individual performance related pay and quantifiable objectives, toward more rounded systems of performance management with a stronger developmental focus'. A similar ambiguity concerns the take-up of practices with organisations introducing performance-related pay while others abandon or modify earlier initiatives (Gilman 2009).

The rise in performance appraisal and performance-related pay also has increased the awareness of the challenges and problems involved. A first major criticism concerns the aforementioned variety and inconsistency among objectives as a source of many implementation difficulties (Bach 2005; Redman 2009). It may result in overly ambitious systems whose costs are not justified and may cause conflicts between appraised and appraiser. This can also explain why managers are often not comfortable or competent when conducting appraisals (Redman 2009). Moreover, other factors also may affect appraisal negatively. Various 'distorting effects' can be distinguished, including the *Halo*, *Horns*, *Doppelganger*, *Crony*, *Veblen* and *Impression* effect[1]. In addition, there may be a 'recency' bias and gender or ethnic biases (Bach 2005). These issues may be aggravated by more mundane problems like excessive paperwork and the danger that the performance appraisal becomes a 'ritual bureaucratic exercise' (Redman 2009: 188). Particularly serious is the criticism on the power relations involved in appraisal. Analyses usually uphold a unitary perspective which presents appraisal as neutral and beneficial to all those involved. However, the process may allow for tighter managerial control over behaviour and performance (Townley 1999; Coates 1994). This throws new light on the aforementioned problems. Barlow (1989) suggests that the shortcomings of appraisal allow managers the discretion to promote certain individuals while at the same time legitimizing their decisions by referring to the formal process.

Firms have tried to address these problems by developing more objective forms of performance appraisal. The best known strategy concerns the introduction of management-by-objectives. However, problems like the conflicting purposes and subjectivity of appraisal are likely to remain. In addition, there are the challenges to find a balance between different (types of) objectives, to set objectives that cover the whole job, and to redefine objectives in response to changing circumstances (Kessler and Purcell 1992). It is not always possible to set appropriate objectives as 'there are a number of jobs where the measurable is not meaningful, and the meaningful is not measurable' (Wright 1991: 89). Appraisal may also be complicated because of team work or because outside factors have a ma-

1 Redman (2009: 187) provides the following definitions of the various effects: the Halo effect is 'where one positive criterion distorts the assessment of others'; the Horns effect is 'where a single negative aspect dominates the appraisal rating'; the Doppelganger effect is 'where the rating reflects the similarity between appraiser and appraised'; the Crony effect is 'the result of appraisal being distorted by the closeness of the relationship between appraiser and appraised; The Veblen effect – named after Thorstein Veblen who is said to give all his students a 'C' – refers to an outcome whereby 'all those appraised receive middle-order ratings'; Finally, the Impression effect refers to 'the problem of distinguishing actual performance from calculated "impression management"'.

jor influence on outcomes. Several strategies address these problems, including 'forced contributions' that prevent excessive leniency of supervisors and evaluator training on conducting appraisals and potential distorting effects (Bach 2005). However, these strategies reduce but do not solve the various problems.

Another innovation concerns the introduction of a competency system. Armstrong and Murlis (2004: 291) define competency-related pay as a method of rewarding people 'by reference to the level of competence they demonstrate in carrying out their roles' (Armstrong and Murlis 2004: 291). It differs from performance-related pay because it not just focuses on outcomes but also on *how* they are achieved (Armstrong 1999; Kessler 2008). Several advantages are ascribed to competency-related pay. First, as competencies are related to the entire job, they can provide a detailed appraisal of the achievements and progress of the employee and thus address the danger that management-by-objectives distorts overall job performance. In addition, it supports the provision of feedback and overcomes 'one of the problems of traditional objective-based appraisal systems in which the appraiser is often at a loss as to how to counsel an employee on what they should do differently if the appraisal objectives have not been achieved' (Redman 2009: 186). However, competency-related pay is also not without its problems. A first issue concerns the developing and running costs involved (Redman 2009). More fundamental, the definition, even the spelling, of competencies has proved rather contentious. Brown and Armstrong (1999) distinguish between hard competences as the standards that people are expected to attain and softer competencies as the behaviour that supports competent performance. Insightful is the distinction between the input (capabilities), process (behaviours) and output (performance) aspects of competency/competence (e.g. Armstrong 1999; Neathey and Reilly 2003). It illustrates how the concept may refer to various aspects, with rather different implications, and firms often follow a mixed approach (ibid). Whatever, the precise approach taken, many challenges of performance appraisal like different objectives and the subjectivity of assessment remain.

A final issue is the supposed link between strategy and remuneration and the contribution of performance-related pay to the motivation of employee behaviour in support of business objectives. Authors question the beneficiary effects on motivation as the evidence linking strategy, reward systems and corporate performance remains scarce (Gilman 2009; Kessler 2005). Even when performance-related pay motivates certain employees they may very well constitute a minority and the effect may be outweighed by a de-motivation of others (e.g. Marsden, French and Kobi 2000; Rice 2004). In addition, it is debated how successful organisations are in linking pay to strategy and whether isomorphic pressures are dominant (Kessler 2008). In accordance, the assumption of a direct link between pay practices and employee outcomes may actually hinder insight in the processes involved as '[t]he contested nature of appraisal, the specific managerial objectives sought, and the nature of the context in which it is applied, all have an important bearing on the impact of the appraisal process' (Bach 2005: 306). The development of appraisal and reward systems therefore has to take the social, political and cultural context into account (DiMaggio and Powell 1991; Morishima 1995; Oliver 1997). In addition, we need to recognise other considerations than the alignment of incentives with business strategies. Gilman (2009) lists alternative objectives like a restructuring of the employment relationship, an adjustment to a lack of promotional positions, and the attempt to decentralise collective bargaining or to marginalise trade unions. Labour costs can be important as organisations may introduce performance-related pay because of budget considerations (Rice 2004).

These issues motivate a closer look at the various factors that can determine pay. As illustrated by Koike's (1997) discussion, we can distinguish at least three contingencies for the determination of appraisal and remuneration; namely, personal, job and performance characteristics. Organisations often link their reward structure to two or all three contingencies because they offer different ways to assess 'performance' in a world of bounded rationality:

> "Generally performance refers to outputs and pay can be linked to the achievement of individual or group targets and objectives. However, pay can also be linked to inputs and these are often intimately related to the person, what they, as individuals, bring to the role in terms of skill, knowledge and behaviour. It is at this point that the notions of performance and person overlap. These individual features and abilities might be seen as representing the basis for an assumed or 'promised' level performance." (Kessler 2005: 321)

The three contingencies also throw light on the character of competency systems. Redman (2009) links their adoption to a shift from job-related towards person-related performance criteria. However, the extent of this shift is not a given. Brown and Armstrong (1999) point out how competencies can be used to assess both jobs and individuals. It confirms that organisations have substantial discretion when introducing competency-related pay as it allows them to mix the various contingencies of pay in accordance with the previous reference to input, process and result aspects. We thus see that the practices of performance appraisal and performance-related pay continue to suffer from various fundamental and operational challenges. Important trade-offs exist when developing systems for performance management; for example between the advantages of more detailed appraisal versus the greater costs and manipulating behaviour it may inspire. This is reflected in the assessment of their success. Redman (2009) states how in the early 1990s performance appraisal was already considered 'doomed' (Halachmi 1993) and a practice 'whose time has gone' (Bhote 1994; Fletcher 1993). This has not prevented a general rise in these practices but has affected confidence in their success (Bach 2005). It underlines the remaining challenge in developing successful systems for performance and reward management. The subsequent sections discuss how developments in Japan can provide an answer to this challenge.

3. Japanese Employment Practices and Performance-related Pay

The specificity of Japanese employment practices has been well-documented (e.g. Aoki 1988; Itoh 1994; Koike 1997). Core to firms' personnel management has been the internal labour market defined by a ranking hierarchy 'in which the remuneration paid to an employee depends on his or her rank and internal promotion from lower to higher ranks is based on a certain formalized standard (Aoki 1988: 72). It makes for a dual hirarchy as these ranks are determined through the ability qualification system that does not evaluate employees for their job position but for their acquired skills. The resulting framework motivates through efficiency wages and promotions rather than incentive pay. Efficiency wages are set higher than market wages to provide a financial reward for 'honest' behaviour, for performing in accordance with the requirements of the organisation. If employees are likely to see their income decrease when 'cheating' is detected, they may refrain from doing so. It may not even be necessary to pay higher wages than other firms given the danger of unemployment after dismissal. This holds in particular for the Japanese situation characterised by a strong labour market duality that may force employees to accept work in the much less attractive secondary market of non-regular employment after dismissal (Keizer 2008). Moreover, social norms strengthen the ambition to maintain employment in a country where the practice of lifetime employment has developed into a normative model (Dore 1973). The relevance of efficiency wages is magnified by the provision of career paths that provide 'incentives for loyalty, honesty, and hard work...by the promise of high future wages' (Milgrom and Roberts 1992: 258). The relevance of career concerns is confirmed by Lazear (1979), who interprets seniority wages as an example of 'bonding' where the bond is 'the sum of money that is forfeited in the event that inappropriate behaviour is detected' (Milgrom and Roberts 1992: 189). Young employees are paid less than their productive value in order to create the possibility for high seniority wages above productive value. This motivates them to refrain from shirking and compete for promotions that determine the distribution of future wages. Itoh (1994) therefore speaks of a 'late-selection approach' in which 'career concerns' act as an incentive device. In this context, promotions serve a dual role. They not only assign employees to the roles or positions in which they best contribute to the organisation's performance but also serve as an incentive and reward mechanism.

Personal appraisal has long played a major role in this internal labour market as shown by Endo's (1994) discussion of the appraisal in Japanese organisations known as *satei*. However, this appraisal is specific to the requirements of the personnel system and Endo lists several aspects in which *satei* differed from merit ratings in US companies. It did not only assess 'factors such as (a) past performance that can be assessed objectively but also factors for which no clear objective standards can be established, such as (b) a worker's eagerness to perform his or her job, his or her attitude as a work group and team member, and (c) his or her potential ability to perform jobs more effectively' (Endo 1994: 70). As a matter of fact, the appraisal emphasised the latter two factors and Endo therefore translates *satei* as 'personal assessment'. This not only confirms the focus on personal skills but also the strong incentives it provides. Endo (1994: 77) describes how the system creates strong competition among workers as '*satei* results in a large variance in promotion and monthly pay between workers'. Moreover, its impact appears to have grown because of the rising importance ascribed to ability with the introduction of the ability qualification system at the end of the 1960s to complement the seniority rule – in particular since the system received an important boost during the 1970s when the first oil crisis motivated management to tighten the criteria for promotion and limit pay rises (Holzhausen 2000). This development is confirmed by the data on wage-tenure profiles that show the diminishing importance of seniority on remuneration (e.g. Ariga *et al.* 2000; JILPT 2007a).

The approach may seem overly complicated compared to more straightforward types of incentive pay. However, efficiency wages and career concerns can offer important advantages when perfect monitoring of behaviour and outcomes is impossible. First, efficiency wages tend to provide greater income security for employees than types of performance-related pay, thus motivating risk averse employees to accept lower wages. In accordance, incentive contracts are not always possible as lower-level employees would lack sufficient income in case of poor performance. Secondly, the use of efficiency wages can function with less precise types of appraisal as a relative ranking of employees is sufficient for a system that rewards employees through promotions (Milgrom and Roberts 1992). It also reduces the subjectivity of evaluation and the impact of outside factors as both aspects are often shared among those being appraised. Finally, employers are less tempted to raise performance standards after a period of good performance (the 'ratchet effect') in order to save money (Ibid).

In spite of these arguments there has been a strong increase in the use of performance-related pay in Japan. The early years of the twentieth century saw a long string of Japanese and English publications regarding its introduction (e.g. Fukase 2001; Morishima 2002; Nihon Keieisha Dantairenmei Shuppanbu 2001; Rōmu Gyōsei Kenkyūjo 2000; Utanabe 2000; Yamaguchi and Tsureta 2001). Moreover, the majority of firms have introduced a form of performance-related pay. Research by the JILPT in 2004 found that 57.8 per cent of all firms had introduced *seikashugi*, with the percentage rising to 74.0 per cent among firms with more than a thousand regular employees (JILPT 2005). A survey by the Ministry of Economy, Trade and Industry (METI) in 2003 found that 77 per cent of firms used individual performance as an element for determining salary (Jackson 2007). Two important instruments have been recognised to constitute this development. Under an 'annual wage system', known as *nenpōsei*, wages are determined by comparing the employee's performance to certain goals set at the beginning of the year. This system initially received much attention and achieved important growth in the 1990s but the trend has slowed down and its introduction is often limited to higher management (JILPT 2007b). More widespread has been the introduction of generic management-by-objectives, usually known as *mokuhyō kanri seido*. Matanle (2003) discusses how it was already introduced by certain firms in the late 1960s and early 1970s but had little impact on the personnel management. However, this has changed since the 1990s and by 2001 almost 70 per cent of firms had implemented management-by-objectives while another 22.5 per cent was either planning or studying its introduction (Seisansei Rōdō Jōhō Sentā 2002).

Few doubts exist about the motivation behind the introduction of performance-related pay. Keizer (2009) finds various reasons including the rise in the average age of employees, the decrease in promotional positions, and the imbalance that exists under the combination of the traditional ability-based system and an excess number of senior employees. But these reasons can all be grouped under the need to reduce labour costs. The ability qualification systems in the pre-*seikashugi* period was supply-side oriented as it required that employees who have improved their skills are promoted to positions that make use of these skills and justify the higher wages (Imano 1995). This was long successful but firms have struggled to create the positions required in the context of diminished organisational growth and an ageing population. The introduction of performance-related pay has enabled them to address the resulting rise in labour costs as it rewards employees for their actual contribution rather than the potential productivity of their skills. This motivation is widely acknowledged and performance-related pay has been described as a 'cover for wage restraint' (Vogel 2006: 13) or a way 'to offset the costs of no lay-off policies' (Jacoby 2004: 63).

In spite of the strong trend and the overwhelming and shared motivation in terms of costs, the introduction of performance-related pay raises some important questions. A first issue concerns its integration with the existing employment practices that define the internal labour market. As mentioned, authors like Koike (1997) and Dore (1998) have questioned the possibility to introduce performance-related pay within the Japanese context. A second question concerns the generic challenges of performance appraisal and performance-related pay as discussed in the previous section. Both issues underline the need to critically investigate the introduction of performance-related pay within the Japanese context and the case study of a major electronics firm in the next section will enable us to do so. As mentioned, it provides an excellent example of testing the implications of change because the competency system promises an overhaul of the existing practices. Ability is no longer attributed to individual employees but required competencies are set for the performance of each job.

4. The Introduction of a Competency System

This case study describes the changes in personnel management at a major electronics firm which produces a wide range of products including computer hardware and software, network infrastructures and communication equipment like mobile phones. At the turn of the century the firm was strongly affected by the weak Japanese economy and the strong emergence of Asian competitors with superior cost advantages. Results improved in the following years but sales did not recover and net income remained low or negative. The data for the case study were collected during two studies among Japanese firms in 2002 and 2007 through interviews with representatives of the firm's personnel department and additional personnel documents such as evaluation forms. The case study is included in greater detail in Keizer (2009: 80-91) as part of a discussion on changes in Japanese employment practices.

The firm has introduced two different though highly similar systems for managerial and non-managerial or union employees. This case study focuses on the latter as it can be considered more fundamental to the overall functioning of its personnel management. The current system for non-managerial employees was introduced in 2000 and sets a 'conduct-standards-document' known as 'practice file' for each role/function. This describes the 'competencies' for that specific function. The files have been set after analysing the characteristic behaviour and skills of people who produce good results (best practice) by evaluating the sorts of behaviour (ways of working) that produce results and the skills (qualifications, language abilities, etc.) required. The practice files consist of two major parts: a 'platform practice' and 'professional practice'. The items for platform practice are core competencies common to all non-managerial employees and include the following: (1) corporate ethics or moral; (2) profit orientation; (3) customer orientation; (4) autonomy or self-management; (5) collaboration; (6) challenges; and (7) sense of responsibility or initiative. The precise definition of these items is specific to occupational groups and job grades. The items for professional practice are dependent upon work, position and department. Table 1 offers a partial example of a professional practice. It shows how generic items like ‘model behaviour’ are further specified. This process of specification takes place at the level of the business unit and the department.

Table 1: Partial example of a professional practice

Major item	***Medium item***	***Minor item***	***Behavioural criteria***
Model behaviour	Sales promotion	Grasp of markets	Understands the business strategy of other companies, draws up a competitive sales strategy for our company.
		Planning	Clarifies concepts in a manner that relates to the keynote business strategy.
	Planning, proposals	Information collection	Draws connections between regular conversations with customers and available market trend information, gives shape to customers’ vague needs.
		Distillation of issues	Sets topics not from within own experience and common knowledge but from a stance with a wide viewpoint.
		Proposals	Has a strategy for users and endeavours to always have ‘answers’ that satisfy customers and produce profit to the company.
Qualifications acquired			Data processing expert test, etc.
Training attended			3 of the designated training courses.
Linguistic skills			TOEIC 470 points or higher.

The practice file is core to the evaluation of employees as it defines the standards by which their skills, behaviour and performance are assessed. Figure 1 shows the logic of the evaluation process, together with the link from evaluation to compensation and promotion. The personnel review consists of a competency/career review and a performance review. In the competency/career review the behaviour and skill levels of the employee are evaluated in relation to the requirements as formulated in the practice files. This determines the grade of the employee and thus promotion. Because the fulfilment of requirements is a prerequisite for promotion to the next level, the supervisors' evaluations and consultations with the employees are perceived crucial. For this purpose, both the employee and the supervisor provide their input after which consultation takes place and the review is described as *'a mechanism for competency evaluation, training and career development through dialogue between the employee and the employee's boss'*. The role of the practice file is threefold and repeats the advantages that the literature ascribes to competency systems. It not only provides the criteria for evaluation but also makes employees aware of their own aptitudes and strengths, provides the objectives to improve behaviour in accordance with the practice requirements, and forms the basis for a career-development plan.

During the performance review the employee's performance is assessed against objectives set through a management-by-objectives system. The procedure is as follows. Every six months three to five objectives are set and registered on a management-by-objectives form that is specifically prepared by each business unit. Figure 2 provides a representative example. It shows how the difficulty levels of the various objectives are taken into account. The appraisal produces one of the following outcomes (from high to low): S – A – B – C – D. Percentages are ascribed for the distribution of these assessments with the actual percentages depending on occupational group and job grade. The procedure also allows for a change in objectives or the development of additional objectives during the period under evaluation. Employees initially enter both the results of the previous half-year and the objectives for the upcoming half-year before a consultation is held with their direct supervisor. This provides the input for the actual evaluation and the results are then communicated to the employee.

The lower half of Figure 1 indicates the impact on compensation and promotion. The competency/career review, in reference to the conditions for promotion as determined by the practice files, determines the grade of the employee and thus promotion. Together with the performance evaluation, this 'class rating' also determines the monthly income.

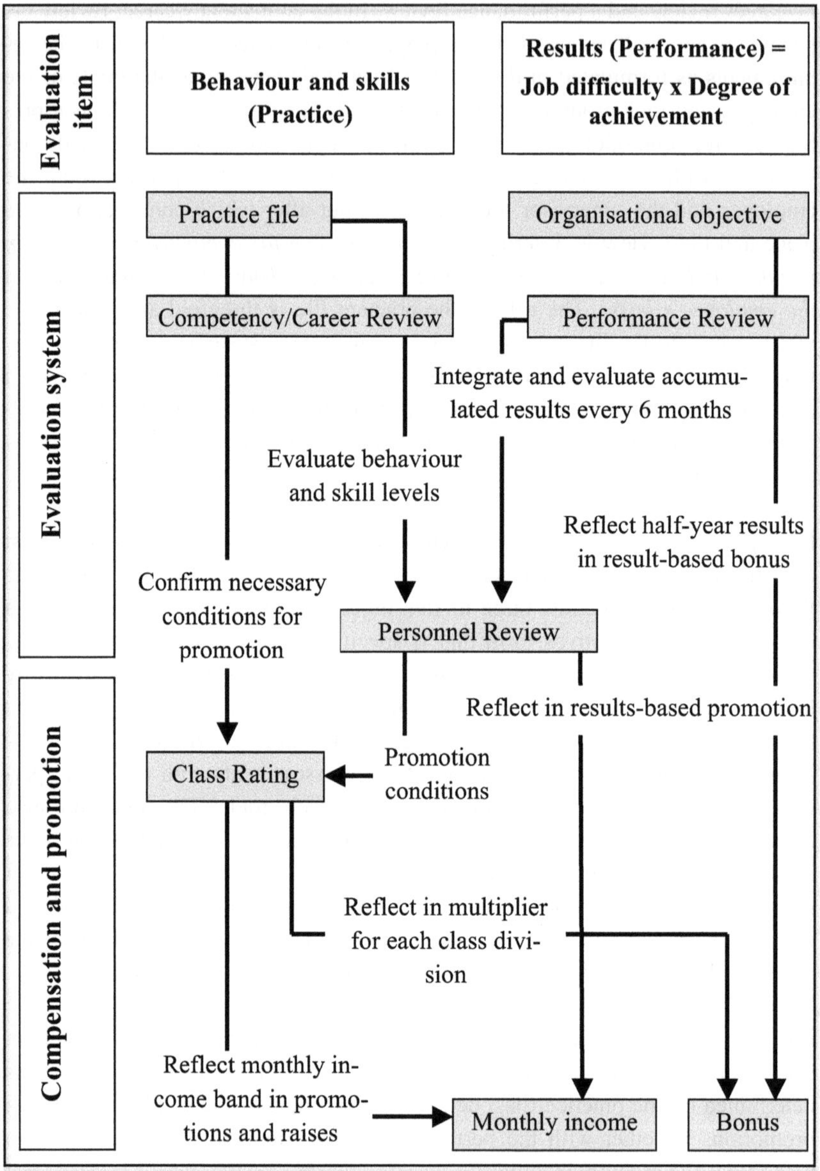

Figure 1: Evaluation and treatment process

<table>
<tr><td colspan="4">OBJECTIVES FOR THE FIRST HALF OF 200X (If the boss judges the objectives to be below the expected level, they shall be revised upward upon discussion. The employee under review shall enter the revisions in the column for objective revisions.)</td></tr>
<tr><td colspan="2">This section to be filled out by employee under review</td><td colspan="2">This section to be filled out by immediate supervisor</td></tr>
<tr><td colspan="2">Main work objectives; Specific content/ objective promotion plan; revisions</td><td colspan="2">Difficulty level of objectives</td></tr>
<tr><td colspan="2">1.</td><td colspan="2">S □ Very difficult
A □ Difficult
B □ Average
C □ Below average</td></tr>
<tr><td colspan="2">Objectives 2 -5</td><td colspan="2">S – A – B - C</td></tr>
<tr><td colspan="2">3.</td><td colspan="2">S – A – B - C</td></tr>
<tr><td colspan="2">4.</td><td colspan="2">S – A – B - C</td></tr>
<tr><td colspan="2">5.</td><td colspan="2">S – A – B - C</td></tr>
<tr><td colspan="2">Comments of immediate superior (enter specific details expected and information to comments of immediate supervisor)</td><td colspan="2">Comments of top superior (enter supplemental supple-mentation of difficulty level)</td></tr>
<tr><td colspan="4">EVALUATION OF RESULTS AND PERFORMANCE IN SECOND HALF OF 200X</td></tr>
<tr><td colspan="2">This section to be filled out by employee under review</td><td colspan="2">This section to be filled out by immediate supervisor</td></tr>
<tr><td>Main work objectives; Specific details results/performance</td><td>Self-evaluation (targeted results/ performance)</td><td>Difficulty level of objectives</td><td>Achievement of results / performance</td></tr>
<tr><td>1.
(No further objectives 2 – 5)</td><td>S □ Achieved more than expected
A □ Sufficiently achieved
B □ Achieved
C □ Nearly achieved
D □ Not achieved</td><td>S □ Very high
A □ High
B □ Average
C □ Below average</td><td>S □ Achieved more than expected
A □ Sufficiently achieved
B □ Achieved
C □ Nearly achieved
D □ Not achieved</td></tr>
<tr><td>Objectives 2-5</td><td>S – A – B – C - D</td><td>S – A – B - C</td><td>S – A – B – C - D</td></tr>
<tr><td colspan="2">Points for improvement / comments</td><td colspan="2">Overall evaluation: S□ A□ B□ C□ D□</td></tr>
<tr><td colspan="2">Immediate Superior's comments (Enter supplementary information concerning achievement of results/performance)</td><td colspan="2">Top Superior - Overall Evaluation – Comments (Enter supplemental information to immediate superior's comments)</td></tr>
</table>

Figure 2: Performance evaluation sheet

The new salary system includes 'broadbanding', a practice that fits the introduction of competency-related pay. It means that 'large numbers of individually rated jobs or job types are clustered into a few, much wider job classifications or "bands"' (Rice 2004: 538). A monthly income band is established for each occupational group and grade. These bands are further divided into three zones and a raise-table is set for each zone. The tables are designed so that as the level rises, the amount of the raise becomes smaller in relation to the evaluation. In other words, a high evaluation will result in a high raise in the lower Zone I but not so much in the higher Zone III. It is important to point out that the process is automatic. In other words, any evaluation (e.g. S or A) automatically translates into a certain salary (given the occupational group, job grade and zone).

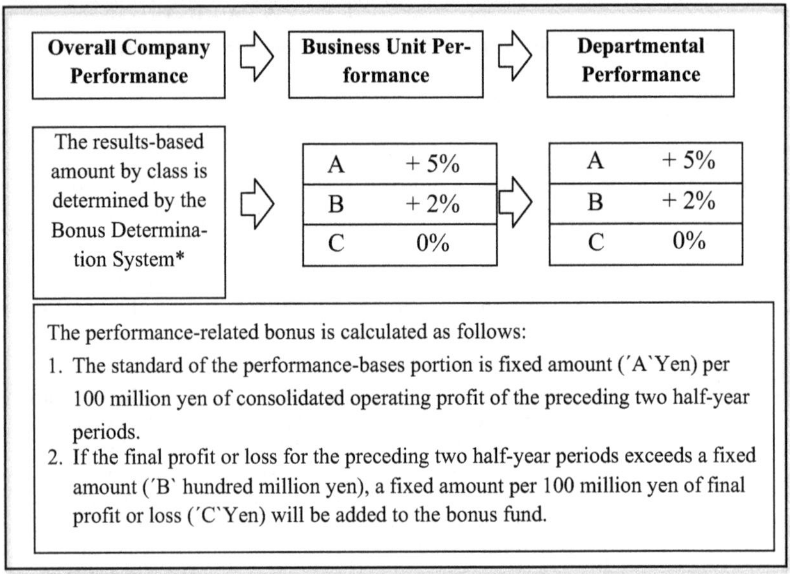

Figure 3: Determination performance-related bonuses union employees

Finally, the performance review co-determines the bi-annual bonuses, which has a fixed and a performance-dependent part. In fiscal year 2007 the fixed part was four times the employee's monthly income. The performance part depends on overall company performance, business unit performance, and departmental (operating division) performance through the procedure as shown in Figure 3.

Before 2006 the variation among business units and departments was larger but it was felt that the employees working in a certain division have little choice to work somewhere else while outside factors are very important in influencing the performance of that division. The higher percentages were therefore seen as diminishing rather than strengthening motivation. The actual allocation of the bonuses over individual members is determined by the supervisor and this makes for an interesting difference with the determination of monthly income where the process is automatic. In the case of bonuses the supervisor has leeway to translate the individual appraisal into a relative ranking because it is very well possible that large numbers of employees will have a similar evaluation outcome (e.g. S or A).

As mentioned, the firm has introduced a rather similar system for managerial employees. Since 2002 these employees are evaluated and rewarded according to a 'job grade' system that focuses on the size of the jobs being filled. As for non-managerial employees, the jobs are evaluated in terms of 'practice' and performance. More in particular, three factors determine the grade of each job: (1) a required professional practice; (2) a leadership practice; and (3) the responsibility for results. The professional practice is determined by choosing the seven most relevant behavioural standards from a list of 13 including, for example, 'cutting loss by being thorough when training', 'resolving problems through trial and error', and 'creating value through creativity and innovation'. Secondly, the leadership practice is defined by seven additional behavioural standards like 'pro-activeness', 'speed', and 'innovation'. Finally, the responsibility for results is specified by distinguishing (1) the preparation of strategies/policies; (2) the execution of work; and (3) the maintenance of the organisation. All these factors also determine evaluation and compensation. An employee's allocation to a certain grade and the position within the salary band is determined by the practice and performance evaluation. Performance objectives are set every six months in accordance with the 'responsibility for results' and their achievement determines the performance bonus. The actual bonus depends on a combination of company, business unit, departmental and individual performance. Average bonuses are distributed to the divisions and then allocated over the individual workers by the supervisor.

In implementing the new personnel system, the firm has paid elaborate attention to the process and quality of appraisal. It was already pointed out that a dialogue between the employee and his or her supervisor is considered crucial to the personnel review. In addition, several factors contribute to the quality of the evaluation. This, for example, includes the elaborate procedure for determining job descriptions; the inclusion of regular communication, coaching, and the development of trust; the explanation of evaluations and comments to the employee by the supervisor; feedback by higher-ranking to lower-ranking supervisors; and a complaint system whereby the personnel department speaks to the employee and supervisor separately. In addition, the firm has introduced various forms of training to improve the skills of supervising managers. A 'Practice Management Course' teaches the important aspects of the personnel system and covers topics like the function of the practice files, the appropriate role and actions to be taken by supervisors in the personnel review, and the implications in terms of salary, bonuses and promotion. In addition, there is specific training on two-way communication for new managers and on managerial coaching.

5. Discussion

The case study firm has introduced major changes in its personnel management of non-managerial and managerial employees. Competencies and management-by-objectives have replaced the ability qualification system. In accordance, the basis for pay has shifted from the individual's skills towards the job characteristics and the achievement of specific objectives. Wages are thus more closely related to actual performance. However, the implications appear not as fundamental as suggested by earlier analyses (e.g. Koike 1997). The 'practice files' take a position between workers and jobs as the successful qualification for platform and professional practices has a rather stable character. The competency/skill review determines the grade of an employee in relation to the practices and these grades are deemed permanent and thus guarantee certain wages. Training and qualifications remain crucial for promotion because of the required qualifications included in the professional practice. Given the close link between practice files and the recognition of individual skills, the shift is therefore not as binary as the distinction between job-based and person-based pay may suggest. This can be directly related to the character of the competency system in-between these types of pay and it can therefore be considered a rather natural extension of the existing employment practices. It agrees with the assessment that competencies can refer to input (capabilities), process (behaviours) and even output (performance) (e.g. Armstrong 1999; Neathey and Reilly 2003). In particular the more behavioural core competencies of the platform practice sit well with the established importance of more subjective factors during *satei*.[2] These aspects constrain the impact of performance on remuneration. A similar argument holds for management employees whose ability in terms of the achieved job grade also tends to be cumulative.

The findings enable an answer to the two questions posed on the introduction of performance-related pay by Japanese firms. The first concerns the integration of the new practices within the internal labour market. The case study illustrates how the flexibility of Japanese employment practices surpasses earlier expectations, a finding that can be considered representative of the developments at other firms. The details of performance-related pay differ substantially among firms but they are confronted with the similar challenge to include performance-related pay among their existing employment practices and the case study therefore allows for analytical generalisation (Yin 1994). However, this flexibility co-exists with stability. The continued support for the practice of lifetime employment means that the internal labour market has remained rather closed to outsiders. Moreover, with a reduction in regular employment, the positions in the internal labour market have become even more precious as they usually remain the sole entrance to a career in management (Keizer 2008). In accordance, the motivation through efficiency wages remains strong. The lack of organisational growth has reduced promotional positions but this is partly compensated for by the reduced percentage of regular employees. The introduction of competency- and performance-related pay has added new factors for evaluation, and thus contributed to the composite character of the appraisal and reward system, but has not fundamentally altered this internal labour market. Moreover, with few complaints about the quality and commitment of employees, the effects of the changed circumstances on the motivation of Japanese employees appear to have been limited. This confirms the current consensus that firms have been relatively successful in adapting their employment practices (e.g. Inagami and Whittaker 2005).

2 Several authors have actually described competency-related pay as an extension of skill-related pay systems (e.g. Brown and Armstrong 1999) and an equivalent to skill-related pay systems that is better suited to managerial, professional and administrative staff (Armstrong 1999).

The second issue concerns the generic challenges involved in performance appraisal and performance-related pay of which some are particularly relevant in the Japanese setting. The organisation of work, characterized by broad job descriptions, fluidity of jurisdiction and teamwork, aggravates the difficulties involved in measuring individual performance and the danger that employees focus on a limited number of objectives at the expense of overall efficiency. Other potential problems such as conflicts between appraiser and appraised and 'distorting effects' like the *Halo* and *Doppelganger* effect are particularly serious in a setting where lifetime employment makes it difficult if not impossible for employees to switch employers.[3] The case study firm has introduced various strategies to address these problems. This holds in particular for the competency system that compensates for the danger that management-by-objectives distorts overall job performance. Moreover, it has brought a new balance between job- and person-based appraisal and remuneration, with performance-related pay just one aspect of the overall personnel system.[4] What results is a 'mixed' model which rewards employees on the basis of skills, behaviours and outputs; an approach similar to the 'pay for contribution' approach as distinguished by Brown and Armstrong (1999). Moreover, the care in the development of the new system, the importance of dialogue in evaluation, and the training to supervisors all contribute to a fair process. The forced distribution in appraisal outcomes addresses the danger of inflation in feedback. An important advantage seems that large Japanese firms, including the case study firm, already had a well-developed system of performance appraisal to build upon (Aoki 1988; Endo 1993). The costs and bureaucracy of the very elaborate systems are substantial but this is therefore not something new. Finally, the firm acknowledges certain limitations of performance-related pay by limiting its introduction among more junior employees. The decision to reduce the percentages for the weighing of business unit and departmental performance is also illustrative of the awareness that misplaced performance appraisal may de-motivate.

3 An infamous example of the dangers is the introduction of performance-related pay at Fujitsu in 1993. As discussed by Jo (2004), this resulted in lower morale as many employees received average or low evaluations and compromised job performance because they focused on the objectives rewarded by the evaluation system at the expense of other responsibilities (Inagami and Whittaker 2005; Tatsumichi and Morishima 2007; Vogel 2006).

4 An important issue concerns the impact of performance on pay. Unfortunately, this is hard to assess. First of all, the impact of performance differs between grades and positions and this makes it almost impossible to give an overall assessment. Moreover, firms are often not willing to share this kind of information and the data is therefore fragmented at best.

Challenges do remain, as the dangers of distorting effects and subjectivity are ever-present. A particular aspect concerns the need for more explicit promotional criteria as required by both the competency system and management-by-objectives. The interviewees during the first study in 2002 expressed concern that this could affect the flexibility of the internal labour market and the motivation it provides. The second study in 2007 suggested that the changes had been well accepted and the competency approach appears to capture the more subjective aspects that tended to characterise the process of *satei*. However, the concerns remain relevant. Moreover, as the focus remains on developed skills and motivation through career concerns, the internal labour market remains supply-side oriented and thus requires the creation of promotional positions. The new criteria for promotion may have addressed the previous lack of sufficient positions but the potential problem still exists – in particular as organisational flexibility may require a certain ambiguity or subjectivity in promotions to enable the firm to adjust to changing circumstances. But this flexibility is limited by the need for objective appraisal procedures. It illustrates an important efficiency trade-off when criteria for evaluation become more explicit. Moreover, it can explain why the implications of *seikashugi* have not been as revolutionary as once expected as it suggests a limit to the introduction of performance-related pay (JILPT 2005). Future developments have to show the extent of this constraint.

6. Implications and Lessons

The current perception of Japanese employment practices is far removed from the critical acclaim in the 1980s and 1990s. Although they continue to inspire 'high performance' management practices (Doeringer *et al.* 2003), the practices have lost their shine in the faltering Japanese economy. However, recent years have seen important innovations in personnel management like the introduction of competencies and performance-related pay. The flexibility in employment practices has been surprisingly large with firms making fairly substantial adjustments while, at the same time, upholding the conventional employment logic based on internal labour markets and long-term employment relations. This suggests a positive assessment of Japanese employment practices. The practices may have lost some of their initial advantages but this can be related to the specific circumstances in the post-war decades when their success was closely tied to the success of the Japanese economy. At the same time, firms like the case study example have developed a highly sophisticated personnel system. It has obviously not solved all the challenges involved in the development of a personnel system but is in many ways as refined as one can expect. The long-term success of the new employment practices remains to be seen and will depend on the wider circumstances within the Japanese economy but firms appear to have acknowledged and addressed the major challenges of performance appraisal and reward.

The case study also illustrates how the outcome remains specific to Japan, a conclusion that is shared by others (Inagami and Whittaker 2005; Jacoby 2004; Vogel 2006). The introduction of competency- and/or performance-related pay may suggest convergence but the innovations are embedded within the internal labour market characterised by long-term skill development and motivation through efficiency wages and career concerns. At the same time, the discussion can offer several insights for the study on human resource management, performance appraisal, competency systems, and performance-related pay. At least three issues stand out. First, the study confirms the need to take all three contingencies of pay – job, person and performance – into account when developing an appraisal and reward system in a world where perfect measures of behaviour and performance are rare. In the case study firm, all three contingencies of pay are covered and it thus shows what such a balance may look like. The relevance of performance is obvious in the use of management-by-objectives which determines the performance-related component of the bonus and also has a minor impact on monthly income. The other two contingencies are covered through the competency system. Its introduction implies a shift in evaluation from personal skills towards job characteristics but this shift is far from complete and the competency system has taken an 'in-between' position between job and person. The latter aspect is particularly interesting as Japanese firms have arrived at the concept of competency-related pay from an opposite direction compared to many Western firms with a tradition of job-based internal labour markets (Doeringer & Piore 1971). The latter tend to reward employees in accordance to the job they hold rather than the skills they have developed. This shows when we compare the developments at the case study firm to discussions that present the adoption of a competency system as a shift from job-related to person-related performance criteria (Redman 2009). The Japanese example can thus provide 'inspiration by extrapolation' about the meaning and implications of competency-related pay.

The other two issues that stand out from the discussion are strongly related. The first concerns the link between the reward system and strategy. The findings illustrate that the doubts about the strength of this relation are warranted. Within the specific Japanese context of the last decade, the introduction of performance-related pay has been almost exclusively motivated by the ambition to control labour costs. This motivation can possibly be rephrased as a change in strategy but it is very different in character to the customary rhetoric of strategic human resource management. It links to a third insight about the relevance of institutional embeddedness in the development of personnel systems. The rise of performance-related pay in Japan makes perfectly clear that firms need to take the social, political and cultural context into account. Its introduction has enabled firms to uphold the core practice of lifetime employment while at the same time providing an acceptable means to address the escalation of labour costs by 'justifying' a reduction in pay and change in promotional patterns (Jacoby 2004). Moreover, the same practices make the changes possible as the continued support for lifetime employment and the internal labour market has substantiated the flexibility to handle the introduction of competency- and performance-related pay. It confirms that the national context shapes the 'strategic space' of firms as conformance with national employment practices offers crucial advantages (see e.g. Hall and Soskice 2001; Marsden 1999). Moreover, the complementary relation between the stability of lifetime employment and the inherent flexibility of internal labour markets agrees with arguments about the trade-offs between different types of flexibility and stability (Aoki 1990; Atkinson 1987; Blyton and Turnbull 2004; Regini 2000).

These aspects underline the complex challenges of performance and reward management. Any approach that presents a direct and dominant causal link with strategy while ignoring aspects like equality and embeddedness underestimates these complexities involved and thus hinders rather than strengthens analysis. Firms need to balance the different objectives of their personnel system and the different contingencies for remuneration. As mentioned by Kessler (2005: 322) 'It is this search for what organizations and other stakeholders feel is the "right balance" between pay and the three contingencies which provides the dynamic for pay developments'. Many Japanese firms, like the case study firm, have engaged with this search in response to their difficult situation in the underperforming Japanese economy. It has produced an impressive mix that combines job-, skill- and performance-related pay. These firms have obviously not solved the fundamental challenges of performance appraisal and performance-related pay but, for that particular reason, can offer important insights in processes of appraisal and remuneration.

7. References

Aoki, M. (1988). *Information, Incentives and Bargaining in the Japanese Economy.* Cambridge: Cambridge University Press.

Aoki, M. (1990). Toward an Economic Model of the Japanese Firm. *Journal of Economic Literature, 28(1)*, 1-27.

Ariga, K., Brunello, G. & Ohkusa, Y. (2000). *Internal Labor Markets in Japan.* Cambridge: Cambridge University Press.

Armstrong, M. (1999). *Employee Reward* (2nd Edition). London: Institute of Personnel and Development.

Armstrong, M. & Murlis, H. (2004). *Reward Management: A Handbook of Remuneration Strategy and Practice* (5th Edition). London: Kogan Page Limited.

Atkinson, J. (1987). Flexibility or Fragmentation? The United Kingdom Labour Market in the Eighties. *Labour and Society, 12(1)*, 87-105.

Bach, S. (2005). New Directions in Performance Management. In S. Bach (Ed.), *Managing Human Resources: Personnel Management in Transition* (4th Edition) (pp. 289-316). Malden, MA: Blackwell Publishing.

Barlow, G. (1989). Deficiencies and the Perpetuation of Power: Latent Functions in Management Appraisal. *Journal of Management Studies, 26(5)*, 499-517.

Bhote, K. R. (1994). Boss Performance Appraisal: A Metric Whose Time has Gone. *Employment Relations Today, 21(1)*, 1-8.

Blyton, P., & Turnbull, P. (2004). *The Dynamics of Employee Relations* (3rd Edition). Houndmills, Basingstoke: Palgrave MacMillan.

Brown, D. & Armstrong, M. (1999). *Paying for Contribution: Real Performance-related Pay Strategies.* London: Kogan Page Limited.

Coates, G. (1994). Performance Appraisal as Icon: Oscar-winning Performance or Dressing to Impress? *International Journal of Human Resource Management, 5(1)*, 165-191.

DiMaggio, P. J. & Powell, W. W. (1991). The Iron Cage Revisited: Institutional Isomorphism and Collective Rationality in Organizational Fields. In W. W. Powell, & P. J. DiMaggio (Eds.), *The New Institutionalism in Organizational Analysis* (pp. 63-82). Chicago: The University of Chicago Press.

Doeringer, P. B., Lorenz, E. & Terkla, D. G. (2003). The Adoption and Diffusion of High-performance Management: Lessons from Japanese Multinationals in the West. *Cambridge Journal of Economics, 27(2)*, 265-286.

Doeringer, P. B. & Piore, M. J. (1971). *Internal Labor Markets and Manpower Analysis*. Lexington, Massachusetts: Heath Lexington Books.

Dore, R. (1973). *British Factory, Japanese Factory: The Origins of National Diversity in Industrial Relations.* London: George Allen and Unwin.

Dore, R. (1998). Asian Crisis and the Future of the Japanese Model. *Cambridge Journal of Economics, 22(6)*, 773-787.

Endo, K. (1994). Satei (Personal assessment) and Interworker Competition in Japanese Firms. *Industrial Relations, 33(1)*, 70-82.

Fletcher, C. (1993). Appraisal: An Idea Whose Time has Gone. *Personnel Management,* 34-38.

Fukase, K. (2001). *Posuto seikashugi no jinzai senryaku* (Talent strategies after performance-related pay). Tokyo: Chūō Keizaisha.

Gilman, M. W. (2009). Reward Management. In T. Redman & A. Wilkinson (Eds.), *Contemporary Human Resource Management: Text and Cases* (3rd Edition) (pp. 138-174). Harlow: Prentice Hall.

Halachmi, A. (1993). From Performance Appraisal to Performance Targeting. *Public Personnel Management, 22(2)*, 323-344.

Hall, P. A. & Soskice, D. (2001). *Varieties of Capitalism: The Institutional Foundations of Comparative Advantage*. Oxford: Oxford University Press.

Holzhausen, A. (2000). Japanese Employment Practices in Transition: Promotion Policy and Compensation Systems in the 1990s. *Social Science Japan Journal, 3(2)*, 221-35.

Imano, K. (1995). *Atarashii jinji kanri no chōryū* (New tides in personnel management), *Nihon Rōdō Kenkyū Zasshi* (Japanese Journal of Labour Research), *426*, 2-14.

Inagami, T. & Whittaker, D. H. (2005). *The New Community Firm: Employment, Governance and Management Reform in Japan*. Cambridge: Cambridge University Press.

Itoh, H. (1994). Japanese Human Resource Management from the Viewpoint of Incentive Theory. In M. Aoki & R. Dore (Eds.), *The Japanese Firm: The*

Sources of Competitive Strength (pp. 233-264). Oxford: Oxford University Press.

Jackson, G. (2007). Employment Adjustment and Distributional Conflict in Japanese Firms. In M. Aoki, G. Jackson, & H. Miyajima (Eds.), *Corporate Governance in Japan: Institutional Change and Organizational Diversity* (pp. 282-309). Oxford: Oxford University Press.

Jacoby, S. M. (2004). *The Embedded Corporation: Corporate Governance and Employment Relations in Japan and the United States.* Princeton: Princeton University Press.

Japan Institute for Labour Policy and Training (2005). Henbosuru jinzai manejimento to gabanansu – Keiei senryaku (Transforming human resource management and governance: Corporate strategies). *Research Report, 33.*

Japan Institute for Labour Policy and Training (2007a). *Japanese Working Life Profile 2007-2008.* Tokyo.

Japan Institute for Labour Policy and Training (2007b). *Yūsufuru rōdō tōkei* (Useful labour statistics). Tokyo.

Jo, S. (2004). *Uchigawa kara mita Fujitsu "Seikashugi" no hōkai* (An insider view of the collapse of "seikashugi" at Fujitsu). Tokyo: Kōbunsha.

Keizer, A. B. (2008). Non-regular Employment in Japan: Continued and Renewed Dualities. *Work, Employment and Society, 22(3)*, 407-425.

Keizer, A. B. (2009). *Changes in Japanese Employment Practices: Beyond the Japanese Model.* London: Routledge.

Kessler, I. (2005). Remuneration Systems. In S. Bach (Ed.), *Managing Human Resources: Personnel Management in Transition* (4th Edition) (pp. 317-345). Malden, MA: Blackwell Publishing.

Kessler, I. (2008). Reward Choices: Strategy and Equity. In J. Storey (Ed.), *Human Resource Management: A Critical Text* (3rd Edition). London: Thompson Learning.

Kessler, I. & Purcell, J. (1992). Performance Related Pay – Objectives and Application. *Human Resource Management Journal, 2(3)*, 34-59.

Koike, K. (1997). *Human Resource Development.* Japanese Economy and Labor Series 2. Tokyo: The Japan Institute of Labour.

Lawler, E. E. (1995). The New Pay: A Strategic Approach. *Compensation and Benefits Review, 27(4)*, 14-22.

Lazear, E. P. (1979). Why is there Mandatory Retirement? *Journal of Political Economy, 87(6)*, 1261-1284.

Marsden, D. (1999). *A Theory of Employment Systems: Micro-foundations of Social Diversity*. Oxford: Oxford University Press.

Marsden, D., French, S. & Kobi, K. (2000). *Why does Performance Pay Demotivate? Financial Incentives versus Performance Appraisal.* Centre for Economic Performance, London School of Economics and Political Science.

Matanle, P. C. D. (2003). *Japanese Capitalism and Modernity in a Global Era: Re-fabricating Lifetime Employment Relations*. London: RoutledgeCurzon.

Milgrom, P. & Roberts, J. (1992). *Economics, Organization and Management.* Englewood Cliffs: Prentice Hall.

Morishima, M. (1995). Embedding HRM in a Social Context. *British Journal of Industrial Relations, 33(4)*, 617-640.

Morishima, M. (2002). Pay Practices in Japanese Organizations: Changes and Non-changes. *Japan Labor Bulletin, April*, 8-13.

Neathey, F. & Reilly, P. (2003). *Competency-based Pay*. Brighton: Institute for Employment Studies. Available at: http://www.employment-studies.co.uk/pdflibrary/mp25.pdf.

Nihon Keieisha Dantai Renmei Shuppanbu (Japan Joint Management Federation Publishing Department, 2001). *Seikashugi jinjiseido jireishū* (Collected cases on performance-related pay human resource).

Oliver, C. (1997). Sustaining Competitive Advantage: Combining Institutional and Resource Based Views. *Strategic Management Journal, 18(9)*, 697-713.

Price, A. (2004). *Human Resource Management in a Business Context.* London: Thomson Learning.

Rebick, M. (2005). The *Japanese Employment System: Adapting to a New Economic Environment*. Oxford: Oxford University Press.

Redman, T. (2009). Performance Appraisal. In T. Redman & A. Wilkinson (Eds.), *Contemporary Human Resource Management: Text and Cases* (3rd Edition) (pp. 175-206). Harlow: Prentice Hall.

Regini, M. (2000). The Dilemmas of Labour Market Regulation. In G. Esping-Andersen & M. Regini (Eds.), *Why Deregulate Labour Markets?*. Oxford: Oxford University Press.

Rōmu Gyōsei Kenkyūjo (Labour Administration Research Institute, 2002). *Saishin jinjikōka jijō* (Latest merit rating situation). Tokyo.

Seisansei Rōdō Jōhō Sentā (Productivity Labour Information Centre, 2002). *Nihonteki jinjiseido no genjō to kadai* (Current situation and topics of the Japanese personnel system). Tokyo.

Tatsumichi, S. & Morishima, M. (2007). Seikashugi from an Employee Perspective, *Japan Labor Review, Spring*, 79-104.

Townley, B. (1999). Practical Reason and Performance Appraisal. *Journal of Management Studies, 36(3)*, 287-306.

Utanabe, K. (2000). *Konpitenshi seikashugi jinji* (Competency performance-related personnel management). Tokyo: Nihon Jigyou Shuppansha.

Vogel, S. K. (2006). *Japan Remodeled: How Government and Industry are Reforming Japanese Capitalism*. Ithaca: Cornell University Press.

Wright, V. (1991). Performance Related Pay. In F. Neale (Ed.), *The Handbook of Performance Management*. London: Institute of Personnel Management.

Yamaguchi, S. & Tsureta, K. (2001). *Seikashugi jinji nyūmon* (Introduction to performance-related personnel management). Tokyo: Chūō Keizaisha (Central Economic Office).

Yin, R. K. (1994). *Case Study Research: Design and Methods* (2nd Edition). London: Sage Publications.

Faceted Intelligence Concept in Japan

Sierk Horn, André Beauducel and Detlev Liepmann

1. Introduction

Intelligence assessment is often referred to as *the* success story of modern psychology. It looks back on a 100-year history of intense research and gradual construct development. Due to the sometimes controversial debates around the nature, content and scope of intelligence and the related research activities complex models of intelligence (Carroll 1993) and extensive inventories are available today. However, complacency is premature. Despite the accepted assumption that intelligence is cause and product of its cultural context the universalistic nature of research streams comes as a surprise (of course this fundamental bias towards generalisation is not only immanent here, but follows the implicit ethnocentricity of most research fields). Even though physiologically cerebral differences are generally be ruled out as academic anecdote (things are not as easy: e.g. Rushton 1995), there is eclectic support for latent Asia-Occident differences in cognitive processes:

- *Cultural differences in hemispheric lateralisation*: Japanese supposedly use more the right hemisphere whereas Westerners are to be described as left-brained (see e.g. Endo *et al.* 1978; Tsunoda 1989). These findings, however, need yet to be re-confirmed and as such should be treated with considerable caution.
- *Holistic information processing*: The predominant mode of information processing in Eastern cultures follows Gestalt-theory while the Western mode of thinking is supposedly logical and analytical (Hiser and Kobayashi 2003).
- *Logographic representations*: The use of Chinese characters that convey meaning and not letters serves as an indicator that alternative perceptions and reasoning processes may exist cross-culturally (Tamaoka 1991). Even though caution is warranted in generalising or stereotyping differences, empirical evidence suggests variations in cognitive processes (Flaherty 1993).
- *Visual Memory Skills*: Empirical evidence suggests that Japanese (and Chinese) score consistently higher than their Western counterparts in tests involv-

ing space, form and shape (Lesser *et al.* 1965), digit symbol and block design of the Wechsler Adult Intelligence Scale (Lynn 1977) and matrices of the Ravens Standard Progression Test (Chan and Vernon 1988) as well as numerical memory span (Flaherty and Moran 2000).

- *Effects of socio-cultural differences*: Eastern cultures such as the Japanese are said to be more collectivistic than Western cultures. Individual behaviour and perception therefore must follow these local rules – with repercussions on information processing.

In his seminal work on culture and intelligence Sternberg (2004) – following in the footsteps of the circular assumption that "intelligence is what is measured by intelligence tests" (Boring 1923) – warns that a psychological concept can only be meaningfully understood within its cultural context. Applying the emic/etic-paradigma of cross-cultural research to both intelligence construct and its assessment, two extreme poles of theoretical positions can be deducted. On the one hand research may follow the basic assumption that intelligence is invariant to cultural influences. This etic research position implies the principal possibility of researching and comparing phenomena in different cultures. The underlying assumption is that intelligence is rooted in precisely the same concepts across cultures. Hence it is culture and time invariable. With this nomothetic argument test inventories may of course be used in different cultural settings.

On the other extreme pole a stringent culture specific research strategy is advocated. This alternative position neglects the universality of phenomena. At the centre of this emic argument is the uniqueness of cultural systems and the need for an isolated research strategy. As criteria are immanent to only one system the insider orientation makes cross-cultural comparisons difficult if not impossible. Following this taxonomic research logic measures used to assess intelligence in one culture are of no use in another. That is the outcomes obtained from using intelligence tests in different cultural settings cannot be compared. The outcomes are either structurally different or – as the actual meaning assigned to the obtained score will differ from one culture to another – the results are misleading in nature. In short, the emic and etic schools of thought differ in their fundamental perspective on the nature of the mental processes and representations, which in social sciences has become known as the "Malinowski dilemma": The universality versus uniqueness of cultural phenomena.

Even though an academic discipline must examine the validity of models in different countries, critical reviews of literature have identified a lack of concern for cross-cultural research in intelligence measurement. We believe that this disappointing status quo is the result of several interrelated factors, including (1) the perplexing cascade of intelligence definitions and types, (2) the lack of academic consent as regards factors and hierarchies, and (3), even when some consent with respect to some general factors emerged (e.g. Carroll, 1993), their remains some debate on the exact definition and meaning of the factors, and (4) considerable methodological complexities involved in intelligence assessment and corresponding multivariate data analyses. It is this finding and the belief in the limitations of single-culture research (and its rash application in different country settings) that sets the stage of this contribution.

The comprehensive work of Carroll (1993) underlines the importance of fluid and crystallised intelligence in the context of intelligence research. However, these factors were originally conceived by Cattell (1963) and have been investigated further by Flanagan and Harrison (1997). Beauducel and Kersting (2002) investigated fluid and crystallised intelligence in the context of the Berlin model of intelligence and Lindenberger and Baltes (1997) discussed similar factors in the context of aging. Thus, the wealth of research on these factors as well as the well-documented nature of fluid and crystallised intelligence makes them highly intriguing for use in a cross-cultural context:

- *Fluid intelligence (gf)* refers to the ability of solving abstract relational problems and inductive reasoning. This includes skills such as spatial and visual imagery, rote learning and memory as well as understanding contextual implications. Due to its primary focus on the perception of complex relations of the sort that are not taught its modus operandi is assumed to be relatively free of cultural differences. Therefore Horn (1988) concludes that fluid intelligence per se has developed outside acculturation processes.
- *Crystallised intelligence (gc)* manifests in individual knowledge and the ability to sensible thinking. As a reflection of cumulative learning experiences it involves understanding relations or solving problems which depend on knowledge acquired as a result of formal teaching and/or other cultural experiences. Rooted in systematic influences by the cultural framework, knowledge and sophistication (general knowledge, word comprehension and

numerical abilities e.g.) crystallised intelligence is closely related to acculturation processes, i.e. it develops inside the acculturation processes.

This second hierarchical level fluid and crystallised intelligence have been identified as powerful dimensions (Horn and Cattell 1982; Carroll 1993). They help to dismantle the interrelations that transcend underlying mental processes, hence their importance in a cross-cultural context. More specifically, facet theory was used as a conceptual framework for a theoretical refinement of the concept of fluid and crystallised intelligence. In this way problems relating to the purely hierarchical concept of fluid and crystallised intelligence (Beauducel *et al.* 2001) have been overcome. By means of the faceted conception it is possible to disentangle verbal, numerical, and figural content variance within fluid and crystallised intelligence.

The integration of gf–gc theory and the dynamic interaction between these two factors makes the "Intelligence-Structure-Test 2000/2000R" (Amthauer *et al.* 1999; Liepmann *et al.* 2007) a very powerful and versatile tool for intelligence assessment. The importance of fluid and crystallised intelligence in an intercultural context on the one hand and the advanced features of the IST 2000 R on the other provide for an invaluable exploration and extension of the intelligence concept. Especially, the separation of verbal, numerical, and figural intelligence from the fluid and crystallised intelligence variance will help to further intelligence measurement in a cross-cultural context. With an eye to the key concern of extending the gf-gc theory to other countries, the faceted concept of gf and gc is currently evaluated in the Western hemisphere (England, Germany, Italy, Czech Republic, Lithuania, Beauducel, *et al.* 2008). In particular, the promising results raise the question whether the instrument designed to measure the intelligence construct is invariant also in a Euro-Asia context. Our knowledge about possible systematic construct differences is still sparse, particularly in the light of this Asian perspective.

Due to several factors the research team has identified Japan as a formidable test environment to assess the faceted concept of gf and gc in an Asian context. First, Japan has a world-renowned education system with one of the highest literacy rates. Second, in an international comparison Japan continually over-performs at the student aptitude test of the OECD (Programme for International Student Assessment, PISA). Third, due to the insular location of the Japanese archipelago and its historic seclusion the population is comparatively homogenous. Few subcultures and almost no long-settled immigrants guarantee high external validity. Fourth, the relatively small population size (127 million in comparison to the People Republic of China's 1.3 billion or Indonesia's 242 million) and its alleged homogeneity make the sampling procedures manageable. Fifth, the Japanese languages use four different writing systems, including ideograms and logograms. Anticipating earlier findings on mental processes, the data set will provide a basis not only for an analysis of figural and spatial reasoning or verbal knowledge vis-à-vis Western samples, but also for deriving generalisations as regards antecedents of the intelligence construct. The complex figural signs may stimulate figural information processing within verbal communication in Japan. In consequence, verbal and spatial-figural intelligence may be strongly related or even confounded in Japan. The project investigates how the Western intelligence structure containing a separate verbal and figural-spatial factor maps on the Japanese structure, where these factors could be confounded. Sixth, with few exceptions (e.g. Doi 1989) insights into the psychological agenda of Japanese are rare in Western literature.

The contribution of our study is threefold.

(1) With a shared frame of reference the paper aims at the broadest level at extending the intelligence construct (and its measurement) cross-culturally. In doing so we posit that from a structural perspective a model that has been developed in German samples can be replicated in a Japanese sample.
(2) The faceted perspective of the Intelligence-Structure-Test, with its verbal, numerical and spatial-figural sub-tests facilitates an exploration of cultural differences at the content (factor) level. Pertaining to inherent cultural idiosyncrasies we expect the Japanese writing system to impact on the intelligence factors in the following way:
    - Higher overlap between verbal and spatial figural facets
    - It is even considered that verbal and figural intelligence might constitute a single factor in the Japanese sample
(3) Although substantial changes in the relations between verbal and figural intelligence are expected in the Japanese sample, the faceted structure of the model is expected to protect fluid and crystallised intelligence against the cultural differences are expected for verbal and figural intelligence, because in the faceted model, verbal and figural intelligence are orthogonal to

fluid and crystallised intelligence. It is therefore expected that fluid and crystallised intelligence have the same structure (loadings and correlations) in the Japanese and in the German sample.

2. Methodology

As cultural differences and construct equivalences can only be meaningfully understood if there are at least two cultures, the research team follows the integrative notion of construct validation, bridging the gap between the etic and emic camps. Here potential (in)variance is measured stepwise, from metric, scale and factor assessments to dimensionality and construct equivalence. This sequential procedure therefore ascertains the comparison across cultures. It will help to identify cross-cultural commonalities of intelligence (as hypothesised in the Intelligence Structure Test IST 2000 R) and test its model fit and reliability both empirically and theoretically. In other words, this approach follows the idea of a general yet flexible concept comparability between cultures, that allows for a systematic and gradual (partial) validation of the intelligence construct in a different cultural setting. The data of the Japanese sample will be compared to an analogous, i.e. in terms of age range, education background equivalence subsample from Germany, the birth place of the original inventory. The German sample used for comparison consists of 2.208 participants. Due to its versatility factor analysis will be used to test sequentially cross-national measurement invariance. In a first step the structure of the Japanese data will be explored with a dimension analysis (PCA, principal component analysis) using SPSS. This data reduction technique will offer first insights into the variability of the observed variables (task groups) in the case of Japan. Here the replication of the structure of the content abilities is of particular interest. Using LISREL 8 in a next step confirmatory factor analysis (CFA, Jöreskog and Sörbom 1993, 2002, which is commonly used in test development) will be employed to determine if the factors and the loadings of the tasks groups (indicator variables) reconfirm the intelligence structure from a cross-cultural perspective (number of factors, factor correlations etc.).

The approach presented here complies with the psychometric notion of intelligence as a hierarchically structured construct with a general intelligence (g) and second order factors (intelligence as composite of separate, distinct aptitudes).

Beyond the hierarchical structure assessment the cross-cultural exploration will also include an analysis of the internal consistency for the sub- and aggregated scales. In this way, the stability of the proposed construct and its test components can be determined for the case of Japan.

2.1 Introduction to the Facet Model of Fluid and Crystallized Intelligence

Intelligence is a complex theoretical trait construct (for detailed information on the historical development of the intelligence construct see Nettelnstroth 2003). Especially, academic intelligence is among the most influential paradigm in intelligence research. It is usually grounded in and assessed via structural theories. Central to this research paradigm is the use of exploratory and/or confirmatory factor analyses. In this way correlates and underlying dimensions can be identified or verified. These statistical procedures help to simplify and refine relationships between variables. First attempts to analyse the structure of intelligence can be found in Spearman's Two-Factor theory, which follows the assumption of a general intelligence factor ("g"). This general intelligence explains variances across numerous sub-tests. Area specific factors ("s") indicate performances solely in sub-categories (e.g. mathematics etc.). They explain the remaining variance. Therefore, "s" factors are hierarchically subordinate to the general intelligence factor "g". Negating this general intelligence factor Thurstone (1938) introduced the concept of independent primary factors. Pertaining to separately measurable skills verbal comprehension, word fluency, numeracy, space, memory, perceptual speed, reasoning were at the centre of his structure model. In this way intelligence is represented rather in a skill profile than in a single value, thereby questioning the hierarchy assumption of Spearman (1904). The "American School" tried to unify these diverging and conflicting intelligence conceptualisations. A milestone was the introduction of the hierarchical structure model by Cattell (1963) and Horn and Cattell (1966). Based on successive factor analyses they introduced three hierarchical intelligence layers. The higher the factors are in the hierarchy the more general skills they involve. First order factors include six primary skills (verbal, spatial, logic and numeric abilities as well as fluency and memory). At the secondary hierarchical level the concepts of fluid and crystallised intelligence are located. While the former describes inherited, from learning processes independent abilities, the latter comprises abilities based on previous experiences, i.e. learnt behaviour. Finally, as a correlate of fluid and crystallised intelligence, third order factors entail general wisdom/life experiences. The secondary factors have proved to be very effective ability projectors: Both factors are more specific than the general intelligence and are particularly useful to clarify relationships that otherwise are hidden by "g". Fluid intelligence stands not only for the capacity to learn and generate knowledge, but also for reasoning, deduction and the understanding of complex tasks. Hence, so-called culture free tests (excluding general and learnt knowledge) are particularly suitable to identify fluid intelligence. Crystallised intelligence in contrast comes to light via tasks referring to individual development and learning. It describes breadth and depth of knowledge, experiences, judgment competence, communications skills and the understanding of (local) customs. "Systematic influences of acculturation' (Horn 1988) are identified with a culture-specific assessment such as verbal comprehension, idea awareness and reasoning (logic, numeric, general). A clear-cut differentiation between these important factors at the second hierarchy level is, however, not straightforward. Studies show a correlation between fluid and crystallised intelligence. Many inventories reveal a substantial assessment overlap in their sub-tests. In short, while the distinction between these two factors is widely accepted, the assessment of the same is still fiercely debated.

2.2 Introduction to the Research Instrument

Instead of equating fluid intelligence with figural tasks and crystallised intelligence with verbal material, the Intelligence Structure Test IST 2000 R combines these with content facets comprising verbal, numerical and spatial-figural tasks, thereby offering a solution to this "contamination". In this way crystallised intelligence is framed as the ability to solve culture-specific cognitive problems, that is, to organise and apply culture-specific knowledge, including communication and pragmatism. It also reflects knowledge at the factual and process level. In contrast to this, fluid intelligence is characterised as fundamental, i.e. non-cultural and therefore primarily biologically determined information processing capacities of an individual. The IST 2000 R assesses this factor with tasks independent from a content-specific profile and is based on a modular approach. It comprises a basic module and knowledge test. The former consists of nine task groups that contain 20 individual tasks, ranked according to their difficulty. To each sub-test a time frame is allocated (power test). Before the start of each task group the test supervisor introduces the task using examples, which show how to solve the problems posed. This basic module assesses the content factors verbal, numerical and spatial figural intelligence (each with three task groups). The latter assesses the degree of learnt knowledge. It comprises 84 tasks (multiple choice) consisting of verbal, numerical, and spatial-figural questions (equally weighted with 28 questions). The topics covered include geography/history, art/culture, mathematics, sciences, economics and general knowledge. Each subject area is linked to the key intelligence facets as Table 1 illustrates.

Table 1: Knowledge test subject/facet matrix of the IST2000 R

	Verbal	Numerical	Figural	Sum
Geography/History	5	4	5	14
Economics	4	5	5	14
Art/Culture	5	5	4	14
Mathematics	5	4	5	14
Sciences	4	5	5	14
General/Daily Routine	5	5	4	14
Sum	28	28	28	84

The content facets are evaluated according to the sub-test design of the basic module, by subsuming the nine task groups to three scales. The verbal intelligence is calculated via the task groups one to three. In the first task group participants are asked to complete sentences wherein one word is missing (sentence completion, SC). Out of five alternatives only one choice correctly completes the sentence. The time allocated to this task group is six minutes. In the second task group the participants are presented three words (verbal analogies, VA). They have to identify a certain connection between the first and the second word. The similar analogy needs to be completed by the third word and one of the five alternatives. The time allocated to this task group is seven minutes. The third task group comprises six words out of which two words needs to be identified that share a generic term (verbal commonalities, VC). The participants have eight minutes to complete this task group.

The numeric intelligence is assessed via task groups four to six. The time allocated for all three task groups is 10 minutes. Task group 04 comprises 20 mathematical problems (calculation, CA). In task group 05 participants are asked to complete a numerical sequence (number series, NS). To do this they need to identify the sequence rule, If this rule is adhered to, the sequence can be continued and the number that is next in line identified. The sixth task group contains equations, where the numbers must be connected via basic arithmetic operators (addition, subtraction, multiplications, division) so that the result of the equation is correct (mathematical signs, MS).

Task groups seven to nine assess spatial-figural intelligence. The first of these task groups comprises 10 two-dimensional figures, five figures for 10 tasks (abstract pieces, AP). Each of the tasks shows one of the given figures cut up into several pieces. The participants are ask to identify one of the given figures, that can be created by putting the individual pieces of the task together. The time allocated for task group 07 is seven minutes. The set-up of task group 08 is similar, however, here the participants are presented with 10 cubes (cubes, CU). Each cube comes with six different signs. Only three sides are viewable. Each task shows the given cubes in altered position, so that the correct match must be identified. Participants have nine minutes to complete the 20 tasks. Each of the final 20 tasks (task group 09) shows three figures arranged in a matrix (matrices, MA). They are set up according to a certain rule, which the participants need to identify. In adhering to the inherent rule, the task can be completed by choosing one of five different figures. The time allocated to this task group is 10 minutes.

Next to the calculation of the verbal, numerical and figural intelligence the IST 2000 R allows for an aggregation of the scales. The resulting value represents reasoning or cognitive processes describing logic thinking. The knowledge module described above helps to identify verbal, numerical and figural knowledge as well as the calculation of overall knowledge (aggregated over the three knowledge facets). The reliability estimations of the scales range from a=.82 to a=.94 (Cronbach's Alpha). By combining the basics module and the knowledge test the IST 2000 R allows for the calculation of values for fluid and crystallised intelligence.

With the geographical extension and the inherent cross-cultural evaluation the translation and adaptation process is of ultimate importance. As the instrument also entails a verbal part (next to numerical and figural sub-tests) a stringency that ensures a comparability of translation and therefore data is paramount. A high accuracy has been accomplished by a dual strategy of independent translation into Japanese and re-translation into German (the original language of the diagnostic instrument). This method was given preference over translation processes discussed in Simmet-Blomberg (2000, use of English master-copy, single bi-lingual native speaker). Employing a more direct and independent translation process ascertained not only the detection of mistakes but also the appreciation (and communication) of finer lingual nuances. As language is a key to understanding culture, the use of two bi-lingual translators with different cultural backgrounds (Japan and Germany) strengthened to a great extent the cross-cultural validity of the instrument. The pre-test phase helped to further fine-tune aspects of the Japanese version.

Table 2: Sample tasks of the Japanese IST 2000 R version

次のシンボルのうち、英国ポンドを表すものはどれですか？

What is the symbol of the British pound?

a)	b)	c)	d)	e)
ß	£	Ľ	$	Ł

モダンクラシックギターの弦は何本でしょうか？

A modern classic guitar has how many strings?

a)	b)	c)	d)	e)
4	6	8	10	12

The IST 2000 R is used to determine fluid and crystallised intelligence by aggregating and differentiating knowledge (distinction between reasoning and knowledge). As knowledge is to a high degree culture-bound the German version needed to be adapted to a Japanese environment. Adaptation ranged from simple changes (instead of asking for then symbol of the Japanese Yen the Japanese participants were asked for the symbol of the British pound) to item localisation (correct answer for speed limits). In some cases there was need to change the question all together (without abandoning the question category). For example the literature question ("The Man and the Sea") was changed into a question asking for the author of "Norwegian Wood". As the reasoning part the structure and content of the knowledge test remained therefore unchanged. Table 2 illustrates the Japanese version of verbal, numerical and figural knowledge tasks.

2.3 Participants

The data was collected in Japan between January and July 2007. 542 participants aged between 18 and 51 were tested with the Japanese version of the IST 2000 R. Table 3 summarises the age and gender distribution. The mean age is 20.9 years and the standard deviation is 3.2 indicating a high age-homogeneity of the sample. From an education level perspective participants were recruited from both undergraduate and postgraduate degree programs. Moreover, the data set also included managers of a Tokyo-based recruiting company. Furthermore, the sub-division opens up the possibility of fine-tuning the analysis particularly for the younger age brackets. All participants were Japanese native speakers. From a geographic perspective and with the purpose of strengthening external validity, the data was collected in the Kantô, Kansai, Chûbu as well as Tôhoku region, thereby spreading the sample across the Japanese main peninsula. Also, the highly nuanced Japanese education system was reflected in the sampling procedure. First and second-tier universities (ranking) were included in the sample, ranging from prestigious universities in Tokyo, to short-term (tanki daigaku) and/or more vocational universities. In this way, a comparative analysis with a view to sub-group education homogeneity is possible.

*Table 3: Age and gender distribution**

Age	Female	Male	Total
18-21	190	227	417
22-29	40	67	107
30-51	10	8	18
Total	240 (44.3)	302 (55.7)	542 (100)

* Percent values in brackets.

The Japanese test participants took the basic module of the IST 2000 R and the knowledge test. The basic module consists of nine reasoning tasks (three verbal, three numerical and three figural). Each task involves 20 items. The speed and power aspect of the IST (i.e. the capture not only of ability but also the speed capabilities) was also implemented by allotting the same time frames to each task group as in the original version. The total time for the basic module was 92 minutes. All 542 participants took this basic module of the IST 2000 R, which provides detailed information about the skill profile. 195 of the participants also took the knowledge test of the IST 2000 R, which consists of art-literature, geography-history, mathematics, science and everyday life questions (all multiple choice), which correspond to the three sub-groups of the reasoning tasks. In this way fluid and crystallised intelligence and with it acculturation and culture-free skills can be calculated. The participants have 40 minutes time to answer the 84 questions. All participants were offered extensive feedback on their test results, which they could access online (this feedback facet helped fundamentally with the recruitment of participants).

3. Empirical Evidence

The starting point of the structural assessment of the Japanese version of the Intelligence Structure Test IST 2000 R is the correlation matrix of the basic module. Table 4 shows the relationship between the sub-tests for both the German (upper matrix) and the Japanese sample (lower matrix). For both group the numerical task groups (calculations, number series, numerical signs) show the highest correlations.

In both groups the lowest correlations can be found between the verbal task sentence completion and cubes (German sample r=.17; Japanese sample r=.11). No differences between the two samples can be detected. The matrix also is non-heterogeneous, so that the data therefore seems suitable for further exploration.

This correlation matrix of the nine task groups of the basic module (content facets) is the basis for exploring the factorial structure of the Japanese version of the I-S-T 2000. Table 5 illustrates the factor loadings and Eigenvalues of the principal component analysis. The results for the German sample are also represented in brackets. Because of the expected interrelations between the verbal, numerical and figural tasks an oblique rotation (oblimin solution) seems appropriate.

*Table 4: R-Matrix of the nine sub-tests (Japanese and German sample)**

Task Group	SC	VA	VS	CA	NS	SI	FS	CU	MA
Sentence Completion	---	.37	.35	31	.25	.25	.19	.17	.20
Verbal Analogies	.30	---	.59	.54	.51	.45	.36	.21	.26
Verbal Similarities	.23	.29	---	.46	.47	.40	.35	.25	.26
Calculations	.20	.35	.26	---	.66	.66	.37	.28	.23
Number Series	.22	.29	.17	.52	---	.62	.41	.33	.29
Numerical Signs	.15	.2	.21	.57	.59	---	.40	.32	.23
Figure Selection	.17	.35	.24	.29	.27	.33	---	.46	.31
Cubes	.11	.21	.20	.27	.30	.32	.50	---	.23
Matrices	.14	.21	.19	.21	.23	.27	.35	.33	---

* lower matrix Japanese sample (N=542), upper matrix German sample (N=2280).

Table 5: Principal component analysis (Oblimin solution)

Task Group		Verbal	Numeric	Figural
Sentence Completion		**.50 (.48)**	.03 (.02)	-.05 (.05)
Verbal Analogies		**.59 (.75)**	.03 (.14)	.07 (-.09)
Verbal Similarities		**.41 (.73)**	.00 (-.01)	.11 (.05)
Calculations		.17 (-.11)	**.65 (.80)**	-.04 (.07)
Number Series		.03 (-.08)	**.72 (.66)**	-.01 (-.10)
Numerical Signs		-.11 (.07)	**.83 (.82)**	.08 (-.05)
Figure Selection		.13 (.03)	-.05 (.07)	**.70 (.67)**
Cubes		-.10 (-.07)	.05 (.04)	**.71 (.64)**
Matrices		.07 (.22)	.05 (-.03)	**.42 (.38)**
Factor Correlation	Numeric	.51 (.67)	----	
	Figural	.49 (.50)	.54 (.54)	----
Eigenvalues:				
German Sample		4.00 1.10 .93 .73 .63		
Japanese Sample		3.35 1.11 1.09 .77 .72		

In both samples a three factorial structure emerges with similar factor loadings on the latent variables Verbal (for task groups 01-03), Numeric (for task groups 04-06) and Figural intelligence (for task groups 07-09). All Eigenvalues are above 1. This prima facie comparison underlines that the factorial structure of the Japanese version is replicating the component results of the German sample. As expected also for the Japanese sample inter-factor correlations indicate some overlap of the content facets.

Further evidence of the cross-cultural homogeneity of the factor structure gives the subsequent reliability analysis. As Table 6 illustrates all reasoning scales show a satisfactory and the aggregated reasoning scale a high internal consistency for the Japanese sample, equivalent to the German base values. Again, the results mirror a good cross-cultural fit of the hierarchically structured intelligence conception as assessed by the I-S-T 2000 inventory.

Table 6: Reliability estimates (Cronbach's Alpha)

	German	Japanese
Verbal Reasoning	.86	.67
Numerical Reasoning	.95	.94
Figural Reasoning	.88	.84
Reasoning	.95	.92

The subsequent investigation of the complete faceted structure of intelligence was based on the sub-sample of 195 Japanese participants (55% females; age in years: M=22.2, SD=3.7, range: 18-41). Since the Japanese participants were all qualified for university entrance, a corresponding sub-sample of 477 German participants (56% females; age in years: M=27.1, SD=8.5, range: 17-60) that were also qualified for university entrance was selected for group comparisons. The German sub-sample was drawn from the data sets used by Liepmann *et al.* (2007) for the development of the IST 2000 (R). The percentage of female participants is similar in both groups. There are, however, significant differences in age ($t_{667.61}$=10.41; $p < .001$). In order to account for the age differences, age was controlled in the subsequent analyses.

The results of the first multiple-groups confirmatory factor analysis based on maximum-likelihood estimation are presented in Figure 1. Like in Beauducel *et al.* (2001) the correlations of the content factors (verbal, numerical, and figural intelligence) with the gf- and gc-factor were fixed to zero in order to identify the faceted model. According to Beauducel *et al.* (2001) interval restrictions were used in order to estimate the loadings of the multiple factors of the faceted model. The freely estimated loadings were therefore restricted to be larger than 0.3 and smaller than 2.5, whereas those inter-factor correlations that were freely estimated, were restricted to be larger than 0.0 and smaller than 1.0. In order to compensate for the significant age difference between the German and Japanese sample, the observed variables were controlled (residualised) for age. All loadings, all inter-factor correlations, and all error terms were constrained to be equal in the German and in the Japanese sample. As can be seen in Figure 1, the factor loadings are substantial and the model has an acceptable fit. This indicates cross-cultural robustness of the faceted model of gf and gc.

In order to test the specific hypothesis on cross-cultural differences in intelligence further, the equality constraint for the correlation of the verbal with the figural intelligence factor was removed in a second step. Thus, verbal and figural intelligence were allowed to correlate differently in the German and the Japanese sample. The remaining model specifications were exactly as in the previous model. In this model, the correlation between verbal and figural intelligence was .31 for the German sample and .86 for the Japanese sample. The χ^2-difference between the latter model and the previous model was significant, indicating that the latter model is a more correct approximation of the data (χ^2_{diff}= 7.30; df_{diff}= 1; $p < .01$), more specifically, that the correlation between verbal and figural intelligence is indeed significantly larger in the Japanese sample. Since the remaining model parameters were nearly identical to those of the previous model, it is not necessary to present a figure for this model.

The very large correlation between verbal and figural intelligence in the Japanese sample was a reason for further analyses, based on the Japanese sample only. A model, in which the factors for verbal and figural intelligence are collapsed to a single factor was investigated in the Japanese sample.

The model specification was the same as for the first model, with the only difference that both the verbal and the figural variables load on factor three, which constitutes a verbal/figural factor. There were no cross-cultural equality constraints, since the model was only investigated in the Japanese sample. The

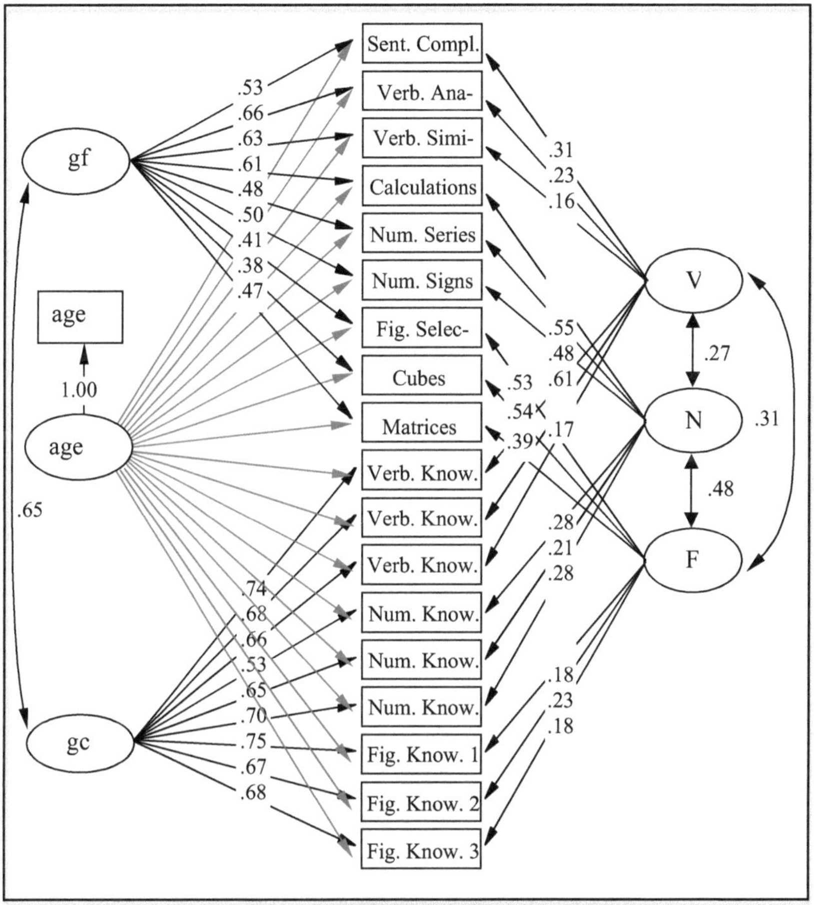

Figure 1: Multiple-group CFA for German and Japanese samples

Note: all loadings, interfactor-correlations and error terms were constrained to be equal in both samples; Model fit: χ^2= 871.61; df= 285; p < .001; RMSEA= .067; CFI= .96. Age is defined as a factor that is perfectly related to the observed variable "age". The loadings of the observed variables on the factor age are not presented.

model has an excellent fit (see Figure 2). Since the age differences between samples needs not to be partialled out, the model presented in Figure 2 was also calculated without controlling for age in the observed scores. The model has a good fit (χ^2= 140.74; df= 115; p = .052; RMSEA= .030; CFI= .99) and the model parameters are so similar to those in Figure 2 that an additional figure was not necessary. Thus, the results presented in Figure 2 do not depend on partialling out age. The models indicate that, at least in the present Japanese sample, verbal and figural intelligence can be conceived as a single ability.

It should, however, be noted that the loadings of the figural reasoning tasks (Figure Selection, Cubes, and Matrices) on the verbal/figural factor were not very large (see Figure 2). This indicates that figural reasoning in the reading

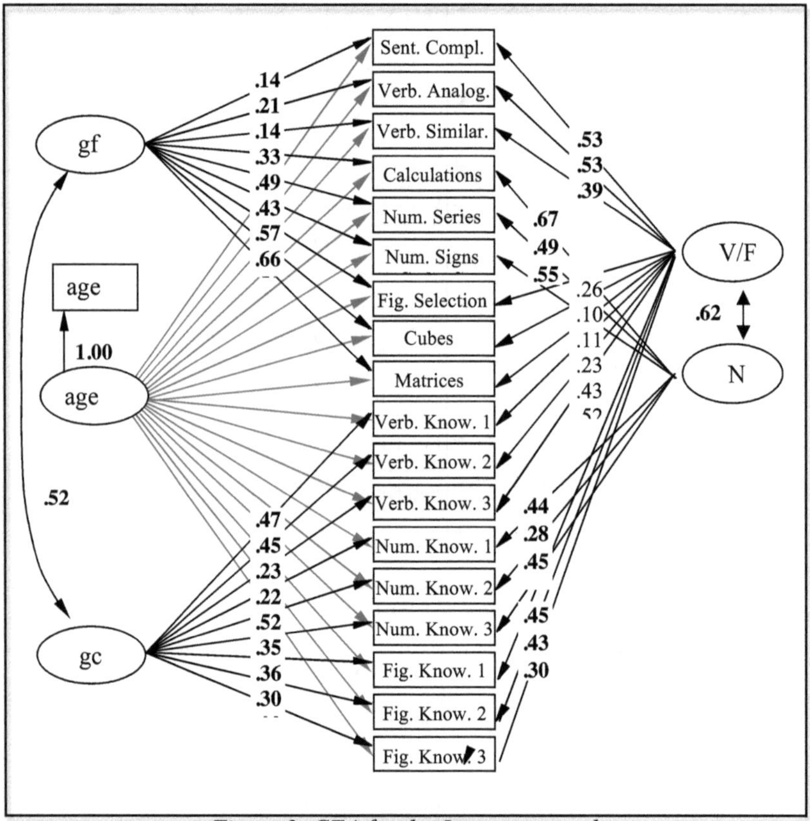

Figure 2: CFA for the Japanese sample

Note: Model fit: χ^2= 139.81; df= 115; p = .058; RMSEA= .029; CFI= .99. Age is defined as a factor that is perfectly related to the observed variable "age". The loadings of the observed variables on the factor age are not presented.

process is probably not the main reason for the large correlation between figural and verbal intelligence in the Japanese sample. The basis for the close relation between verbal and figural intelligence seems to be more related to the knowledge domain, since both the verbal and the figural knowledge variables load substantially on the common factor.

Even when this result was not explicitly expected, it seems quite reasonable that the figural aspects of the Japanese writing system are not so much related to figural reasoning processes, but to figural knowledge, because reading and writing are highly automatic processes. Automatic processes generally do not involve substantial amounts of reasoning, which might explain the small loadings of the figural reasoning tasks on the verbal/figural factor.

The correlation between verbal and figural intelligence within the reasoning tasks was investigated by means of a separate CFA model. The complete sample of Japanese participants (N=542; 44% females; age in years: M=20.9, SD=3.2, range: 18-51) performed the nine reasoning tasks and was therefore used for the subsequent analyses. All participants were qualified for university entrance. A multiple group CFA model comprising a verbal, numerical, and a figural reasoning factor was calculated for this, and the previously described German sample. The salient loadings and the inter-factor correlations were freely estimated. Age was controlled in the observed variables since the age difference between the German and the complete Japanese sample was again significant ($T_{590.37}$=14.87; P < .001). When cross-cultural equality constraints were imposed on the loadings, the inter-factor correlations and the error terms, the model-fit was only moderate (χ^2= 293.68; df= 69; p < .001; RMSEA= .080; CFI= .96). Model fit was significantly improved when the error terms were allowed to be different for the Japanese and the German group (χ^2_{diff}= 77.67; df_{diff}= 9; p < .01).

The model with different error terms for the groups is presented in Figure 3. In the next step the model in Figure 3 was modified in that the correlation between verbal and figural intelligence is allowed to be different for the groups. The increase in model fit was not significant (χ^2_{diff}= 0.19; df_{diff}= 1; p = .94), indicating that the correlations between verbal and figural intelligence is not significantly different in the two groups.

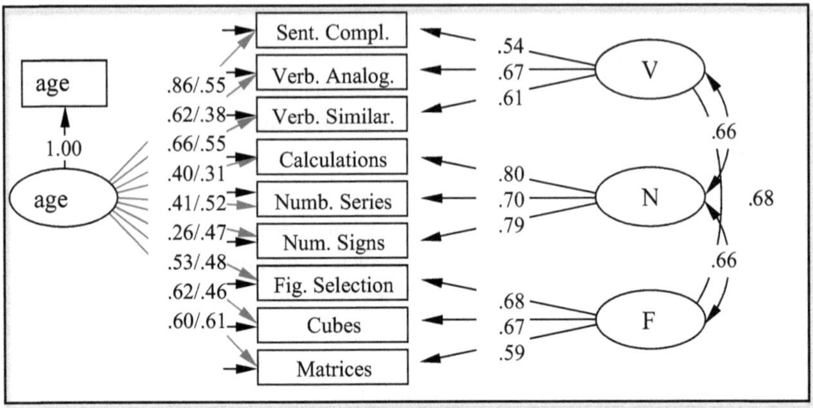

Figure 3: Multiple-group CFA for German and Japanese samples

Note: All loadings and interfactor-correlations were constrained to be equal in both samples; Model fit: χ^2= 216.01; df= 60; p < .001; RMSEA= .072; CFI= .97. Age is defined as a factor that is perfectly related to the observed variable "age". The loadings of the observed variables on the factor age are not presented. The error variances of the German sample are presented before the slash and the error variances of the Japanese sample are presented behind the slash.

4. Discussion

Research on intelligence already fills libraries, yet a broad consensus on concept universality is not in sight. If "culture" is assumed to be the result of a learning and multiplicator process (where societal miniature solutions are passed on from one generation to the next, cf. Kluckhohn and Strodtbeck 1961), then without empirical evidence the psychological construct "intelligence" must remain strongly embedded into an intrinsic cultural setting. A closing of this interpretative loophole of theory and inventory can only be achieved by assessing their validity via cross-country comparisons (preventing respondent artefacts, cultural bias etc.). This cross-cultural extension is even more important as the academic discipline in itself continues to enhance the structure of intelligence and the associated inventories. After all, intelligence is a fundament of personality, influences development and professional biographies and with it the overall lifestyles of individuals. As intelligence has become the epicentre of meritocratic societies a convincing assessment inventory becomes even more important. The increasing international vista of human resource management is a case in point here. The present study has therefore decisively contributed to the further development and refinement of the intelligence construct. In developing the above discussion it tried to find an answer to the question whether an intelligence inventory developed in the Western hemisphere can be applied in an East Asian context. This Euro-Asian perspective is especially important for the generalisabilty of the intelligence concept as earlier empirical findings indicate substantial differences as regards cognitive processes.

As regards the relevant constructs, the choice fell on fluid and crystallised intelligence. From a methodological point of view a faceted model of fluid and crystallised intelligence was investigated. In the faceted model fluid and crystallised intelligence are conceptualised as orthogonal to the three content factors, verbal, numerical, and figural intelligence (Beauducel *et al.* 2001). This allows to investigate the cross-cultural robustness of fluid and crystallised intelligence independently from cross-cultural effects that might occur in the content factors. The respective model is represented by the intelligence structure test IST 2000 R, developed by the co-authors, due to its theory driven construction, its high internal consistency and scale reliability as well as its persuasive capture of fluid and crystallised intelligence, and most importantly its proven track record of consistency in a European context (Amthauer *et al.* 2001, 2005, 2007). To date little is reported in Western literature on Japanese psychology in this respect and next to the timeliness of this extension, makes for an even more interesting comparative environment from an Asia-Occident perspective. As the writing system and verbal components – key aspects of academic intelligence – have been singled out as a potential influence factors, a cross-cultural extension to Japan has proved useful to further our understanding of the structure of intelligence, particularly our understanding of differences between and similarities of individuals from diverging cultural habitats.

A key question in extending the intelligence theory, its associated constructs and assessment instruments (and with it the discipline itself) is whether or not it exhibits adequate construct equivalence for a meaningful applicability in a different cultural context and/or for cross-cultural comparisons. The empirical findings suggest that the cross-cultural construct invariance for fluid and crystallised intelligence as hypothesised and assessed with the intelligence structure test IST 2000 R can be assumed. Moreover, the three content factors verbal, mathematical and spatial figural could be clearly reproduced. The first hypothesis pertaining to the three constituting intelligence pillars can therefore be confirmed. In multiple group CFA a model with equal parameters for the Japanese and the German sample fitted well to the data. From a structural perspective, the intelligence construct shows high congruency as regards the underlying dimensions and points towards equivalence of facets, inter-relationships and hierarchies. As anticipated the IST 2000 R underlined its robustness also for non-European setting. At the same time a translation and content equivalence of the research instrument itself has been achieved, confirming the importance of a team-assisted translation process.

Subsequent analysis of correlation of verbal intelligence with spatial-figural intelligence also brought multifarious insights on idiosyncrasies and influences of the writing system (here Japanese) to light. At the most abstract level, empirical evidence points towards a higher intersection of verbal and figural components of intelligence. Multiple group CFA revealed that the correlation between verbal and figural intelligence was significantly larger in the Japanese sample than in the German sample. The a priori assumption of systematic influences of figural intelligence on the verbal skill profile has therefore been confirmed. With the centrality of symbolic representations in the Japanese language (i.e. Chinese characters) verbal skills are contaminated with figural information processing. This was most prominently shown in a CFA for the Japanese sample, in which the verbal and figural intelligence factor were collapsed to a single factor. The model with a verbal/figural intelligence factor fits well to the data, thereby confirming our second hypothesis that the Japanese writing system has a substantial impact on the correlation between verbal and figural intelligence. Moreover, the cross-cultural models as well as the model with the collapsed verbal/figural factor show that fluid and crystallised intelligence are cross-culturally robust when they are assessed within a faceted model of intelligence. As expected in our third hypothesis, the cross-cultural differences were entirely captured by the content facet so that fluid and crystallised intelligence were cross-culturally confirmed. This points to the advantages of a faceted concept of fluid and crystallised intelligence as they have been discussed earlier (Schulze *et al.* 2005).

It should, however, also be noted that the contamination of verbal and figural intelligence was primarily due to the knowledge component involved. When the multiple-group CFA was performed for the reasoning tasks only, no difference between the Japanese and the German sample occurred for the correlation between verbal and figural intelligence. Despite the strong overlap of verbal and figural intelligence in the total model for the Japanese sample, verbal and figural intelligence are distinct factors in the context of the reasoning tasks. Thus, the contamination of verbal and figural intelligence stems from the knowledge domain. It can be assumed that the impact on the writing system on the correlation between the factors should be related to highly over-learned processes.

5. Outlook

Intelligence is an evolving construct. Despite the history and legacy of research in intelligence this study has raised numerous questions as regards the validity of psychological constructs in general and the intelligence construct in particular in the light of their cultural embedding. If an inventory is used in a different cultural context any conclusions based on country-of-origin measurements and assumptions must be deceptive. Only the empirical support of construct equivalence (and not presumed prima facie) enables a meaningful scale deployment in different cultural habitats. After all, cross-cultural differences may evidence “true” differences but may also reflect systematic biases brought forward by erratic construct variances. In short, it is vital to ensure that what is intended to be tested is actually measured (and apples are compared with apples and not oranges). In this sense this study tried to break through Boring’s (1923) circular diktat of the idiosyncrasies and limitations of intelligence tests. Addressing the critical issue of cross-cultural extension to East-Asia (or rather the lack thereof) the study has found many answers to the measurement of the intelligence concept. The findings provide valuable insights for both theory and practice, most notably the structural equivalence of intelligence in the case of Japan as assessed with the IST 2000 R. Convincing evidence has been brought forward that it indeed yields measures of the same attributes for fluid and crystallised intelligence, thereby defusing doubts about the applicability of the theory in an East-Asian context. Moreover, the power of the faceted model of intelligence was shown, since it allows to protect fluid and crystallized intelligence against cross-cultural instabilities that occur on the level of the content factors verbal and figural intelligence. Given the multitude of challenges in cross-cultural research by no means all questions have sufficiently been answered or indeed have come to the open. One aspect is the inherent limitation of this exploratory study: The sample is currently pear-shaped with the majority of participants in the younger age brackets. While this caused no additional challenges for the present study (age was statistically controlled in the analyses) an extension to elder age brackets would make for an even better theoretical grounding. A bigger variety of participants would in turn also extend the scope of the educational background and therefore substantiate the findings.

It is important to note that the aim of the study was not to make qualitative comparisons between the samples. While a structural comparison is possible (etic research assumption), single-country analyses are currently only available using the standardised values and norms of the original German data set. Particularly with a view to the sensitiveness of intelligence testing an inventory tailored to each culture is therefore mandatory. Following the emic argument of the uniqueness of cultural systems standard values and test norms need to be developed for each habitat. Bringing etic (structural equivalence) and emic (single country analysis) streams together, the development of norms specific to Japan seems advisable. Reflecting diverging skill nuances only in this way a meaningful analysis for Japanese test participants (calculation of IQ score etc.) can be achieved. This means that as a next step the database must be substantially extended. Now that the general equivalence of intelligence has been confirmed for the case of Japan, this would open up the possibility of shedding further empirical light on cultural influence factors. Here, it would be interesting to examine whether the research findings warrant a Japan-specific sub-scale development that allows for a discrimination between verbal and spatial-figural intelligence components. The authors also observed differences in the problem solving speed during the data collection. Japanese participants were significantly quicker in answering the verbal sub-tests (and to some extent the mathematical task groups) than their German counterparts. This may indicate that the Japanese script system indeed influences the perceptual speed, which deserves further scrutiny. Closely related to this, the effect of the Japanese education system on individual performance is another important avenue of future investigation. Beyond the further exploration of fluid and crystallised intelligence the presented faceted approach should be therefore related to existing intelligence inventories (or aspects thereof) and other indicators commonly used for skill assessments in Japan (e.g. SPI).

The present study has successfully taken the up the cudgels for interdisciplinary research. The authors highlighted the application potential for Japanese social science research and with it the scope for cross-fertilisation between different research disciplines. The inherent emic/etic-paradigm – a key dilemma of cross-cultural analyses – has been successfully addressed by means of quantitatively oriented field research and empirical exploration. This may well open new streams of applied research with regional and linguistic expertise as an important component.

6. References

Ackerman, P. L.& Heggestad, E. D. (1997). Intelligence, Personality, and Interests: Evidence for Overlapping Traits. *Psychological Bulletin. 121(2)*, 219-245.

Amthauer, R. Brocke, B., Liepmann, D. & Beauducel, D. (1999). *Intelligenz-Struktur-Test 2000* (Intelligence-Structure Test 2000). Göttingen: Hogrefe.

Amthauer, R., Brocke, B., Liepmann, D. & Beauducel, D. (2001). *IST-2000. Test di Struttura dell'Intelligenza* (Intelligence Structure Test). Firenze: Organizzazioni Speciali.

Amthauer, R., Brocke, B., Liepmann, D. & Beauducel, D. (2005). *Test Struktury Inteligence. I-S-T 2000 R* (Intelligence Structure Test I-S-T 2000 R). Praha: Vydalo Testcentrum.

Amthauer, R., Brocke, B., Liepmann, D. & Beauducel, D. (2007). *Intelekto Strukturos Testas 2000 R* (Intelligence Structure Test I-S-T 2000 R, Vilnius). Göttingen: Hogrefe.

Beauducel, A., Brocke, B. & Liepmann, D. (2001). Perspectives on Fluid and Crystallised Intelligence: Facets for Verbal, Numerical, and Figural Intelligence. *Personality and Individual Differences, 30(6)*, 977-994.

Beauducel, A., Liepmann, D., Brocke, B. & Horn, S. (2008). *Intelligence-Structure-Test IST 2000 (English Version)*. Göttingen: Hogrefe.

Beauducel, A. & Kersting, M. (2002). Fluid and Crystallised Intelligence and the Berlin Model of Intelligence Structure (BIS). *European Journal of Psychological Assessment, 18(2)*, 97-112.

Borg, I. J. & Lingoes, C. (1987). *Multidimensional Similarity Structure Analysis*. New York: Springer.

Boring, E. G. (1923). Intelligence as the Test Measures it. *New Republic, June*, 35, 35-37.

Carroll, J. B. (1993). *Human Cognitive Abilities. A Survey of Factor-analytic Studies*. Cambridge: Cambridge University Press.

Cattell, R. B. (1963). Theory of Fluid and Crystallised Intelligence. A Critical Experiment. *Journal of Educational Psychology, 54(1)*, 1-22.

Chan, J. & Vernon, P. E. (1988). Individual Differences Among the Peoples of China. In H. I. Sidney, & J. B. Berry (Eds.), *Human Abilities in Cultural Context* (pp. 340-357). Sidney, New York: Cambridge University Press.

Costa, P. T. & McCrae, R. R. (1992). Four Ways Five Factors are Basic. *Personality and Individual Differences, 13(6)*, 653-665.

Doi, T. (1989). *The Anatomy of Self: Individual versus Society.* Tokyo: Kodansha.

Endo, M., Akinori, S. & Tadao, H. (1978). Functional Asymmetry of Visual Fields for Japanese Word, in Kana Writing and Random Shape-recognition in Japanese Subjects. *Neuropsychologica, 16(3)*, 291-297.

Flaherty, M. (1993). Are Japanese Kanji Processed like Pictures? *Psychologica, 36(3)*, 144-150.

Flaherty, M. & Moran, A. (1996). Visual Memory Skills in Japanese and Caucasians. *Perceptual and Motor Skills, 82(3, Pt 2)*, 1319-1329.

Flaherty, M. & Moran, A. (2000). Absence of a Numerical Memory Span Advantage in Japanese Kanji. *Perceptual and Motor Skills, 90(1)*, 272-278.

Flanagan, D. P. & Harrison, P. L. (1997). *Contemporary Intellectual Assessment: Theories, Tests, and Issues.* New York: Guilford.

Guilford, J. P. (1967). *The Nature of Human Intelligence.* New York: McGraw-Hill.

Guilford, J. P. (1980). Fluid in Crystallised Intelligences: Two Fanciful Concepts. *Psychological Bulletin, 88(2)*, 406-412.

Hiser, E. & Kobayashi, J. (2003). Hemisphere Lateralization Differences: A Cross-cultural Study of Japanese and American Students in Japan. *Journal of Asian Pacific Communication, 13(2)*, 197-229.

Hofstede, G. (2001). *Culture's Consequences: Comparing Values, Behaviours, Institutions, and Organizations Across Nations.* London: Sage Publications.

Hofstede, G. (2005). *Cultures and Organizations: Software of the Mind.* New York: McGraw-Hill.

Horn, J. L. (1988). Thinking about Human Abilities. In J. R. Nesselroade, & R. B. Cattell (Eds.), *Handbook of Multivariate Experimental Psychology.* New York: Plenum.

Horn, J. L., & Cattell, R. B. (1966). Refinement and Test of the Theory of Fluid and Crystallised General Intelligences. *Journal of Educational Psychology, 57(5)*, 253-270.

Horn, J. L. & Cattell, R. B. (1982). Whimsy Misunderstandings of gf-gc Theory: A Comment on Guilford. *Psychological Bulletin, 91(3)*, 623-633.

Horn, S. (2005). *Interkulturelle Kompetenz im Zugang zu japanischen Konsumenten* (Intercultural Competence in Accessing Japanese Consumers). Wiesbaden: Deutscher Universitäts-Verlag.

Jöreskog, K. G., & Sörbom, D. (1993). *LISREL 8-User's Reference Guide.* Chicago: Scientific Software International.

Jöreskog, K. G. & Sörbom, D. (2002). *LISREL 8.53.* Chicago: Scientific Software International.

Kluckhohn, F. R. & Strodtbeck, F. L. (1961). *Variations in Value Orientations.* Evanston, Ill.: Row, Peterson.

Liepmann, D., Beauducel, A., Brocke, B. & Amthauer, R. (2007). *Intelligenz-Struktur-Test 2000 R, erweiterte Auflage* (Intelligence-Structure Test 2000 R, Extended Edition). Göttingen: Hogrefe.

Lindenberger, U. & Baltes, P. B. (1997). Intellectual Functioning in Old and Very Old Age: Cross-sectional Results from the Berlin Aging Study. *Psychology and Aging, 12(3)*, 410-432.

Lesser, G. S., Fifer, G. & Clark, D. H. (1965). Mental Abilities of Children from Different Social Class and Cultural Groups. *Monographs of the Society for Research in Child Development, 30*, 1-115.

Lynn, R. (1977). The Intelligence of the Japanese. *Bulletin of the British Psychological Society, 30*, 69-72.

Nettelnstroth, W. (2003). *Intelligenz im Rahmen der beruflichen Tätigkeit* (Intelligence in the Context of Occupational Activity). Digitale Dissertation. Freie Universitaet Berlin. Available at: http://www.diss.fu-berlin.de.

Rushton, J. P. (1995). Construct Validity, Censorship, and the Genetics of Race. *American Psychologist, 50(1)*, 40-41.

Schulze, D., Beauducel, A. & Brocke, B. (2005). Semantically Meaningful and Abstract Figural Reasoning in the Context of Fluid and Crystallised Intelligence. *Intelligence, 33(2)*, 143-159.

Simmet-Blomberg, H. (2000). *Interkulturelle Marktforschung im Europäischen Transformationsprozess* (Intercultural Market Research in the European Transformation Process). Stuttgart: Schäffer-Poeschel.

Spearman, C. (1904). General Intelligence, Objectively Determined and Measured. *American Journal of Psychology, 15(2)*, 201-293.

Sternberg, R. J. (2002). Cultural Explorations of Human Intelligence Around the World. In W. J. Lonner, D. L. Dinnel, S. A. Hayes, & D. N. Sattler (Eds.),

Online Readings in Psychology and Culture. Centre for Cross-Cultural Research, Western Washington University, Bellingham: Washington. Available at: http://www.wwu.edu/~culture.

Sternberg, R. J. (2004). Culture and Intelligence. *American Psychologist, 59(5)*, 325-338.

Tamaoka, K. (1991). Psycholinguistic Nature of the Japanese Orthography. *Studies in Language and Literature, 11(1)*, 49-82.

Thurstone, L. L. (1938). *Primary and Mental Abilities*. Chicago: The University of Chicago Press.

Tsunoda, T. (1989). Hemispheric Dominance in Japan and the West. In Klivington, K. A. (Ed.). *The Science of the Mind*. Cambridge: MIT Press.

Wechsler, D. (1991). *Wechsler Intelligence Scale for Children* (3rd Edition). San Antonio: Psychological Corporation.

Applied Perspectives on Recruiting and Work Assessment in Japan

Sierk Horn, Detlev Liepmann and André Beauducel

1. Introduction

Historically, much has been made of the Japanese employment system. Crises are, however, a litmus test for the efficiency of social institutions and act in many cases as a change agent. In the wake of the burst of the bubble economy and the longest recession Japan has experienced in the post-war era, there was little doubt about the necessity of major reform of the Japanese economic system in general, and the Japanese corporate system in particular – including the once glorified (but in many cases overestimated)[1] lifelong employment, seniority based promotion and corporate unionism. Deregulation measures, the influx of foreign direct investment and the rise of entrepreneurship have changed Japan's work environment dramatically. While the organisational structures and management systems that will emerge to replace the J-system (Aoki 1990, 1994) are in flux, the consistent model of Japanese human resource management has seen a decisive caesura. The organisation and structure of the Japanese market have changed substantially since the turn of the millennium. The world finance crisis in 2007 further accelerated shifts in Japanese employment practises.

While many companies clung onto the traditional employment pillars until late into the last decade, the leitmotif of long-term commitment and development of human capital is now being replaced by more flexible approaches – resulting in a more diversified human resource spectrum. Aoki *et al.* (2007) categorise three emergent types of Japanese firms, representing either hybrid forms of Western- and Japan-style employment practises or traditional firms that are yet to wholeheartedly embraced change. Despite this ongoing softening of hierarchical and

1 Many studies overlook that these facets of Japanese work life is only applicable for a small percentage of the overall Japanese workforce. The reality for employees of small and medium-sized corporations (SMEs) and non-core staff of big corporations, which make up the lion share of Japanese working population, is substantially different to the stylised J-model with *Shûshin Koyô* (lifelong employment), *Nenkô Jôretsu* (seniority based promotion) and *Kigyônai Rôdô Kumiai* (corporate unionism) at its core.

largely closed human resources, this trajectory of change is likely to continue with unclear outcome. Labour markets are becoming more permeable. Evidence suggests that the seniority principle is being gradually replaced by a meritocratic system in which a result-orientation is given preference to the potential performance of employees (Anon. 2004; NKS 2008; for cases of design and impact in the electronics sector see Itô 2006). This in turn casts of course doubt on the traditional focus on non-individualistic group-think (and with it one of the corner stones of human resource philosophies if not raison d'etre of Japanese firms). Therefore the work profile and ultimately the expectations vis-à-vis employees have changed dramatically. Obvious sign of this shift in labour relations is the introduction of an achievement system (*Seika Shugi*) as short-term wage determinant (Tatsumichi and Morishima 2007) and with it performance-oriented gratification systems[2] (cf. NKS 2007: 20). More and more emphasis is put on the skill formation of employees and (labour) market oriented qualification benchmarks. As by-product these efficiency-seeking measures will also lead to more transparent organisational hierarchies and career paths. While somewhat underrepresented in Western literature (where the debate focuses primarily on seniority based wages, exceptions are for example Keizer 2005, 2007) performance has always played a role in Japanese labour relations, most notably in the form of biannual bonus payments. With these new measures, however, a shift will occur away from group-performances (bonus payments are based on the overall economic success of the corporations), so that individual achievements come more into the lime light. Competition, assessment and with it interpersonal comparability are reversing the motto "the nail that sticks out gets hammered in" (*Deru Kui Ha Uttareru*). In short, employees in Japan wake up to a work environment significantly different from the core employment pillars blueprinted and caricaturised ("worker bees") ad nauseam in Western literature. Triggers of the redesign of labour relations in Japan are the hyper-aging Japanese society (*Kôreika Shakai*), the influx of technology (information technology, robotics to name just a few) as well as push and pull factors of globalisation (competition due to inward FDI and outsourcing). While Japanese firms will maintain long-term employment, implications of the changing competitive environment for the Japanese employment system are far-reaching. Important pre-requisites of the Japanese employment system, including a) age balance of employees (with the

2 A recent study by the Japan Institute for Labour Policy and Training reveals that the majority of Japanese firms plan to introduce a wage system that reflects also the achievement of employees (JILPT 2004).

younger employees forfeiting salary with the prospect of higher returns in the future), b) high economic growth (to support wage increases) and c) long-term survival of firm (trust in commitment) have been decisively eroded. Therefore, instead of contractual stability (with an implicit life-long vista and increasing wages) especially young Japanese employees face a shortage of jobs, short-term contracts, a flattening of wage curves and job-insecurity.

2. Rationale: Changes in Japanese Recruiting Practises

The "market value" of employee skills has been conventionally impeded by a stringent in-house orientation. With the focus on general knowledge of social institutions (education system), vocational skill formation[3] was the preserve of corporations. In this way, a system developed, in which skills were tailored to corporations and therefore non-transferable in external labour markets (cf. Demes 1998). Hence, Japanese employees rather identify themselves with a corporation than with their profession. If inherent aspects of Japanese recruiting and promotion process – the focus on educational credentialism (*Gakureki*), networking orientation (*Senpai-Kôhai* relationships) and outplacement to affiliate companies (*Shukko*) – are alleviating, the traditional logic of multi-skilling, generalist know-how and flexibility (with its latent focus on team efforts) comes to an end. The system of interdependence between employee and corporation is being replaced by a system of independence. For the individual this translates into the necessity to build up an awareness of the development of specific skill profiles, too. It is not a question of if but rather a question of when the human resource management à la Japonaise has had its day. There is growing literature to suggest that the implementation of widespread changes to the re-organisation of Japanese human resources is bearing fruit (Holzhausen 1998; Dirks *et al.* 2000; Park 2003; Waldenberger 2006). Deep knowledge, specific expertise and job applicability are already key ingredients of today's Japanese work environment as various reports by relevant labour institutes suggest (Itô 2006). Today the majority of Japanese firms are using Management by Objectives (*Mokuhyô Kanri*) and continuous assessment of its employees to monitor achievements (MHLW 2004, MHLW 2006), challenging entrenched thinking purported particularly in Western literature. While this transformation of the Japanese work

3 Graduates undergo an extensive on-the-job training. Job-rotation and constant secondments are manifestations of the multi-skilling approach of Japanese firms.

place is already well under way, a dimension not yet fully explored is the impact of new human resource management techniques on recruiting and promotion (assessment) in Japanese firms. This is inasmuch surprising as selection and retention processes particularly in this transformation period are vital for the long-term survival of firms. After all, a more flexible labour market must mean a decisive break from past recruiting, training and promotion practises. In turn, the important aspect of how this ongoing change influences experiences and behaviour at the individual level is in this context underrepresented.

Traditionally, Japanese firms recruited from colleges and universities each year. With their focus on in-house, on-the-job training throughout an employee's career the specific skill set was less important than the fit between firm and applicant or the stable company's relationships with colleges and universities[4]. Therefore modern assessment techniques that help to identify skill profiles of applicants have been less important in Japan. Embedded into overall shifts towards a meritocratic employment environment corporations are, however, forced to professionalise their recruiting and promotion practises. Selection techniques, such as database profiling, assessment centres or personality tests, commonly used in the West increasingly find their way to Japan. The following examples illustrate the substantial shifts in Japanese recruiting practises:

- Japanese corporations traditionally emphasise relationships with colleges and universities. These ties grant continuous access to top-performers. While this informal networking is still in place (Kikuchi 2006)[5], a gradual change from biographic towards skill-based selections is under way. Nowadays many firms make use of internet application processes, in which desirable skill profiles can be easily filtered out. While this still leaves open the option of selecting feeder institutions, the recruiting system becomes more transparent and permeable. Companies such as Mitsui offer not only a web based CV applications, but prior to this also online personality tests, that help to evaluate the skill-personality mix of potential applicants (including feedback to

4 During the economic miracle of the 1950s and 1960s with its short supply of skilled labour Japanese firms forged close ties with feeder universities to secure qualified personnel. This meant that small and medium sized enterprises (SMEs) have had traditionally problems of accessing top-graduates. Only in times of slow growth were they able to attract a sufficient number of qualified students. This resulted in an anticyclic recruiting pattern.

5 In fact this informal network seeking is central to the application cycle. Prior to interviews applicants contact peers that are already working in the prospective company (usually referred to as *Gakubatsu* or university cliquism), to gain insights into recruiting patterns and job potential.

the candidates). Career advisors in universities find it therefore increasingly difficult to "place" their students with corporations based on informal contacts. Some universities go even as far as organising promotion tours to advertise the skill profile of their students.

- Recruitment agencies witness a renaissance. Traditionally a foreign bastion, Japanese have started to make use of external services to identify and headhunt suitable candidates. Showing an increased willingness to pay for specialist know-how, they break with the tradition of relying solely on new male recruits that are nurtured in-house to become future leaders[6] (JIL 2008). This goes hand in hand with the rising ratio of postgraduates of the Japanese workforce (MEXT 2007). Further signs of this fundamental change can be found in the increased mobility of the labour force itself. On the one hand Japanese firms become more flexible and open up career tracks for the female labour force (*Sôgô Shoku*). In this way they start to tap into a highly qualified yet so far under-represented employee segment (Macnaughtan 2006). On the other hand Japanese employees themselves become more open towards changing jobs (Higashino 2005) creating new opportunities for foreign firms, that traditionally only played an outsider role in the Japanese labour market (cf. Esser 2003 on the strategy of foreign SMEs the to recruit Japanese personnel).

3. Conceptual Framework

The changing labour environment forces human resource departments in Japan to re-visit the criteria for staff selection and personal development. With the implementation of the result oriented *Seika Shugi* new assessment and career planning systems become paramount. As staff retention particularly of younger employees[7] gets increasingly difficult Japanese firms complement their recruiting interviews with paper and pencil tests for a more grounded decision process.

6 While this is certainly not new for technical expertise, this can now also be found in managerial mid-career recruits.

7 This change however is a double-edged sword. According to a NHK documentary (2007) the staff retention among new recruits has reached an all time low. In contrast to the artistic "freeter" (*Furîtâ*), a growing Japanese youth segment without fulltime employment, many young employees are impatient with their slow career progress. Wanting to make full use of their qualifications an increasing number of graduates switch jobs within a few years of employment. This phenomenon has become known as "*Dai Ni no Shinsotsu*" or "Second Graduate" shedding light on the repercussions of the slow growth economy.

However, only few local inventories exist. The most famous is the SPI / SPI 2 (Synthetic Personality Inventory). Originally developed by Recruit agency in 1974 (modelled after the Minnesota multiphasic personality inventory, MMPI) this combined aptitude and personality inventory is very popular in Japanese job assessments. This is however not limited to "classic" job applicability (language skills, mathematics, sciences, English skills). It consists of measuring emotions (stability, adaptation abilities towards people and organisation), behaviour (activism, sociableness, perserverance), enthusiasm (motivation, diligence, attitude) and character (interests, concerns, opinions, judgement) (URL 2008). Specialist foreign providers have reacted to this (market) niche and have started to offer tailored assessment packages in Japan. For example SHL has recently introduced their Occupational Personality Questionnaire (OPQ) that looks at behavioural aspects and their impact on performance and work competence. Similarly, foreign headhunting companies bring their expertise to Japan in using in-house test batteries for candidate assessment. However, many human resource managers remain sceptical as regards these inventories. During a four-month stay in Japan (April to July 2007) the author conducted expert interviews in leading Japanese and European companies, career advisors at universities as well as recruiting agencies. While many show an interest in this new form of personnel assessment they distrust the predictability of paper and pencil tests, thereby confirming earlier findings reported in Iwawaki and Vernon (1988). As the majority of firms make use of these tests many career centres at universities offer courses to prepare graduates for the application situation[8]. Some companies such as Fujitsu offer online training packages for Recruit's SPI test. Updated and available at the beginning of each year's recruiting cycle, Recruit itself publishes preparatory material for its hit product. Next to the potential distortion of the test results, it is the test procedure itself that many professional human resource managers criticise. The general tenor was that personality tests "help to support the decision process, but cannot fully replace it" (CEO of Tokyo-based recruitment company, interviewed in June 2007). In this context a perceived non-accuracy oscillated the discussion on psychometric assessments. The interviewees, that employ assessment inventories in Japan estimate a hit-ratio between 70-80 per cent. This at least partially explains a reserved attitude towards psychometric testing in Japan.

---

8 Some universities have developed their own inventories which stand in competition with external providers. For a small charge students have the chance to sit the psychometric tests which are likely to be used by firms.

From the reconfiguration of the Japanese work environment and the ongoing scepticism vis-à-vis quantitative competence screening arises the need for objective and accurate employee profiling with high predictability. The efficient provision of information is important for all fields of human resource management such as career counselling, personnel selection, performance assessment or personnel development. As performance becomes the epicentre of a meritocratic work environment a convincing assessment inventory becomes even more important. An ability analysis will give human resource professionals in Japan the opportunity to adequately assess the status quo of the workforce. This is of particular relevance for foreign firms operating here. Within the – old –network-oriented system many Western firms had not only little access to high performing personnel[9] but suffered also from a mis-match between the idiosyncrasies of the Japanese labour market (and the expectations of prospective employees) and their performance oriented work conception à la American. In many cases these aspects paired with culturally reinforced mis-conceptions often result in latent dissatisfaction with the local workforce. The evolving labour system and shrinking labour force leads to a (more) level playing field and at the same time to fiercer competition for human resources. By taking a fresh and timely look at psychometric profiling in Japan this study will inform the debate on human resources in Japan. While many correlates of job performance can be employed (social origin, social competence, behavioural aspects, motivation etc. as described above these are commonly assessed in Japanese inventories) a stable denominator of work-related success is intelligence (Nettelnstroth 2003). This psychological construct is therefore deemed as most reliable prognostic personality facet in the diagnosis of occupational aptitude and personnel selection. The use of intelligence tests promise quick and uncomplicated insights into the abilities of screened candidates. Particularly tests that provide detailed information on performance-relevant aspects (next to the overall intelligence level) are increasingly popular among human resource professionals. As contingencies of intelligence will differ for job categories (e.g. numeracy for accountants etc.), these tests open up the possibility of more transparent selection criteria by matching candidate and job profile.

9 In corporate image rankings foreign firms continue to do badly in Japan (cf. newest ranking compiled by NKK 2007). This complements the overall and traditional trend that Japanese employees prefer working for Japanese firms.

Modern intelligence inventories are, however, currently not available in Japan. For intelligence testing of adults foreign batteries such as the Wechsler-Test are widely used. Their clinical grounding and cultural bias makes them a suboptimal choice in the context of human resource assessments. In developing the above discussion the research team decided to employ the Intelligence Structure Test (I-S-T 2000) with a view to shed light on skill profiles of Japanese employees. As a standard test instrument in the Western hemisphere its key modules verbal, numerical and spatial-figural competence as well as reasoning are ideally suited to shed light on occupational aptitudes. While the intercultural extension to Japan and structural equivalence is discussed elsewhere (see previous chapter), the additional benefit is that this approach enables a powerful comparison with data from Germany (the origin of the inventory) as regards the constituting facets verbal, numerical and spatial-figural abilities.

4. Research Hypotheses

Using the modular approach of the Intelligence Structure Test we expect culturally reinforced skill profiles to emerge. In contrast to Western cultures idiosyncrasies of the Japanese language (writing system) will stimulate the ability as regards spatial-figural information (Foster 1990). Numerous studies point towards cross-culturally high cognitive ability to process visual information (e.g. Bagley 1994; Flaherty and Moran 1996; Lesser *et al.* 1965; Tamaoka 1991). Japanese will show a high competence in dealing with figural and illustrative material, grasping proportions of surface and space and creating logical relations between figures. This should also result in high scores at the aggregate level. We therefore assume that Japanese will score higher than Western candidates in the spatial-figural reasoning.

The Programme for International Student Assessment (PISA) regularly assesses fundamental knowledge and skills in more than 40 countries. Since the first test round in 2003 Japanese students have continuously been among the top-performers in mathematical proficiency. While German and UK students also rank above the OECD average, the score difference is substantial, confirming earlier findings of a high numerical proficiency of Japanese students (e.g. Uemoto and Haslerud 1959, Husen 1967 or Comber and Keeves 1973). Miura (1987) and Miura *et al.* (1988) report evidence that differences in numerical rep-

resentation may be responsible for the better performance in mathematical tests (see also Flaherty and Moran 2000 or Kuraishi *et al.* 1958). Analysing the mathematics curricula Stigler *et al.* (1982) conclude that Japanese students are introduced to more complex mathematics at an earlier age than Taiwanese or American students. We therefore assume that Japanese participants will exhibit a high calculating/mathematical ability, high level of abstract thinking and distinct competence in creating logical relationships between numbers. At the aggregate level Japanese candidates should reveal a high mathematical proficiency.

The Japanese literacy rate is very high despite its complex writing system (e.g. Sakamoto and Makita 1973, Saito 1982), which consists of 4 simultaneously used scripts. According to the United Nation's human development index (HDI) 99 per cent of Japanese can read and write. Although socio-cultural reasons are yet unclear (rigorous education system, high personal motivation, see e.g. Yamada 1984 on Kanji education) this places Japan among the world's most literate nations. Similarly, a general consensus on Japanese language processing has not been reached. Comparative psycholinguistic experiments have produced inconclusive results. While various studies report a high suitability of the Japanese script for language processing (e.g. Jones and Chisato; 1988 Makita 1969; Shimamura 1987; Shimomura and Yokosawa 1991) other studies are more cautious in their conclusions (e.g. Hirose 1994; Sasanuma 1992; Kess and Miyamoto 1999, Stevenson *et al.* 1982). With the use of the verbal module of the I-S-T 2000 some explorative light will be shed on the status quo of Japanese literary skills. High scores in the verbal field reflect good association with language-related material, a high level of language acquisition and competence in creating relationship between terms. All international indicators point towards similar skills of Japanese and Western candidates. We therefore assume that despite the complex language system, no significant literacy differences between Japanese and Westerners exist.

Fuelled by intense competition the Japanese education system has a traditionally a rigorous focus on memorisation and knowledge building (see also Cummings 1980). The main learning motivation is to achieve high scores in the university entrance exams (*Nyûgaku Shiken*) and with it access to feeder institutions for prestigious corporations. As immense knowledge is expected, many students attend after-class cram schools (*Juku*) to complement the regular school curriculum. This all-or-nothing mentality culminates in the Japanese saying "Sleep four hours, pass – sleep five hours, fail" (*Yontô Goraku*). This contrasts the Humboldtian ideal with its emphasis on developing personality and individuality that is the basis of many Western societies and we assume that Japanese test participants score higher when it comes to learnt knowledge.

5. Methodology

Intelligence is a complex trait construct grounded in differential psychology. The most influential paradigm – academic intelligence – is commonly assessed via psychometric inventories. While a consensus on definition, content and scope of intelligence has not yet been found, it is commonly accepted that intelligence describes independent abilities contributing to human performance. Pertaining to the assumption of separately measurable skills these abilities are represented in verbal, numerical and figural aptitudes. Due to the well-documented predictability on performance-related outcomes this conceptualisation (and derogatives) is extensively used in education and business.

5.1 Introduction to the Research Instrument

The inventory deployed in the present study is the Intelligence Structure Test 2000R. Based on a modular approach it measures verbal, numerical and figural intelligence via nine sub-tests. Anticipating over-simplification (i.e. measuring abilities with a single scale) each area is assessed via three task groups. Verbal intelligence is measured through sub-tests on sentence completion, verbal analogies and similarities. The numerical intelligence sub-tests include numerical calculations, number series and numerical signs. Figure selection, cubes and matrices are employed to assess figural intelligence. All nine task groups consists of 20 individual tasks. To each task a specified time frame is allocated (power test). The overall assessment time is about 90 minutes (for detailed information on the set-up of test and underlying test theory extant literature is available: Beauducel *et al.* 2001 and Liepmann *et al.* 2007).

Developed from the work of Amthauer (I-S-T 70) the completely revised I-S-T 2000 has become standard inventory for ability and aptitude assessment. Due to its convincing internal consistencies (with Cronbach's Alpha ranging between .86 and .95 for the English version), validity (correlations with other aptitude tests such as the d2 test, WAIS-R) and versatility the battery is currently translated into in 10 languages. Next to the base module (reasoning) the I-S-T 2000 also comprises a further sub-test, which assesses the degree of learnt knowledge. It comprises 84 tasks (multiple choice) consisting of verbal, numerical, and spatial-figural questions (equally weighted with 28 questions). In this way a differentiation between fluid intelligence and crystallized intelligence[10] is possible.

The cross-cultural extension to Japan is the first attempt to test and establish the I-S-T 2000 in a non-Western environment and first analyses have shown promising cross-cultural consistencies. Cross-cultural research is always problematic, and instrument equivalence is of utmost importance. This is particularly true for psychometric inventories. The translation of inventories is usually the weakest link of meaningful comparisons. Therefore great care has been taken in translation and where necessary local adaptation (colloquialism etc.) was emphasised. Particular challenges as regards the verbal sub-tests such as inherent ambiguities in languages, idioms and culture bound concepts (e.g. "grandfather clock") have been addressed. As knowledge is culture-bound some items of the knowledge test also needed to be adapted to the Japanese habitat.

While items around geography and mathematics are more or less universal ("What is the capital of Texas?" etc.) literary and art questions are more difficult to adapt. Figure 1 gives an example of this localisation process (further examples of this 'localisation' can be found in the previous chapter).

A high accuracy has been achieved within a six months process of independent translations into Japanese and re-translation into German (the original language of I-S-T 2000), pre-testing and fine-tuning of the Japanese inventory.

10 The I-S-T 2000R stands in the tradition of structural intelligence models. Hierarchical models of intelligence were first introduced by Cattell (1963) and Horn (1988). Within their triarchic layering system first order factors describe six primary skills (verbal, spatial, logic and numeric abilities as well as fluency and memory). In this model the general "g" factor is conceptualised as the two part construct fluid and crystallised intelligence and located at the secondary hierarchical level. The former comprises inherited, from learning processes independent abilities, that help to draw inferences. The latter describes abilities that make use of previous experiences, knowledge and skills. As both factors are very effective ability projectors, the hierarchical models are very useful as selection criteria.

With what was the following symbol originally associated with? 

a)	b)	c)	d)	e)
psychedelic drugs	ecological way of thinking	an eastern religion	astrology	the hippie movement

Adapted version:

次のシンボルは何を連想するものでしょうか？* 

a)	b)	c)	d)	e)
幻覚剤	エコロジカル的思考	西洋の宗教	占星術	ヒッピー運動

* What is the following symbol associated with?
(a: psychodelic drug; b: ecological way of thinking; c: Western religion; d: astrology; e: Hippie movement) – in both cases c is the correct answer.

Figure 1: Item adaptation in Japanese version of the I-S-T 2000 (example)

5.2 Sample(s)

The sample was drawn in Japan between January and July 2007. 542 participants aged between 18 and 51 took part in the study. The mean age of the overall sample is 20.9 years. All participants were Japanese native speakers. A high age- and educational homogeneity can be assumed. The data set includes both graduate and post-graduate students from universities in the Kantô, Kansai, Chûbu as well as Tôhoku region. Reflecting the Japanese education system first-, second- and third-tier universities were included in the sample, ranging from prestigious universities in Tokyo, to short-term (*Tanki Daigaku*) and/or more vocational universities. Also early career managers of a Tokyo-based recruiting company were surveyed. With a view to the group comparability as selection criteria the qualification for university entrance was used. This university entrance criteria was used for drawing a corresponding sub-sample of 477 German participants (56% females; age in years: M=27.1, SD=8.5, range: 17-60) from the data sets used by Liepmann *et al.* (2007) for the development of the I-S-T

2000. The percentage of female participants is similar in both groups. Table 1 summarises the age distribution for both sub-samples.

*Table 1: Age and gender distribution**

Age	Japanese	German
-21	417 (76.9)	209 (29.6)
22-29	107 (19.8)	257 (38.9)
30-	18 (3.3)	195 (29.5)
	542 (100)	661 (100)

* Percent values in brackets

6. Empirical Findings

In the previous chapter we have identified similarities in the factorial structure of our German and Japanese sample. At the most abstract level of skill profiling (score of right questions across three sub-tests) no significant differences could be found between the Japanese and the German group (sig. = .440). The subsequent test for effects also revealed no relevant discrepancies between the two groups (d = .04). Figure 2 illustrates the mean values for both the Japanese and German sample on each of the nine I-S-T 2000 sub-scales. The *-signs signal significant differences between the two test groups (t-test). The Japanese sample scores significantly higher on the CA, SI, FS, CU and MA scales. In contrast the German sample shows significantly more correct answers on the SC, VA and VS sub-scales. No differences are to be reported for the NS sub-scale. These findings are reconfirmed on the aggregate level, reflecting substantial differences in verbal, numerical and spatial-figural abilities. The t-tests for the three facets (nominal, raw values) show significant group differences on the 0.01-level. Table 2 illustrates the aggregate group comparison. The effect sizes for each facet highlights substantial differences, particularly as regards the verbal skills of the Japanese and German sub-groups. The reported magnitude (0,98) indicates a non-overlap of 51 per cent of the two distributions. Despite these differences at the sub-test level, a high skill coherency is to be reported for the Japanese and German sub-groups. The effect size is negligible, confirming the overall cross-cultural robustness of the test instrument.

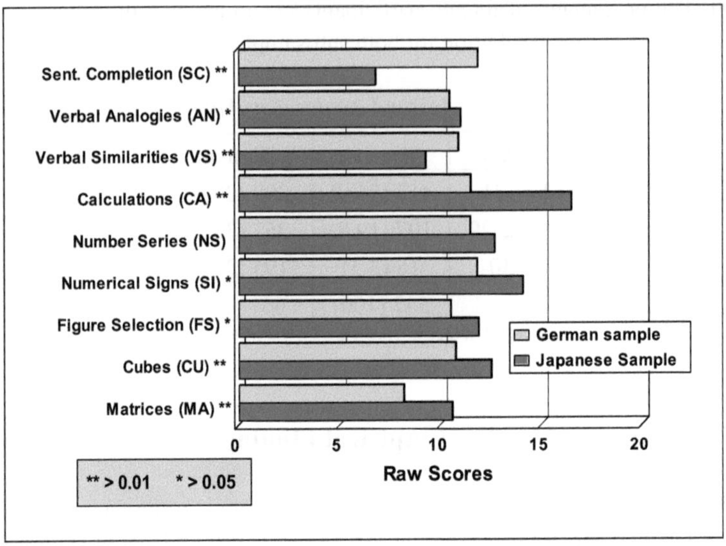

Figure 2: Sample means (I-S-T 2000-sub-scales)

Our assumptions pertaining to good numerical and spatial-figural skills among Japanese test participants have therefore been confirmed. In contrast to the comparative sample from Germany, Japanese individuals have scored considerably higher (overall value) both in terms of spatial figural and numeric reasoning. Limited knowledge about language abilities between German and Japanese led to the conservative a priori assumption of no significant differences.

The data exploration revealed, however, de facto substantial sample differences with the German participants scoring higher than the Japanese, mirroring the findings of the sub-scale analysis. These findings are inconsistent with our a priori assumption of similarities in verbal proficiency.

The knowledge module comprises 84 tasks (multiple choice) consisting of verbal, numerical, and spatial-figural questions (equally weighted with 28 questions). The data of 195 Japanese and 661 German test participants are

Table 2: Group comparison of aggregate I-S-T 2000-scales (standardised)

	Japanese Sample		German Sample		Effect Size (d)
	Mean	SD	Mean	SD	
Verbal **	-,539	,591	,442	1,049	,981 (Big)
Numerical **	,181	,894	-,148	1,057	,329 (Small)
Spatial-Figural **	,199	,879	-,163	1,063	,362 (Small)
Total	-,024	,786	,020	1.146	,045

** > 0.01

for analysis. Table 3 shows that the former sample scores lower on all three knowledge related aspects. Particularly the verbal facet shows substantial differences between the two sub-groups mirroring the findings from the basic module. In contrast to the reasoning part of the I-S-T 2000, here the Japanese under-perform as regards the numerical knowledge facet. The German subgroup answers more numeric related questions correctly. However, the subsequent analysis on effect sizes shows negligible differences between the two groups. No significant differences are to be reported as regards the spatial-figural knowledge. The analysis of the overall score across the three sub-tests highlights considerable inter-group differences, with the Japanese sub-group scoring significantly lower than the German one. Contrary to the a priori assumption high levels of learnt knowledge are more distinct in the German sub-

Table 3: Group comparison, knowledge test

	Japanese Sample		**German Sample**		**Effect Size (d)**
	Mean	**SD**	**Mean**	**SD**	
Verbal	15,09	3,29	19,50	5,36	,992 (big)
Numerical	13,28	3,06	15,82	5,13	,602 (medium)
Spatial-Figural	15,75	2,90	16,07	5,43	,073
Total	44,12	7,50	51,38	14,71	,622 (medium)

group. At this point it is important to reiterate that the research team has put considerable efforts into minimising cultural artefacts of the knowledge test (as described above). Even though it may be argued that culturally reinforced items are responsible for these differences, the structural analysis (CFA, as reported in the previous chapter) shows no aberrations for the Japanese version of the knowledge test.

Further Data Exploration

Verifying the external validity of the inventory Japanese test participants in the younger age brackets were chosen on the basis of their university affiliation. In this way the highly nuanced Japanese education system was reflected in the sampling procedure, thus enabling a subsequent comparative analysis with a view to potential sub-group education heterogeneity. In the context of university entrance exams as selecting criteria and with it university affiliation as likely ability and motivation predictor, further data exploration looked at group differences between participants from first-, second- and third-tier universities. Universities rankings (AS 2007) were used as grouping variable, resulting in three homogeneous sub-groups. In this way 57 participants have been allocated to top-ranking universities (11.2%), 347 participants to second-tier universities (68.4%) and 103 participants to third-tier universities (20.3%). Variance analysis was employed to test for anticipated group differences. Figure 3 illustrates the findings for the nine sub-tests of the I-S-T 2000 (mean nominal values, count of correct answers).

The *-signs signal significant group differences between the test groups. The first-tier university group scores significantly higher in all nine sub-tests in contrast to the other two groups. Conversely, the second-tier university group scores significantly higher on the SC, VA, CA, NS and SI scales. No differences between the second-tier and third-tier groups have been found on the VS sub-scales and all scales relating to spatial-figural reasoning. The subsequent effect size analysis (Cohen's d) reveals large effects between group A (first tier) and the two other groups. Between group B (second-tier) and group C (third-tier) medium effects can be shown (with the exception of FS, CU and MA).

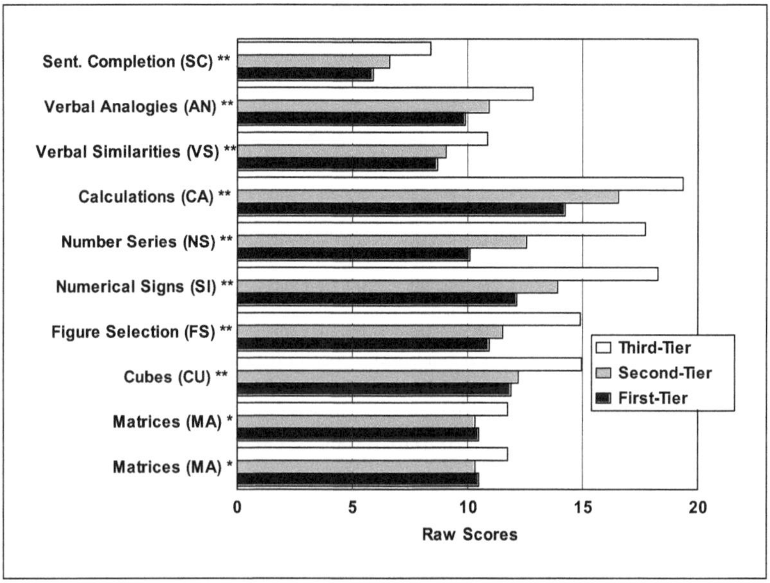

Figure 3: Japanese sample means (I-S-T 2000-sub-scales)

These findings are reconfirmed on the aggregate level as illustrated in Table 4. The substantial inter-group differences in verbal, numerical and spatial-figural abilities highlight the discriminatory value of the Japanese version of the I-S-T 2000. Variance and the subsequent effect-size analysis (with mainly large to medium effects) shows considerable group differences on all three skill facets. However, no significant differences between second- and third tier university affiliation are to be reported for the spatial-figural component (LSD test, no effect). The overall test scores (aggregate of the sub-tests) highlight substantial inter-group differences, with large to medium effect estimates. In sum, all groups show high abilities in the fields of numerical and spatial-figural reasoning (also in a cross-cultural perspective) with the group comprising affiliation to top universities underlining a particularly nuanced skill profile. While these results pertain to the raw scores (number of correct answers), the non-normed indicators must be used with some caution.

The findings of the knowledge test presented in Table 5 further supports the discriminatory value of the Japanese version of the I-S-T 2000. The data is only available for the first- (57) and second-tier (102) affiliated participants.

Table 4: Group comparison of aggregate I-S-T 2000-scales (standardised)

	Tier Group						Effect		
	(A)		(B)		(C)		(A-B)	(A-C)	(B-C)
	Mean	SD	Mean	SD	Mean	SD			
Verbal **	1.01	.78	-.05	.94	.96	-.47	1.07[1)]	1.48[1)]	0.41[3)]
Numerical **	1.07	.48	-.00	.90	1.09	-.58	1.08[1)]	1.65[1)]	0.57[2)]
Spatial-Figural **	.85	.70	-.09	.99	1.03	-.18	0.94[1)]	1.03[1)]	0.09[4)]
Total	1.25	.50	-.06	.89	1.03	-.18	1.31[1)]	1.79[1)]	0.48[2)]

** > 0.01 [1)]Large Effect [2)]Medium Effect [3)]Small Effect [4)]No Effect

The t-test reveals significant group differences. Cohen's d points towards large effect (1.415).

By combining the information provided in the basic module (reasoning) and the knowledge test the I-S-T 2000 allows for the calculation of values for fluid (gf) and crystallised intelligence (gc). The former refers to the ability of solving abstract problems and inductive reasoning. The latter is the reflection of cumulative learning experiences and involves understanding relations or solving problems which depend on knowledge acquired as a result of formal teaching and/or other cultural experiences.

The inter-group comparison identifies substantial differences on the second hierarchy level (cf. Cattell 1963 and Horn 1988, 1966 on hierarchical structure models of intelligence), with the first-tier university group showing higher scores than the second-tier group.

Table 5: Knowledge scores and fluid and crystallised intelligence

	First Tier Group		Second-Tier Group	
	Mean	SD	Mean	SD
Knowledge **	51.07	5,76	40.55	5,38
SWK**	102.37	4,88	94.58	4,42
SWF **	114.85	3,91	107.07	6.45

** > 0.01

7. Discussion and Implications

Japanese human resource management is undergoing substantial change. While institutional perspectives as regards work and employment environment are well documented (and already fill libraries) empirical evidence at the individual level is scarce. This study attempted to tackle the important issue of the influx of performance-orientation into Japanese human resource management from the immanent angle of the performance/skill profiles. Examining emerging meritocratic facets, the findings therefore raise the understanding of Japanese labour relations from the (micro)perspectives of career assessment. Additionally, the cross-cultural extension and use of a European intelligence inventory sheds light on idiosyncratic skill sets of Japanese employees. This latter aspect is especially important for foreign corporations, that traditionally had difficulties in securing qualified local personnel. From the increased access to personnel (due to the improved permeability of the Japanese employment system) arises the nascent need for adequate assessment. Shifts in the labour market have of course also affected recruiting practises and career planning of Japanese firms, which have begun to extend their assessment repertoire to psychometric evaluation. The (to date) limited availability of reliable local inventories is a further gap that this study aspires to close. Earlier work has already reported ample evidence on the good intercultural fit of the hierarchically structured intelligence conception as assessed with the I-S-T 2000 in the case of Japan. A high overlap of factorial structure (PCA, CFA) and satisfactory reliability scores (Cronbach's Alpha) point towards a high internal consistency and therefore general applicability of the research instrument. The findings presented here help to further our understanding at group-level, i.e. cross-cultural homogeneity of skill profiles. It is important to note, however, that this exploration does not to make qualitative comparisons between the samples. While a structural comparison has already been successful (etic research assumption), single-country analyses are currently only available using the standardised values and norms of the original German data set. Following an emic research postulate (particularly with a view to the sensitiveness of intelligence testing), the underlying question is whether a tailoring of the I-S-T 2000 inventory (normation) is mandatory.

The arrival of performance orientation at the individual level in the Japanese work world must be accompanied by a new design of achievement measurement. While the current discussion of achievement primarily focuses measurable outputs (Management by Objectives) there is an increasing concern about identifying and predicting the skill profile of suitable candidates. Psychometric assessment offers multifarious techniques of screening the potential of (future) employees. Among these intelligence enjoys particular popularity in recruiting and career planning. This psychological construct is not only a stable predictor of work-related success, it also looks on a more than 100 year history of gradual development, making it one of the success stories of modern psychology (Nettelnstroth 2003). Academic intelligence (the most influential paradigm) is therefore one of the most reliable prognostic personality facets in the diagnosis of occupational aptitude and personnel selection. Among the numerous inventories the Intelligence Structure Test is one most often employed assessment tools in Europe (due to its versatility and reliability). Its modular structure offers insights into the verbal, numerical and spatial-figural reasoning abilities both at the task and aggregate level – important building blocks of intelligence (and therefore success factors). As contingencies of intelligence will differ for job categories, the I-S-T 2000 is especially suitable for making Japanese skill sets transparent. Albeit the non-significant results at the aggregate level (overall score) the findings provide ample cues for cross-cultural differences between Japanese and German test participants (which were chosen as anchor sample) which will be discussed below.

Verbal facet: Research streams have engaged with Japanese language acquisition, differences in the decoding of the four Japanese scripts, differences in information processing, hemispheric lateralisation or visual representations. However, our knowledge about the Japanese writing system and intelligence is limited. Contrary to the a priori assumption substantial group differences have been detected. The aggregated sub-tests revealed that Japanese test participants scored significantly lower than members from a comparable Western sample (German). The large effect size suggests that Japanese may have a less developed association with language related materials. The ability of language acquisition may also be less pronounced, as is the competence in creating relationships between terms. The test results are, however, in line with findings from Iwawaki and Vernon (1988), who report higher scores on non-verbal and spatial than verbal tests. However, explanations for these differences must remain at this stage speculative. Even though the test instrument has been rechecked for its accuracy, numerous aspects may be responsible for these findings, including idiosyncrasies of the Japanese language itself, test situation (power test) or the style of the tasks. The intermittent use of various script systems (Kanji, Kana, Romaji) may also be responsible for the discrepancies between the Japanese and German samples. The test instructor observed very fast answer strategies by the Japanese test participants (most of the candidates used only half of the time allocated to the three verbal task groups), i.e. there seemed to be a very high (but unjustified) confidence in language abilities. It is important to note, that the hierarchical structure of the I-S-T 2000 can be confirmed (both in terms of verbal reasoning and verbal knowledge), albeit a high overlap of verbal and spatial-figural intelligence. The findings from a comparative angle lend further support as regards the considerable influence of cultural aspects (i.e. writing system) on the intelligence structure. It therefore reconfirms the inherent need for an emic extension and standardisation of the I-S-T 2000 in the case of Japan.

Numerical facet: The assumption pertaining to the high mathematical skills of Japanese test participants has found broad support. At the aggregate level a small effect size confirms practical differences between the Japanese and German groups. The subsequent analysis revealed that it is particularly task group 04 (mathematical equations) in which the Japanese test participants score considerably higher (more correct answers) than the German comparative group. The effect size (0.76) highlights large differences in the answer behaviour of the two groups. Task group 05 (number series) does neither show significant differences nor a sufficient effect size, whereas in task group 06 (numerical signs) statistical analysis revealed considerable differences at the 0.05 level. In sum, the Japanese participants have exhibited distinct competences as regards calculating/mathematical ability, abstract thinking and the creation of logical relationships between numbers. As per above at this stage a cross-cultural comparison must remain arbitrary, but the findings support the performance results of Japanese students at PISA. While the debate about underlying reasons would exceed the scope of the present study, human resource professionals can generally expect a high mathematical proficiency among potential Japanese applicants from a practical perspective. For recruiting or selection purposes a standardisation of the data seems mandatory (emic approach). Only in this way a meaningful intra-cultural classification can be achieved. Subsequent projects may not only look at the reasons for the mathematical performances (e.g. education system, employment of Kumon method) but also involve further scrutiny of differences in task presentation (Japanese symbols vs. Arabic number system), variations of speed for problem solving or controlling for the Japan-specific quinary counting system (grouping digits in myriads, i.e. 10,000 etc.). The inclusion of more advanced mathematical problems to strengthen the intra-cultural discriminatory value of the Intelligence Structure Test may also be considered in future research.

Spatial-figural facet: The findings reveal a nuanced Japanese skill set in dealing with figural and illustrative material and are therefore largely supportive of earlier studies which attest comparatively high cognitive abilities to process visual information. The test participants demonstrated a high performance as regards grasping proportions of surface and space and creating logical relations between figures. Even though the results of the t-test is relativised by the small effect size at the aggregate level differences between the Japanese and German groups have been confirmed. The modular approach of the Intelligence Structure Test helps to identify the origin of the diverging answer behaviour. The subsequent analysis at the sub-test level shows that it is particularly task group 08 (Cubes) and task group 09 (Matrices) in which the Japanese test participants score considerably higher than their German counterparts. The small to medium effect sizes highlight relevant differences in the answer behaviour of Japanese test participants. Task group 06 (figure selection) does show significant differences but not a sufficient effect size (.17). The assumption pertaining to the high visual skills of Japanese test participants has therefore found broad support. These findings are consistent with earlier empirical evidence in the context of related intelligence tests (Wechsler Test reported in Lynn 1977, and the Ravens Standard Progression Test reported in Chan and Vernon 1988). At the same time they also underpin earlier evidence of a high overlap of verbal and spatial-figural intelligence (see findings in previous chapter). The Japanese writing systems involve a substantial amount of figural information processing and leads to high performances of spatial-visual reasoning. In line with the discussion above the limitations of this "presumed etic" research approach are also valid here. The findings highlight the need for a standardisation for a meaningful intra-cultural skill assessment. Subsequent projects may further explore the impact of the Japanese writing on visual information processing. This may involve variations of speed in task presentations (controlled display with tachistoscope), the inclusion of memory tasks or the cross-cultural exploration of visual reasoning via electroencephalography (EEG).

Knowledge test: The findings do not support the assumption of a deeper general knowledge of Japanese test participants vis-à-vis their German counterparts. To the best of our knowledge cultural task artefacts can be ruled out, as the questions pertaining to verbal, mathematical and spatial-figural knowledge are to be presumed "culture-free" (e.g. geographical knowledge, world music etc.). Also, a confirmatory factor analysis points towards the successful translation and adaptation of the knowledge module into Japanese. In this sense the rigorous focus on memorisation and knowledge building may be fuelled by and directed towards university entrance exams. An alternative explanation could be the situational nature of knowledge (e.g. availability of knowledge at certain points in time). One important influence factor may, however, have been the small sample size of only 195 participants that took the knowledge test next to the basic module. Additionally, in terms of group consistency the sample is skewed towards second-tier universities. While the German subsample was highly homogenous (the German system provides an easier classification of test participants such as secondary school, university qualification etc.) the Japanese group consistence may have lead to some contamination. Even though the factor structure of the faceted intelligence concept – including the important dimensions fluid intelligence (gf) and crystallised intelligence (gc) – has been confirmed, the acculturation aspect that manifest in the knowledge test deserves further scrutiny in the future. As problem solving depends on knowledge acquired as a result of formal teaching and/or other cultural experiences, crystallised intelligence is closely related to acculturation processes. Hence, an extension to more Japan-specific knowledge tasks may help to shed light on systematic influences of the cultural framework and its inherent cumulative learning experiences (general knowledge, word comprehension and numerical abilities etc.).

With the Japanese employment system being in flux, the present study has successfully taken up the challenge of analysing change at the individual level. In the light of the increasing need for adequate assessment methods, we highlighted the application potential of the Intelligence Structure Test for Japan. The findings have helped to identify a performance/skill set of Japanese university graduates and young employees. As the outcomes obtained from intelligence tests in different cultural settings cannot be directly compared – the actual meaning assigned to the obtained score will differ from one culture to another and the results may be misleading in nature – the study has shown the normation/standardisation necessity in the case of Japan. In this sense the findings send out a cautionary note, not to simply apply Western assessment standards in Japan. Instead finetuning and adaptation of the inventory (normative sampling) seems mandatory to further strengthen the intra-culturally discriminatory value of personality tests such as the I-S-T 2000. Despite these inherent and important limitations the findings helped to identify strengths and weaknesses of Japanese test participants, which from an applied perspective maybe instrumental for cross-culturally sensitive recruiting and selection processes. After all, in this way the skill set of employees with diverging cultural background has become accessible and potential misinterpretations have been addressed. This is particularly relevant for (but not limited to) the human resource management of foreign firms as to date no empirically grounded assessment tool is available and potentially false assumptions/expectations constitute the relationship between local and expatriate staff. As a diagnostic instrument, corporations operating in Japan would greatly benefit from the I-S-T 2000 – especially in the light of the sensitivity of recruitment of personnel. The candidate profiling can be used to impartially identify employee strengths and weaknesses as part of an assessment/selection. This study therefore advanced our knowledge of skill differentiation in a society where inherent assumptions of equality and homogeneity are strong undercurrents.

8. References

Anon. (2004, 30. September). Seika shugi dônyû sara ni fuandai (Introduction of performance system: Further uneasiness). *Yomiuri Shinbun.*

Aoki, M. (1990). Toward an Economic Model of the Japanese Firm. *Journal of Economic Literature, 28(1)*, 1-27. M. Aoki, & R. Dore (Eds.), *The Japanese Firm. The Sources of Competitive Strength.* Oxford: Oxford University Press.

Aoki, M., Jackson, G., & Miyajima, H. (2007). *Corporate Governance in Japan.* Oxford: Oxford University Press.

Asahi Shinbun (2007). *Daigaku rankingu 2008* (University ranking 2008). Tokyo: Asahi Shinbun Shuppansha.

Bagley, C. (1984). Cultural Diversity, Migration and Cognition Styles. In G. K. Verma, & C. Bagley (Eds.), *Race Relations and Cultural Difference: Educational and Interpersonal Perspectives* (pp. 217-246). New York: St. Martin's Press.

Brown, J. (2003). The Self-enhancement Motive in Collectivist Cultures. *Journal of Cross-Cultural Psychology, 34(5)*, 603-605.

Cattell, R. B. (1963). Theory of Fluid and Crystallised Intelligence. A Critical

Experiment. *Journal of Educational Psychology, 54(1)*, 1-22.

Chan, J., & Vernon, P. E. (1988). Individual Differences among the Peoples of China. In S. H. Irvine, & J. W. Berry (Eds.), *Human Abilities in Cultural Context* (pp. 340-357). Sidney, New York: Cambridge University Press.

Comber, L. C. & Keeves, J. F. (1973). *Science Education in Nineteen Countries*. Stockholm: Almquist and Wiksell.

Cummings, W. K. (1980). *Education and Equality in Japan*. Princeton: Princeton University Press.

Dai, H. (2005, September). Japan's Changing Labour Market. *JETRO Japan Economic Monthly*.

Demes, H. (1998). Arbeitsmarkt und Beschaeftigung (Labour Market and Employment). Deutsches Institut für Japanstudien (Ed.), *Die Wirtschaft Japans* (pp. 135-164). Berlin: Springer.

Dirks, D., Hemmert, M., Legewie, J., Meyer-Ohle, H. & Waldenberger, F. (2000). The Japanese Employment System in Transition. *International Business Review, 9(5)*, 525-553.

Esser, M. (2003). The Changing Labour Market in Japan and its Impact on the Personnel Management of Small Size Companies. In W. Dorow & H. Groenewald (Eds.), *Personalwirtschaftlicher Wandel in Japan (pp. 223-231)*. Gabler: Wiesbaden.

Flaherty, M. & Moran, A. (1996). Visual Memory Skills in Japanese and Caucasians. *Perceptual and Motor Skills, 82*, 1319-1329.

Flaherty, M. & Moran, A. (2000). Absence of a Numerical Memory Span Advantage in Japanese Kanji. *Perceptual and Motor Skills, 90(1)*, 272-278.

Foster, M. (1990). A Cross-cultural Study on Hemispheric Asymmetries in Tachistoscopic Recognition of Kanji Characters. *Tôhoku Psychologica Folia, 49*, 1-14.

Hirose, T. (1984). Kanji oyobi kana tango no imiteki shôri ni oyobosu hyôki no kôka (Effects of script frequency on semantic processing of kanji and kana). *Shinrigaku Kenkyû, 55(3)*, 173-176.

Holzhausen, A. (1998). *Das japanische Beschäftigungssystem in der Krise* (The Japanese Employment System in Crisis). Wiesbaden: Gabler.

Horn, J. L. (1988). Thinking about Human Abilities. In J. R. Nesselroade & R. B. Cattell (Eds.), *Handbook of Multivariate Experimental Psychology*. New York: Plenum.

Husen, T. (1967). *International Study of Achievement in Mathematics*. Stockholm: Almquist and Wiksell.

Itô, K. (2006). *Gendai no rômu kanri* (Contemporary labour management).

Tokyo: Minerva Shobô.
Iwawaki, S. & Vernon, P. E. (1988). Japanese Abilities and Achievements. In S. H. Irvine & J. W. Berry (Eds.), *Human Abilities in Cultural Context (pp. 358-382)*. Cambridge University Press: Cambridge.
JILPT (Japan Institute for Labour Policy and Training, 2008). *Japanese Working Life Profile 2007/2008*. Available at: http://www.jil.go.jp.
Jones, E. A. & Chisato, A. (1988). The Processing of Japanese Kana and Kanji Characters. In D.C. de Kerckhove, & C. J. Lumsden (Eds.), *The Alphabet and the Brain (pp. 301-320)*. Berlin: Springer.
Jöreskog, K. G. & Sörbom, D. (1993). *LISREL 8-User's Reference Guide.* Chicago: Scientific Software International.
Jöreskog, K. G. & Sörbom, D. (2002). *LISREL 8.53*. Chicago: Scientific Software International.
Keizer, A. (2005). *The Changing Logic of Japanese Employment Practise.* Rotterdam: Erasmus Research Institute of Management, Erasmus University.
Keizer, A (2007). Flexibility in Japanese Internal Labour Markets. *Bradford University School of Management Working Paper Series, 07(1).*
Kikuchi, S. (2006). *Jiko bunseki – hajimeru shûshoku katsudô* (Self-analysis, starting job search activities). Tokyo: Nihon Jitsugyô Shuppansha.
Kuraishi, S., Umemoto, T., Yasuhara H. & Okuno, S. (1958). Psychological Studies on Learning in School Subjects: The Developmental Study on the Relations between Achievement in Arithmetic and Intelligence Factor. *Japanese Journal of Education Psychology, 6*, 159-167.
Lesser, G. S., Fifer, G. & Clark, D. H. (1965). Mental Abilities of Children from Different Social Class and Cultural Groups. *Monographs of the Society for Research in Child Development, 30*, 1-115.
Lynn, R. (1977). The Intelligence of the Japanese. *Bulletin of the British Psychological Society*, 30, 69-72.
Macnaughtan, H. (2006). From 'Post-war' to 'Post-bubble'. Contemporary Issues of Japanese Working Women. In P. Matanle, & W. Lunsing (Eds.), *Perspectives on Work, Employment and Society in Japan (pp. 31-57).* Palgrave Macmillan: Houndsmills.
MEXT (Ministry of Education, Culture, Sports, Science and Technology, 2007). *Statistics: University and Junior college.* Available at: http://www.mext.go.jp.
MHLW (Ministry of Health, Labour and Welfare, 2004). *Koyô kanri chôsa* (Labour management survey). Tokyo.

MHLW (Ministry of Health, Labour and Welfare, 2006). *Basic Survey of Human Resources Development*. Tokyo.

Miura, I. T. (1987). Mathematics Achievement as a Function of Language. *Journal of Educational Psychology, 79(1)*, 79-82.

Miura, I. T., Kim, C. C., Chang, C-M. & Okamoto, Y. (1988). Effects of Language Characteristics on Children's Cognitive Representation of Number: Cross-cultural Comparisons. *Child development, 59(6)*, 1445-1450.

Nettelnstroth, W. (2003). *Intelligenz im Rahmen der beruflichen Tätigkeit* (Intelligence in the context of work). Digitale Dissertation. Freie Universitaet Berlin. Available at: http://www.diss.fu-berlin.de.

NKK (Nihon Kôkoku Kenkyûjo, 2007). *Nikkei kigyô imêji chôsa* (Japanese firms' image survey). Tokyo: Nihon Keizai Shinbunsha.

NKS (Nihon Keizai Shinbun, 2007). Zenshain nattoku wo mesasu (Seeking the agreement of the workforce). In Nihon Keizai Shinbunsha (Ed.), *Nihon keizai shinbun*. Tokyo, 22 November, 20.

NKS (Nihon Keizai Shinbun, 2008). Tekizai tekisho' de sôryokuzen (Total war with 'the right person at the right post'). In Nihon Keizai Shinbunsha (Ed.), *Nihon keizai shinbun.* Tokyo, May, 1.

Park, S-J. & Kim, W-P. (2003). Ohne Daichi versus Carlos Ghosn: Zum Paradigmenwechsel von Unternehmensstrategien in Japan (Ohne Daichi versus Carlos Ghosn: Paradigm Shift in Corporate Strategies in Japan). In W. Dorow & H. Groenewald (Eds.), *Personalwirtschaftlicher Wandel in Japan* (Changes in Japanese Human Resource Management) (pp. 95-113). Wiesbaden: Gabler.

Saito, H. (1982). Kanji no yomi ni kansuru jôhô shôri katei (Information processing in kanji reading). *Jidô shinrigaku no shinpo*, *21*, 328-351.

Sakamoto, T. & Makita, K. (1973). Reading in Japan. In J. A. Downing (Ed.) *Comparative Reading* (pp. 440-465). New York: Macmillan.

Shimamura, A. P. (1987). Word Comprehension and Naming: An Analysis of English and Japanese Orthographies. *American Journal of Psychology, 100(1)*, 15-40.

Shimomura, M. & Yokosawa, K. (1991). Processing of Kanji and Kana Characters within Japanese Words. *Perception and Psychophysics*, *50(1)*, 19-27.

Stevenson, H. W., Stigler, J. W., & Lucker, G. W. (1982). Reading Disabilities: The Case of Chinese, Japanese and English. *Child Development, 53(5)*, 1164-1181.

Stigler, J. W., Lee, S., Lucker, G. W. & Stevenson, H. W. (1982). Curriculum and Achievement in Mathematics: A Study of Elementary School Children in Japan. *Journal of Educational Psychology, 74(3)*, 315-322.

Tamaoka, K. (1991). Psycholinguistic Nature of the Japanese Orthography. *Studies in Language and Literature, 11(1)*, 49-82.

Tatsumichi, S. & Morishima, M. (2007). Seikashugi from an Employee Perspective. *Japan Labour Review, 4(2)*, 79-104.

Uemoto, T. & Haslerud, G. M. (1959). Response and Attitude of American and Japanese Children to Number Situation. *Bulletin of Kyoto University, Faculty of Education*. 69-96.

URL (2008) http://www.recruit-ms.co.jp/service/service_detail/org_key/A001/

Waldenberger, F. (2006). The Evolution of the Japanese Employment System in Comparative Perspective. In P. Matanle, & W. Lunsing (Eds.), *Perspectives on Work, Employment and Society in Japan* (pp. 8-30). Palgrave Macmillan: Houndsmills.

Yamada, J. (1984). Kodomo ni totte kanji to wa: Kanji no Kyôikugaku (Kanji for children: kanji education). In H. Kaiho (Ed.), *Kanji wo kagaku suru* (Making kanji scientific). Tokyo: Yuhihaku.

Changes in Japanese Companies' Personnel Management Practices Relating to Female Employees: From the Early 1980s to the Early 2000s[1]

Kuniko Ishiguro

1. Introduction

More than twenty years have passed since the Equal Employment Opportunity Law (EEOL)[2] was enacted in Japan in 1986. The government has been proposing and implementing policies for promoting the utilisation of female employees since the 1990s[3]. It seems, however, that Japanese women's overall position in society, as well as in companies, is still lagging behind that of other developed countries. For example, according to the Gender Empowerment Measure of the United Nations Human Resource Development Report, Japan is 57th out of 109 countries: despite the fact that in the Human Development Index it ranks 10th among 182 countries (UNDP, 2009). Thus, according to the Ministry of Health, Labour and Welfare (2010), average wages of female workers were 78.3 per cent of men's in 2009. Overall rates of female workers holding managerial positions are also low. Among *kakarichō* (chief[4]), only 13.8 per cent were women in 2009 (ibid.), 7.2 per cent of *kachō* (section manager) were women, and only 4.9

1 This chapter is based on re-edited extracts from an unpublished PhD thesis submitted to the University of Sheffield, K. Ishiguro (2008) *Generating Equal Employment Opportunities: The Work and Life of Female Managers in Japanese Companies.*

2 The Equal Employment Opportunity Law was enacted in 1986. The official name is the 'Law on Securing, Etc. of Equal Opportunity and Treatment between Men and Women in Employment' (*Koyō no bun-ya ni okeru danjo no kintō na kikai oyobi taigū no kakuho tō joshirōdōsha no fukushi no zōshin ni kansuru hōritsu).* In practice, the EEOL was enacted as a radical revision of the Working Women's Welfare Law (*Kinrō Fujin Fukushi Hō*), adopted by the Diet in 1972. For detailed information on the passage of the law, see for example Lam (1992, 89-100), Okutsu (n.d.) and Shinotsuka (1995, 65-68).

3 For detailed information on the government's efforts in developing a gender-equal society, refer to the website of the Gender Equality Bureau, Cabinet Office: http://www.gender.go.jp/index.html.

4 Although it is impossible to translate position titles in Japanese organisations into English due to the difference in management practices, I have used the English translations from the Basic Survey on Wage Structure (see http://www.mhlw.go.jp/english/database/db-l/b-explanation.html for further explanation).

per cent among *buchō* (director), though these numbers are indeed an improvement on those of the past.

Given the number of media reports on the backward situation of female workers in Japanese companies, has there not been any effort to improve women's working conditions? This study analyses Japanese companies' management practices regarding female regular workers from the early 1980s to the early 2000s based on the cases of three major Japanese companies – an electronic company (Company A), a bank (Company B) and a company in the service industry specialising in education and publishing (Company C).

In summary, the three cases lead us to understand that economic and financial situations, as well as status of domestic employment market, are among the major factors in deciding companies' management policies and practices. From the early 1980s to the early 2000s, Japan experienced economic turmoil – the so-called bubble economy in the late 80s, the burst of the bubble economy in the early 90s and the subsequent "lost decade" during the 90s. Companies were forced to change various aspects of management practices, also in relation to female workers.

However, this does not equal a dramatic change in management practices involving female employees. Recruitment policies in the Japanese business world are still decided by the trend in male university graduates as well as the situation of the labour market and the company's position within it.

Apart from this, the initiatives of company leaders have also exerted strong influence over management practices. The values instilled by the leaders were enhanced by interactions among all employees, creating strong corporate cultures and thereby affecting the perceptions of managers and the public in relation to female employees.

The cases of the three companies illustrate various interesting features of employment practices in Japanese companies. These vary according to their respective industries, and the skills and abilities required of employees. The companies' personnel management policies are affected by these differences as well as by their financial situation. Company C seems to provide all the necessary elements for facilitating advancement of female employees in the organisation, while the other two companies, until recently, did not appear strongly motivated in this respect.

In the remainder of this study, we will first briefly depict scenarios of women and work in Japan. The next section moves on to the cases of three companies, which will subsequently be analysed with an eye to the distinctive features of women and personnel management practices in Japan, as well as changes during the past twenty years.

2. Women and Work in Japan

The legal system in relation to women and their position in Japanese society has been gradually changing over the last two decades. Important milestones include Equal Employment Opportunity Law (EEOL, 1986), the Child Care Leave Law (1991), and the Basic Law for a Gender-equal Society (1999). These important legislative milestones have, however, been continuously challenged, namely as obstacle to business development or cultural values (Yamamoto, 1987; Ō ba, 1988, Imada, 1996). Female employees themselves are generally portrayed to have adopted one of three stances: support, opposition and indifference. Currently, women comprise 42.5 per cent of the total labour force in 2009 (Statistics Bureau, 2010). Of these working women, 86.4 per cent are employed (Cabinet Office, 2008: 70). However, gender inequality in Japanese companies still persists in wage differences between women and men, and women's lower representation in managerial positions. The high ratio of non-regular workers among Japanese women (53.3% in 2009, Statistics Bureau, 2010) has also had serious social repercussions (Ishiguro, 2008).

From a range of economic theories on discrimination, theories on statistical discrimination (Piore, 1971; Arrow, 1972; Goldin, 1990, 88; Phelps, 1972; Kawaguchi, 1997), and internal labour markets and the related concept of the dual labour market (Piore, 1971; Doeringer and Piore, 1971, cited in Osterman, 1984; Piore, 1975 cited in Lam, 1992, 31-44) are most often used to explain causes of gender inequalities in Japanese companies. The representative works of Koike (1988, 1999) and Yashiro (1980) strongly support the theorisation of statistical discrimination in Japanese companies: a) women serve on average fewer years than men; b) whilst some women do work longer, it is difficult and costly to identify them and c) jobs which require high levels of proficiency need mid- and long-term on-the-job training (OJT) (Koike, 1988, 80-85, 1999, 194-195). The author asserts that both a) and b) are seen in many countries besides Japan; however, condition c), namely the necessity for mid- and long-term OJT has been a core competency of Japanese companies, consequently the hurdles for women have become higher in Japan (ibid.). Yashiro (1980, 89-90) summarises thus: a) gender wage differences are caused by differences in productivity, which are due to different training investment opportunities, not by employers' taste for discrimination or their emotional preferences; b) the main cause of 'statistical discrimination' in allocating training opportunities is that women's job separation rates are higher than men's, which means women do not receive as much training, job assignment, or job rotation as men; c) statistical discrimination is applied not only to new graduate employees, but also to new employees with experience; consequently there are considerable wage gaps among middle-aged experienced employees.

Tomita (1988, 144-165) stresses the necessity to reconsider the application of statistical discrimination theory, as he did not find any correlation between high job separation rates and gender differences in employment management. Osawa (1993, 109-117) draws attention to the possible importance of the dual labour market in Japanese companies. A case study of a department store in Japan by Lam (1992), cites the influence of the internal labour market on gender inequality. Yashiro, who has been a proponent of the theory of statistical discrimination, also argues that the particular feature of Japan's strong internal labour market exacerbates gender inequality (Yashiro, 1980, 6, 75-81).

In addition, Osawa (1998, 106-145) specifies the reason for gender inequality in the Japanese employment market: the career patterns of male company employees. She asserts that the main cause of the wage differential is the long length of service of male workers. Under sustainable company growth, which was supported by the indirect financial system, long-term employment and seniority-based employment became the rationale of Japanese companies (ibid, 148-149)[5]. With these distinctive employment practices, companies in Japan could operate their businesses using different rules from those in other countries; consequently providing long-term job security for men (ibid, 7-8, 148-149). Japanese compa-

5 By hiring a young labour force Japanese companies were able to lower their personnel costs (Osawa, 1998, 148-149).

nies invest greatly in their employees from the beginning and are wary of investing in women, who will not work as long as men. However, the situation began to change with the increase in women's service years. This led to further disparities. Since companies do not invest much in women, the difference in productivity between men and women widens in line with the length of their service (ibid, 115-119). The longer women stay in a company, the greater the pressure that salaries, which - following the Japanese logic of lifelong employment and promotion by age - increase according to service years, put on the company's personnel costs.

Empirical research has helped to shed further light onto the unrealised employment potential of women in organisations. The main findings on gender inequality from labour research in Japan can be summarised as follows:

1) gender division of work allocation due to different patterns of work arrangement by industry and by company, and consequent differences in career formation by gender (Wakisaka, 1993; Tomita, 1991)
2) gender differences in allocating tasks and consequent differences in opportunities for skill and ability development by OJT (Rengō Sōgō Seikatsu Kaihatsu Kenkyūjo, 1996; JIWE, 2002)
3) personnel management systems, represented by the *kōsubetsu jinji kanri seido* (dual career track employment system), which segregate employees into *sōgōshoku* (career track) and *ippanshoku* (non-career track) roles (Koike, 1988)
4) issues around women balancing family roles with work (JIWE, 2002, 2005)
5) inefficiency of systems such as child-care leave which are intended to support women's continuation in work
6) differences of supervisors' attitudes and behaviours in guiding, evaluating and motivating employees, based on the gender of subordinates (Yashiro, 1992; Nihon Rōdō Kenkyū Kikō,1997)
7) persistent problems of discrimination in companies which follow conventional values and practices (Matsushige, 1998)

These problems are also observed in statistics compiled by the MHLW (Figure 1).

If we compare each set of data in chronological order, changes did occur from 1986 to 2000. However, women's incompatibility with conventional working patterns and styles in companies, and the need for more service years and longer working hours, seem to be potent issues for companies. In addition, employers strongly believe that it is difficult for women to balance work and family responsibilities.

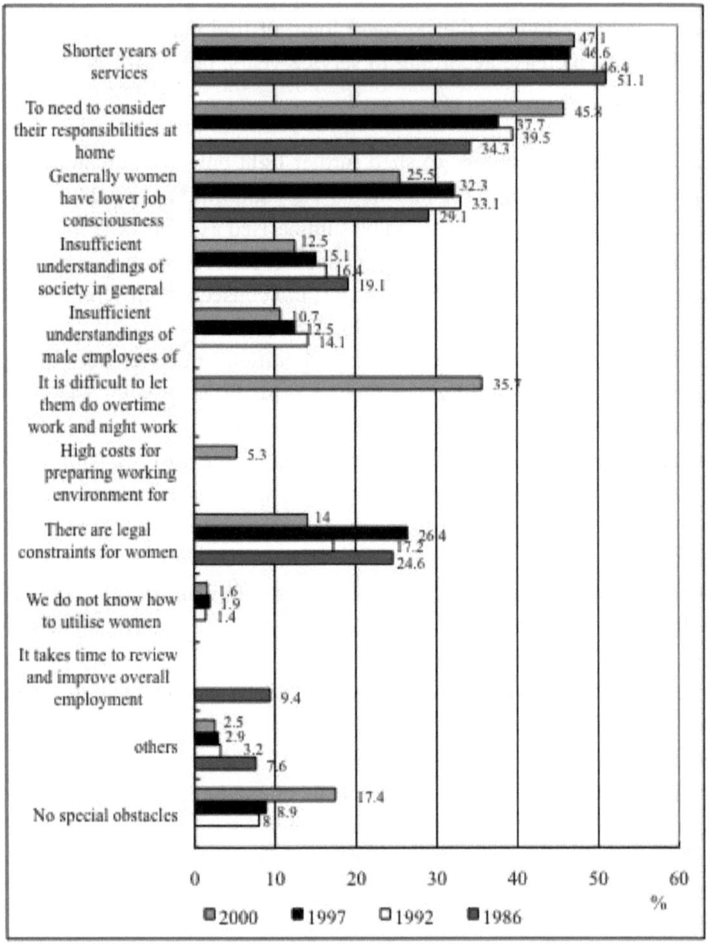

Figure 1: Obstacles to companies' utilisation of female employees

Source: MHLW (2004), *Heisei 15 nenban Hataraku Josei no Jitsujō*, available at http://www.mhlw.go.jp/houdou/2004/03/h0329-1a.html#gaiyou

Although the topics and disciplines vary, our review suggests a firmly established gendered employment system. In addition, government and employers actively joined in the process of institutionalisation of the system. The union's lacklustre support of women's advancement is well documented (e.g. Broadbent, 2003; Asakura, 2004; Kinoshita, 1998; Weathers, 2005a and b; Schoppa, 2006). Despite legislative improvements, gender inequality continues to be the reality for many Japanese people.

In order to understand the situation surrounding women and work, we need micro level analysis of employment and management practices in Japanese companies. Kimoto (2003, 28-30; 2005, 29-32) also argues the necessity for case studies which approaches reality in the employment process by using gender perspectives, while at the same time improving on macro analysis. She argues that:

> Case studies are required because the actual organisation of capitalism in Japan, and the various conditions that sustain this organisation both in Japan and abroad, are changing, with the result that the structure of job segregation by gender is also showing subtle signs of change. Another reason is that company society, with its variations, cannot be bundled together as a whole. It is necessary to conduct careful investigations as to what combination of conditions changes the way in which individual industries, companies and workplaces respond. These types of case studies will enable us to recognise the direction of future changes and the various factors that underlie restructuring. 'Men's labour studies' have accumulated a body of case studies, which although overwhelmingly concentrated on analyses of manufacturing industry, reach right down to the level of various companies and workplaces. Taking a lesson from this, it is imperative that we begin to see more case studies enriching women's labour studies. (Kimoto, 2005, 31)

Asami also supports the idea of the necessity of in-depth research using case studies, in conducting her research into career formation of female clerical workers: '… it hinders our understandings if we come to the conclusion that the roles of female clerical workers are 'routine and secondary' without observing and analysing their work and career' (Asami, 2006, 4). There are three good examples of case studies which investigate women's work and management in contemporary Japanese organisation in the retail industry. As has been mentioned, Lam's study reveals institutionalised discrimination against female employees by using the case of *Seibu* department store (Lam, 1992). Lam examined the company's personnel policies and personnel management practices and contributory factors to institutionalised discrimination against female employees, such as hiring, career systems, career planning and promotion, job rotation and mobility and training, by interviewing numerous employees and managers as well as conducting questionnaire surveys. Kimoto conducted close examination into female employees and management through case studies within a department store and a supermarket (Kimoto, 2003). Kimoto examined policies on female employees including company rules such as maternity leave and child care leave, salary structures and personnel management practices such as hiring, placement, and promotion. Like Lam, she also conducted interviews to elucidate the ways those policies and practices are actually operated. From both cases, she found organisational problems which have made the advancement of female workers to managerial positions difficult (ibid, 195-203). Another study is Broadbent's case study of a supermarket where she conducted participant observation (Broadbent, 2003). Their findings led to insightful analyses, proving the effectiveness of using case studies for research into gender issues in organisations.

3. Case Studies

With the help of case studies, we intend to chart actual cases of work and women in Japan in order to analyse gender relations in the employment process in Japanese organisations. This section presents the cases of three companies. Table 1 provides general information on the case companies.

Company A

Company A was established in 1935, and it has grown to become one of the biggest electronics companies in Japan, currently covering businesses such as software and services, computer and communication platforms, electrical devices and other related operations. The company was developed during the early *Shōwa* period through the shift to nationalisation of the automatic telephone switchboard. Afterwards, the company expanded in line with the development and production of computers, radio communication equipment, semiconductors, office computers and business information-communication network systems.

Table 1: General information on the companies

	Company A	Company B	Company C
Industry	Electronics	Bank	Service (Education and Publishing)
Sales Consolidated FY 2005 (Approx.)	¥5,000 billion ($42 billion)	¥1,000 billion ($8 billion) *Total Income	¥350billion ($ 3 billion)
Net Income Consolidated FY 2005 (Approx.)	¥70 billion ($600 million)	¥400 billion ($3 billion)	¥16 billion ($ 130 million)
Number of regular employees March 2006 (Approx.)	160,000 (group, worldwide) 35,000 (headquarters)	16,000 (group) 8,000 (Company B)	12,000 (group) 1,800 (headquarters)
Percentage of women among regular employees	15.9% (2004)	33.3% (2004)	55.5% (2006)
Percentage of women among managers	n/a, but below the average rate in companies in the survey of the MHLW	5.4% (2004)	32.3% (2005)
Union	Federation of labour unions of group companies.	Unions in group companies.	Union in branches of an overseas subsidiary.
Characteristics of work/skills	Three main types of employees: factory workers / engineers (need specialised skills) / white-collar	Only white-collar employees (Sales, loan, clerical, administration)	Creative / intellectual production work including editing, research, marketing, in addition to sales / administration

Source: Company Documents; Annual Reports

Figure 2: Changes in numbers of employees (Company A)

Company A employed a total of 160,000 employees in locations worldwide, including the headquarters of the group which has about 35,000 employees at the end of fiscal year 2005. The consolidated net sales for the fiscal year 2005 were approximately 5,000 billion yen, with operating income of 180 billion yen and net income of 70 billion yen (Annual Report).

The electronics industry has greatly contributed to Japan's economic growth. By focusing on hi-tech growth, the industry rode out two oil shocks and the 1985 appreciation of the Japanese yen due to the Plaza Accord. The growth of the semiconductor market also maintained their business growth. However, Company A's sales stagnated in the 1990s and the 2000s. In response to the first crisis in the early 1990s, the company was forced to change its management strategies drastically, including personnel management practices. In terms of the employment structure, the percentage of female workers was around 40 per cent in the 1950s; however, it has been gradually decreasing, and had fallen to only 16 per cent by 2004. This decrease is mainly due to the change in factory work from assembly to processing which demands fewer female employees. In addition, females employed in administrative work have been replaced by temporary workers, causing a decrease in numbers of female regular employees since 1994 (Figure 2)[6].

There have been drastic changes in recruitment activities as well. In the 1980s, companies in the electronics industry enthusiastically started hiring female university graduates with majors in humanities as systems engineers in addition to students with majors in science. However, owing to the economic stagnation in Japan and consequent decline in company performance, numbers of new graduates hired have decreased steeply since the early 1990s. As Figure 3 shows, except for engineers, numbers recruited have been at a very low level since 1993. Recruitment from junior college and high school, in particular, became negligible, clearly indicating a shift in the employment policy to replace administra

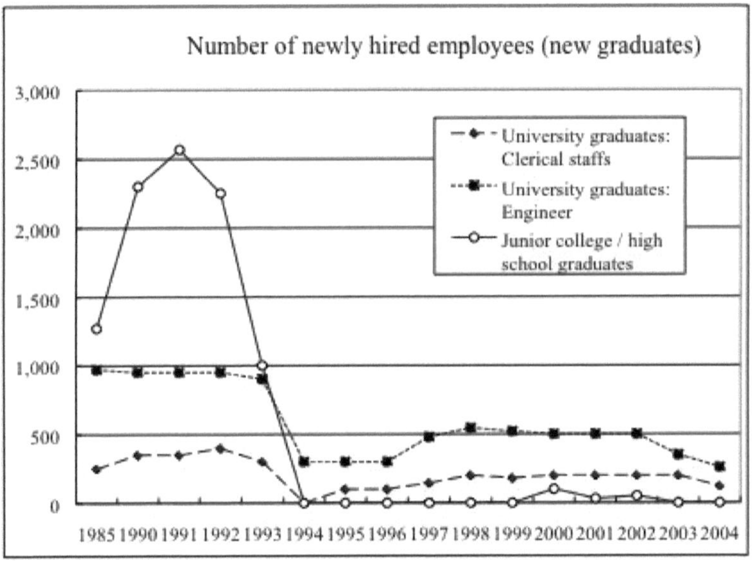

Figure 3: Trend in numbers of newly hired employees (new graduates, Company A)

6 There are three main types of employee in the company – clerical staff, engineers, and factory workers. The ratio of factory workers shifted from about 50 per cent in 1970 to around 20 per cent in 2004 due to the shift of the work in factories from assembly to processing (HR manager, Company A).

tive/clerical workers with temporary workers. Only core employees have been hired as regular employees. Other personnel management programmes were also forced to change in order to reduce personnel costs and increase business efficiency, most notably the introduction of a pay-per-performance system and related changes in the personnel management programmes.

In terms of gender differences among employees, both average age and average service years show a tendency for a greater increase among female employees (Table 2 and Table 3). The average age of female employees increased by almost eight years between 1982 and 1998 (male employees: four years and eight months). Consequently, the age differences between men and women decreased from about eight years to four years and five months. Similarly, women's years of service increased by seven years and four months while men's service years increased by five years and three months. The difference between men and women decreased from six years to three years.

Table 2: Average age by gender[7] (Company A)

Year	**1982**	**1985**	**1990**	**1995**	**1998**
Male	33. 1	32. 5	34. 0	36. 3	37. 9
Female	25. 5	25. 3	27. 3	30. 4	33. 4

Source: Financial Reports: various years

Table 3: Average service years by gender (Company A)

Year	**1982**	**1985**	**1990**	**1995**	**1998**
Male	11. 9	11. 3	12. 6	14. 9	16. 2
Female	5. 8	5. 5	7. 4	10. 3	13. 2

Source: Financial Reports: various years

Despite the narrowing gap in average age and service years between men and women, changes in average monthly salary by gender do not reflect as much improvement (Figure 4). Salaries of women were 50.1 per cent of those of men

7 Before 1982, the financial report presented average age and service years of clerical/engineering work employees and shop floor employees separately. The report stopped presenting data by gender altogether in 1999.

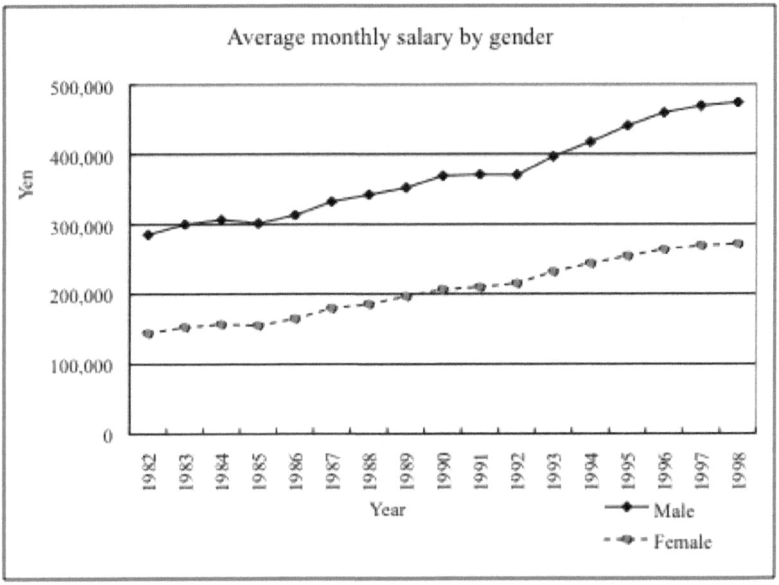

Figure 4: Average monthly salary by gender (Company A)

Source: Financial Reports (various years)

in 1982, improving to 57.3 per cent in 1998. If we look at the increase in percentage from 1982 to 1998, the salary increase for female employees was 88 per cent, while male employees' salary increased by 66 per cent. Salaries of female employees have indeed improved; however, there is a bigger gap in terms of the amount and, compared to the narrowing gaps in average age and service years, we can observe that there are still significant gender differences in financial rewards.

Some of the reasons for this phenomenon may be related to the examination of women and work in the previous section, as well as the changes in the economy, society and the company's management system: 1) under the previous salary system whereby salaries were determined more by age and length of service than job/duties, women who were younger and had fewer service years in general received lower salaries than their male counterparts, and it has taken them a long time to catch up with men; 2) as fewer women have tended to major in science and engineering, consequently, men occupy the majority of posts in the area of technological development, which has been the core of the company's competency in the market. As a result, women on average have had fewer opportunities to be utilised at the core of the company than men, as well as receiving lower salaries than men; 3) Even though the company shifted to twenty-four hour operation due to the changes in the process lines, women were, in the past, prohibited from doing night work. As a result, female workers at the factories were replaced by male workers. Although the prohibition of night work for women was lifted by the revision of the Labour Standard Law in 1999, many factories with assembly lines had already moved overseas; 4) with the shift of factory operations overseas, many women have lost the opportunity for employment within Japanese operations.

At Company A, there has not been a decisive turning point for the advancement of female employees. At the time of the implementation of the EEOL, no change in personnel management was made. Company A started hiring female university graduates in the 1970s, when very few of the big Japanese companies opened the employment door for female university graduates. In addition, there has been no discrimination between the salaries of men and women as long as they were appointed to positions at the same level on the basis of their educational attainment. Although the company thought it had already provided equal treatment for men and women in the eyes of officialdom, this does not mean that there have been no gender gaps within the company. The company's case shows many characteristic aspects of gender relations in Japanese organisations during the period from the 1970s to the 1990s. Although it was not possible to obtain numerical evidence, it is a common understanding among people in the organisation that there have been many barriers to prevent women from pursuing their careers as effectively as their male counterparts.

Firstly, as speed of career progress in the organisation was basically defined by *shokunō* (job ability) and *shikaku* (qualification): which were based on educational attainment, under the old personnel system (*shokunō shikaku seido*: ability-based grade system), women, who generally had fewer educational qualifications than men, needed many years to catch up with male colleagues with undergraduate degrees. Secondly, even though the company started hiring university graduates from the beginning of the 1970s, many women left due to marriage, child bearing and rearing within four years of joining. Not only was there insufficient employment tenure for women, but also the company's reluctance to invest in women's careers was apparent. Thirdly, the overall atmosphere in the company and long hours working style of core male workers, which an HR manager expressed as '*fuyajō* (a castle that never sleeps)', were inevitably incompatible with the family responsibilities of women. In sum, even though there was not a formal system of gender discrimination in the company, the ability-based grade system, the differences in educational attainments between men and women and consequent gender segregation in classifying job ability and qualification, the incompatibility of working styles within the company and women's shorter service years all made it difficult for women to be promoted to higher positions.

A significant change in personnel management systems within the company began in the early 1990s. The company pioneered the introduction of the pay-per-performance system. It was not targeted specifically at improving women's career advancement. However, it resulted in the removal of one of the barriers to women by shifting to a grade system by which individuals' performances became more important than personal attributes. In addition, like other companies in the industry and other big Japanese companies, Company A developed preferential conditions for women, including the introduction of a child-care leave system. However, other aspects such as the long working hours and the company's encouragement of strong competition among employees under the pay-per-performance system, at the same time restricted women's advancement in the company. There have been no apparent positive initiatives to improve women's career advancement. It appears that Company A has not assisted the advancement of female employees as much as the other two companies surveyed.

Company B

Company B was established in 2002 in the midst of the wider post-bubble financial reorganisation in Japan. Following the collapse of the bubble economy, and especially since the second half of the 1990s, a large-scale industrial reorganisation involving big city banks has been in progress.

The banking industry financially supported manufacturing industries, contributing to Japanese economic growth by means of indirect financing and by sending executives to companies during the economic growth period. However, the banks' strong role and influence among Japanese companies started declining in the late 1980s due to companies' shift from indirect to direct financing and the liberalisation of the financial market. With the collapse of the bubble economy, problems surfaced in the financial position of many banks. In March 1992, the Ministry of Finance announced that the total bad debt held by the main banks was eight trillion yen (60.2 billion US dollars), although it was to increase to 12.7 trillion yen (95.5 billion US dollars[8]) (Miwa, 2002, 213). The accumulated amount of bad loans had ballooned to almost 70 trillion yen (583.3 billion US dollars[9]) by March 1999.[10]. The collapse of the financial institutions started with local small banks at the beginning of the 1990s. However, the serious collapse began in 1994 (ibid)[11]. In 1998, the government injected 1.42 trillion yen (10.7 billion US dollars[12]) of taxpayers' money into seventeen banks, implemented via the *Kin-yū Saisei Hō* (Financial Revitalization Law) and *Kin-yū Kenzenka Hō* (Financial Restoration Law), set up the Financial Reconstruction Commission and appointed a Minister to be in charge of the commission (ibid, 214)[13]. In 1999, a further 7.5 trillion yen (62.2 billion US dollar[14]) was injected into fifteen banks including major city banks. At the same time, Prime Minister Hashimoto pursued the Japanese version of '*Kin-yū Biggu Ban* (financial big bang)' (ibid, 214-215). However, the original purpose of the Japanese 'Big Bang' financial reforms, of reorganising Japanese financial markets according to international standards, has not been achieved. Rather, it had the effect of accelerating affiliations and consolidations among Japanese financial institutions (ibid, 215).

Therefore tracing back banks' histories in Japan is complicated. All the big banks in Japan, including forerunners of Company B, have been involved repeatedly in mergers. Consequently, they had been consolidated into only four

8 1 US $ = 133 JPY (At March 1992 prices (Bank of Japan (BOJ), 2008))

9 1 US $ = 120 JPY (At March 1999 prices (BOJ, 2008))

10 including regional banks, second class regional banks, cooperative banks and credit cooperatives (Miwa, 2002, 213)

11 Representative examples are the bankruptcies of Nichiei Finance (1996), Nissan life Insurance, Sanyo Securities, Hokkaido Takushoku Bank and Yamaichi Securities (1997) (Miwa, 2002, 213-214).

12 1 US $ = 133 JPY (At March 1998 prices (BOJ, 2008))

13 For information on the changes in organisations concerned with financial administration since the early 1990s, please refer to Financial Services Agency (2006, http://www.fsa.go.jp/common/about/suii/index.html).

14 1 US $ = 120 JPY (At March 1999 prices (BOJ, 2008))

big financial groups by 2006 (Miwa, 2002, 21; Nihon Keizai Shimbun, 2006).

Currently the holding company of Company B has a total of five banks. By March 2006, the group employed about 16,000 employees and the number of branches was 600. Due to the financial crisis, the banks under Company B's

Table 4: Changes in numbers of employees (Company B)

		1980	1985	1990	1991	1992	1995	1997
Company B-i	male	5,288	5,333	5,184				
	female	3,566	2,939	2,062				
	total	**8,854**	**8,272**	**7,246**				
Company B-ii	male	6,787	6,167	5,586				
	female	3,951	3,357	2,384				
	total	**10,738**	**9,524**	**7,970**				
Company B-iii	male				10,705			
	female				4,503			
	total				**15,208**			
Company B-iv	male					10,428	9,540	9,125
	female					4,675	4,148	3,563
	total					**15,103**	**13,688**	**12,688**
Company B-v	male	6,001	6,073	6,116	6,364	6,400	6,061	5,647
	female	4,346	3,264	3,222	3,362	3,431	3,097	2,444
	total	**10,347**	**9,337**	**9,338**	**9,726**	**9,831**	**9,158**	**8,091**
Total	male	**18,076**	**17,573**	**16,886**	**17,069**	**16,828**	**15,601**	**14,772**
	female	**11,863**	**9,560**	**7,668**	**7,865**	**8,106**	**7,245**	**6,007**
	total	**29,939**	**27,133**	**24,554**	**24,934**	**24,934**	**22,846**	**20,779**
	% of female	39.62	35.23	31.23	31.54	32.51	31.71	28.91

Source: Financial Reports: various years

administration had been bailed out by taxpayers' money in 2003, and practically nationalised.

Owing to repeated mergers and financial turbulence since the late 1990s, there is limited availability of data; however we can still observe the characteristics of employment management in the banking industry. Table 4 shows changes in numbers of employees of each forerunner of Company B and totals from 1981 to 1997. In the early 1980s, women accounted for nearly 40 per cent of the employees. The number of women gradually decreased, and it was around 30 per cent in 1997. This may be due to the computerisation of clerical work and the trend for companies to hire non-regular employees for positions which used to be filled by female regular employees.

Similarly, if we look at the changes in average service years, women's years increased year by year (Table 6). The gap in the early 1980s was considerable. For example, average service for men was 16 years 3 months while women's was 4 years 10 months.

Table 5: Average age by gender (Company B-v)

Year. months	**1980**	**1985**	**1990**	**1995**	**1997**
Male	37. 0	38. 8	37. 8	37. 8	38. 2
Female	23. 8	25. 3	26. 2	28. 5	30. 4

Source: Financial Reports: various years

Table 6: Average service years by gender (Company B-v)

Year	**1980**	**1985**	**1990**	**1995**	**1997**
Male	16. 5	17. 11	16. 2	15. 7	16. 0
Female	4. 10	6. 3	6. 5	8. 1	10. 0

Source: Financial Reports: various years

These trends show that there were considerable differences in working patterns in terms of their service years – men's were longer – though this gap became smaller. In terms of average ages and service years, male employees' patterns have not changed in twenty years,[15] presenting a stark contrast to the considerable changes in women's work patterns. The increase in average age and service years of women can be explained as follows: firstly, the banks shifted to hiring women from higher educational backgrounds; consequently women's starting age rose. Secondly, the average age has increased along with the increase in their service years. Thirdly, there has been a possibility that the working environment in the bank, as well as social perception towards working women in general, have gradually changed enabling them to work longer in the late 1990s compared with the early 1980s.

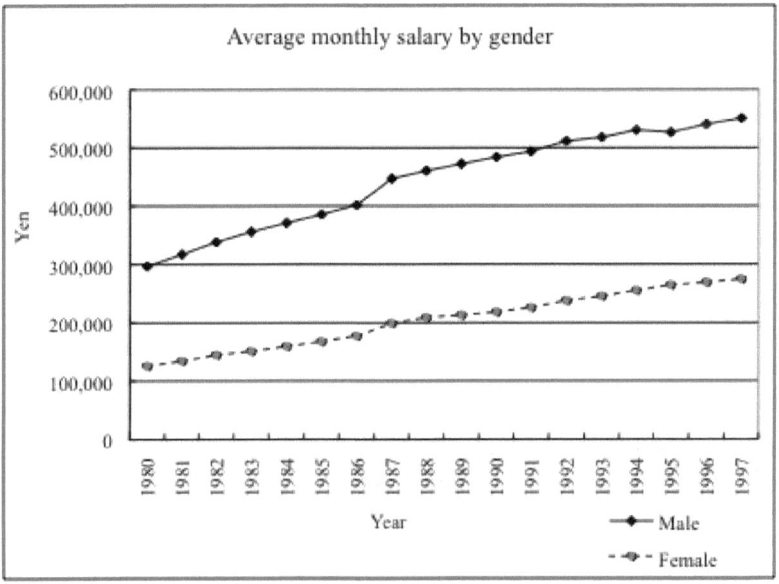

Figure 5: Average monthly salary by gender (Company B-v)

Source: Financial Reports (various years)

15 One thing we should note is an employment practice prevalent in the banking industry of transferring employees who have reached the age of around fifty to subsidiaries or client companies unless they have reached a certain level of the corporate hierarchy such as branch manager or director of a division. This employment practice has enabled banks to sustain their employment structure. I assume that this employment practice is the main reason for the lack of change in men's service years and average age.

Figure 5 highlights, however, a continued trend of the average salary gender gaps by gender. At company B-v, women's salaries were 42.3 per cent of men's in 1980. Actual salary amounts increased dramatically over the twenty years studied, for both sexes; however, the percentage gaps between men and women have not changed. In 1997, women's average salaries were still only 50 per cent of men's. Considering the link between salary, position and service years, women would have little hope of earning a similar salary to men. Women are still short on service years compared to men making it difficult to reach higher positions.

Table 7: Changes in numbers of employees by employee status

		2001	2002	2003	2004	2005
Company B-iv	Regular	13,948	12,143			
	Non-regular	6,071	6,388			
Company B-v	Regular	9,698	8,415			
	Non-regular	4,513	5,064			
Company B (Total)	Regular	23,646	20,558	16,386	11,924	10,360
	Non-regular	10,584	11,452	6,260	7,813	8,368
	Total	34,230	32,010	22,646	19,737	18,728
	% of Non-regular	30.92	35.78	27.64	39.59	44.68

Source: Financial Reports: various years

In the series of mergers the company culture of each bank has changed many times, also accompanied by a change in management practices. Moreover, the data since 2001 shows another interesting employment trend in the bank. Predecessors of Company B were bailed out by taxpayers' money in the late 1990s. Thereafter they followed the financial revitalisation plan laid down by the Financial Services Agency. Restructuring was frantically pursued, especially after the nationalisation of 2003. The total number of employees decreased by 45 per cent from 2001 to 2005. In terms of the number of regular employees, we can observe a general decrease in all banks from 2001 to 2005, which was greater than the total decrease – 56 per cent. In contrast, since 2003, the number of non-regular employees has continuously increased and non-regular employees accounted for 44.68 per cent in 2005 (Table 7).

Company B started recovering its financial position in fiscal year 2004, possibly due to the shift from regular to non-regular employees and lower costs[16]. Modified management practices in the organisations help to contextualise these unusual and drastic changes in employment structure.

Company B has implemented drastic restructuring since it was bailed out in 2003, based on the reduction of personnel costs (including encouragement of early retirement, cutting salaries by 30 per cent, and stopping bonuses), selling assets, including company dormitories and houses, and the elimination and consolidation of branches and subsidiaries, in addition to the disposal of non-performing bank loans (interviews from managers). As a result, profits started recovering from 2004. Its operating income amounted to 1,000 billion yen, and net income was 400 billion yen (3.3 billion US dollars) in fiscal year 2005.

Company B, when compared with Company A and, as we shall see, Company C, shows differentials in gender relations and personal management systems at the company level. Unlike Company A, which revealed both equality and inequality in its personnel management systems, Japanese banks have been well known for marked gender segregation in the past. This is symbolised by the introduction of the dual career track employment system (*kōsubetsu jinji kanri seido*).

In the banking system, core employees (who are usually male university graduates) are generally assigned to a retail banking branch. They move from branch to branch at two- to three-yearly intervals in order to experience main tasks of the banking business, except day-to-day office work. They may occasionally be transferred to the headquarters. However, the core of the banking business is in branch banks (a HR manager uses the term '*genba*' – site or shop floor in the case of manufacturing). Therefore core employees advance through experienc-

16 Weathers (2005a) points out, by referring to recent MHLW investigations, that companies in the financial sector abandoned the dual career track employment system in the early 2000s, and it is not a wholly positive trend as most companies simply replaced clerical-track women with non-regular women.

ing many branches and tasks, with the post of bank manager or director at the top of the hierarchy. Jobs with special skills such as dealer, treasurer, and actuary are assigned to people who have proved particular competence in these fields. Within these normal career paths, female employees were concentrated (or confined) in the day-to-day office work, including customer services and clerical staff roles. For them, there was therefore little chance to develop their careers within the hierarchy.

The situation was, however, changed owing to a fatal crisis for the company in the late 1990s. The company (even after the series of mergers) implemented corporate downsizing, and subsequently unexpectedly high numbers of male core employees in their late twenties and thirties left the company. Consequently, the company needed to fill the vacant positions. A shift from regular employees to temporary employees for clerical jobs also began at the same time, providing a wider range of jobs for female regular employees.

The situation of women was also significantly strengthened by the initiatives of a chairman who joined the company in 2003 from outside the banking industry. In order to survive in the competition among mega banks, Company B needed to distinguish itself by establishing a different set of core values from other banks. Subsequently, the bank started in earnest to promote women's advancement in the company. In 2005, the bank launched a Women's Council under the chairman's control. Since then, the advancement of women has developed dramatically. Simultaneously, the official shift to the pay-per-performance system was made in 2002, although the introduction of the system took place later than in other industries due to urgent personnel agendas involving corporate mergers and downsizing.

Company C

The founder of Company C first started business in 1947. After several successes and failures, he established Company C in 1955. Despite 50 years' history the company is relatively young compared to the other two companies; however, it has already had more than fifty years' history so may not be regarded as a 'young company'.

The company's core business activities have been education and publishing, its main focus being educational correspondence courses. The company has bought out several other companies as well as expanding its original business beyond education and publishing.[17] At the end of fiscal year 2005, the company employed 1,800 employees (12,000 in all group companies) and its sales amounted to about 200 billion yen (consolidated sales were about 350 billion yen, the net profit was 15 billion yen (consolidated, 16.0 billion yen). The company also conducts foreign operations in North America and Asia.

In the early period of the company's history, its business focused on the establishment of education and culture industries centring on mock entrance exams for junior and high school students (1955-1968), and then expanded its activities through distance learning (1969 onward). The company's growth period after the 1970s can be divided into three phases: establishment (1970s to early 1980s); expansion (late 1980s to 1990); and diversification (from 1991to the present). One distinctive characteristic of the company has been the comparatively large proportion of female employees. During the company's growth period, numbers of employees grew dramatically. In particular, the proportion of female employees has surpassed that of male employees since the late 1970s, increasing from around 50 per cent to 60 per cent since then (in 31 March 2006, female employees accounted for 55.5 per cent of total employees).

Factors such as relatively late growth, being a well-known but smaller company, and a unique business development style, led the company to apply a different personnel management strategy from many other companies in Japan. It sought to hire and retain talented women, and developed unique employment management practices to achieve this, and they have occupied the majority within the organisation. In terms of personnel management, even though it was indeed seniority-based, Company C used a salary system called *Yatomi-shiki* (*Yatomi*-style) salary system, which refers to graded remuneration system[18].

The biggest motive for the company in employing more females than males, and

17 Currently the Company C group operates in five main areas of business: education; women and family; seniors; language; and other activities. The core company of the group, Company C, also operates five types of business in publishing: education; language; pregnancy, child bearing and rearing; lifestyle; and nursing care.

18 *Yatomi-shiki* (Yatomi-style) salary system is relatively unknown, but spread mainly among small and medium-sized companies. However, big organisations such as Honda and the National Personnel Authority also applied this system (Yatomi, 1997).

employing female university graduates was simply the company's need, as an emerging company, to optimise their human resources. In an employment market which centred on new graduates, there was great competition to hire the best male graduates from high profile universities. From the 1970s to the 1990s, the most popular companies for male university students were banks, insurance, trading and airline companies. In the 1980s, manufacturing companies such as electronics, automobiles, and telecommunications also launched massive recruitment programmes.

On the other hand, the majority of the companies interested in hiring female graduates before the EEOL were in the retail industry (Nihon Keizai Shimbun, 1984). Moreover, before the enactment of the EEOL, it was difficult to find companies where female graduates could be hired as white-collar employees in exactly the same positions as male graduates. It was always a '*semaki mon* (narrow gate)' for female graduates. In addition to the retail industry, electronics companies enthusiastically started to hire female graduates as system engineers, and securities companies also tried to hire female graduates for their sales divisions during the late 1980s to early 1990s (Nihon Keizai Shimbun, 1990). Female university graduates who sought jobs apart from sales and system engineers needed to set their sights on different industries or on smaller companies. Company C opted to recruit students of equal quality to the male students who chose zaibatsu-type banks, trading companies, and manufacturers.

The nature of the company business also matched this strategy. As one of the female executives of the company stated in an interview[19], women's points of view and characteristics were more suitable than men's to a business that dealt with education, welfare, lifestyle and language. Sensitivity and concern for children and senior citizens are the core products and services of the company. Therefore, the company could achieve growth by utilising women's particular talents.

In the early 1980s, Company C implemented a series of measures in support of women and gender-equal treatment, including the enforcement of a policy whereby all employees were classified as career track employees. In 1986, in response to the increasing variation in women's life plans, three types of em-

19 An interview published on a website of a NPO which supports the promotion of women's full-scale participation' in society.

ployment arrangements were introduced for employees with childcare responsibility:

- Career course (maternity leave) – for six months
- Re-entry course (leave job and rejoin) – after three years
- Route-change course (employment status change) – for three years

In addition, a re-entry course programme was implemented in order to retain talented women. The following three courses are included in the available re-entry programmes:

- A course: leave of absence for three years with continuation of social security
- B course: leave of absence for three years without social security
- C course: leave job and rejoin after three years

Considering the fact that the EEOL was first implemented in 1986 and the implementation of the Child Care Leave Law was in 1992, this company's personnel management programmes seem extremely advanced.

In the latest stage, since 1991, further programmes have been introduced in response to the diversification of employees' lifestyles and based on mid-term life and career plans. The following are the major programmes implemented:

- 1991: Nursing Care Leave
- 1992: Reduction of working hours for child rearing (working hours can be reduced to five or six hours a day (normal working hours: seven hours) for employees who have children below fourth grade of elementary school (ten years old)
- 1995: revision of child rearing support programmes (longer than the mandatory period (one year)) * three years leave was considered too long for women to come back to the office and adapt to the new environment
- 1995: Reduction of working hours for nursing care (to be reduced to five or six hours a day, maximum of one year)
- revision of child care leave programme along with revision of the Child Care Leave Law: duration of the leave should be chosen according to the employee's preference either until the end of March after the child has reached one year or when the child reaches 18 months.

In addition, under the cafeteria benefit plan[20], employees can receive an addi-

20 "A flexible benefit plan which allows employees to choose necessary benefits and services from a

tional allowance from the company if they need nursing care services or home help services due to a stay in hospital or because of their own or a family member's disability.

The company believes that the programmes mentioned above, which were introduced before laws were implemented and provide better conditions for women and even for male employees, have benefited the business in several ways: retention of talented employees; a better image for potential employees, i.e. new graduates; the development of new products and services using employees' experiences of childrearing and nursing care; boosting the company image by engendering high loyalty to the brand among mothers of young children; and enhancement of individual shareholders' perception of the company. Treating female employees equally and supporting their life plans to the same degree as those of male employees has not only played an important role in recruiting talented employees but also improved the company image, whilst the support programmes can be linked directly to the development of the company's products and services. In that sense, Company C's actions to advance female employees stemmed from their business-oriented and strategic standpoint.

Consequently, despite the fact that it is still smaller among major Japanese companies, the Company C has gained as high a reputation as the other two companies, and has become especially renowned for its success in promoting women and its establishment of an impressive pool of talented women. In terms of employment structure and support system for women balancing work and private responsibilities, Company C has been a unique company in many senses. Firstly, women have made up the majority of employees since the late 1970s. Secondly, the support systems for women have been well-developed since before the introduction of the EEOL. Thirdly, the percentage of women among managers is very high. As a result, the company has been regarded as a champion for women's advancement in organisations.

wide-ranging "menu" according to their individual life plan, which include childcare, education, medical services and nursing care to health promotion, financial planning, risk management assistance and housing." (Company Webpage)

4. Analysis

The above three companies' cases illustrate different developmental patterns of utilisation of female employees over the last twenty years. They are in different industries, have different histories, as well as different employment management practices. Thus, they enable us to develop a nuanced understanding of the realities of women and work in Japan.

In the case of Company A, the company started hiring and allocating women as core employees relatively early compared to other big companies in Japan. Therefore, in the perception of the company the required equal treatment of women was already in place. Hence, Company A did not respond particularly to the implementation of the EEOL. Neither has there been an enthusiastic or decisive drive to promote female employees' advancement. One change which improved opportunities for women was the shift of the personnel management practices from *shokunō shugi* (paying salaries according to job abilities) to *seika shugi* (pay-per-performance system), owing to a serious downturn in business in the early 1990s. Although their gendered employment system is not officially institutionalised, Company A's case exhibits a male-centrism that to some extent has prevailed.

On the other hand, examination of Company B and its forerunners reveals significant changes in management policies and practices for women since the 1980s. The institutionalised gendered employment systems worked well in the past for big companies like Company B. The cultural norm of gendered division of labour, ('men are at work, women are at home') reinforced a gendered employment systems. In response to the implementation of the EEOL, banks in Japan introduced the dual career track employment system, leading to a clear segregation between men and women. However, the biggest opportunity for women was brought about by a serious company downturn and large-scale corporate restructuring in tandem with the nationalisation of the bank in the early 2000s. Currently their enthusiasm for including female employees is strong and gradually it has made progress in this area.

The case of Company C presents an entirely different situation for women. From the outset, and throughout its growth period, female employees have been at the core of the organisation. Consequently, the company's management policies and practices for women have advanced far beyond the government's requirements, and perhaps beyond social perceptions. In addition, owing to its weak position in the employment market, Company C needed to act differently from many big companies. The main reason for the company's high standing in terms of utilisation of women is that it hired talented people regardless of their gender. A possible source was the pool of female graduates from high-ranking universities: whom the company sought out rather than employing male university graduates from relatively low ranked universities. During the 1970s and 1980s, female university graduates were hardly ever recruited by private corporations as potential candidates for corporate managers, and Company C stood out in this respect. The championing of women by a founder of the company has influenced management practises until today. Thirdly, even though the core business is education, the company's business has expanded, focusing on various elements of people's lives, including pregnancy, childcare, childbirth and nursing care, making experiences of women instrumental to the development of the company.

As we have seen, it is difficult to lump all three companies together and regard them as a group of "Japanese companies" in terms of personnel management practices for women. Company B's case shows an example of the famous (or notorious) dual career track employment system. This is juxtaposed by the case of Company A with no formal gender discrimination in since the early 1970s. Company C challenges the stereotypical view of Japanese companies' gender induced treatment of female employees.

Can we, then, find any clear changes in companies' personnel management practices relating to women from the early 1980s to the early 2000s? Societal perceptions towards women and work would indeed have changed. However, by examining the three companies' cases, we found that the main sources of changes in companies' personnel management policies are changes in the economic situation and consequent changes within the country's employment market and its industries.

In companies' behaviours, there are simple but very important preconditions for the advancement and utilisation of female employees: demand and supply. There needs to be demand from the company to hire and promote female employees and a supply of female employees with the necessary skill sets and experiences, or the potential to acquire these. In other words, a company needs to provide opportunities for women, and the women also need to seek opportunities, and to respond to the opportunities by exhibiting their capability of pursuing tasks and responsibilities.

In the past, there was little demand for companies to utilise women and only a small supply of women ready and eager to work in the long term like their male colleagues. The reason that Company C was successful was that there was both the demand by the company for talented female employees and a supply of women who had ability and a strong desire to work.

Companies decide their employment policies in view of the situation of the labour market and their position within it. As the analyses of Company B and Company C illustrate, the weakness of their position in the labour market forced them to utilise women. As for Company A, ironically, due to its continuing strength in the employment market, the necessity to utilise women has not (yet) arisen; consequently, the utilisation of women is not as advanced as in the other two companies.

Additionally, the nature of the industry and the required skills and services inevitably determine the human resources needed: especially in the new globalised economy where "speed" is an essential feature. For example, Company A demands that even its white-collar employees keep pace with speedy product development and services in addition to having specialised skills and knowledge.

Consequently, women with family responsibilities or without relevant skills and knowledge are unlikely to be appointed to the core of the organisation. In contrast, Company C's business directly links to women's lives and it requires creative and intellectual skills which may make it more compatible with women with family responsibilities as well as work responsibilities.

In addition to the conditions mentioned above, the relationships between corporate leaders' initiatives, personnel management practices and people's perceptions have also supported the advancement of female employees in Japanese organisations. Figure 6 shows these relationships.

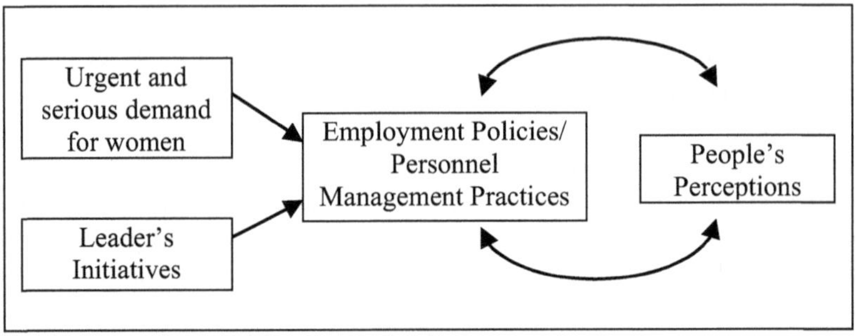

Figure 6: Relationships between conditions in the employment market, leaders' initiatives, personnel management practices and people's perceptions

In both Company C and Company B, there was an urgent and serious demand for women in relation to their overall employment needs. At the same time, there were forceful and decisive initiatives from the leaders of the companies. Under these two strong prior conditions, employment policies and personnel management practices were re-designed. As these policies and practices made their mark, people's perceptions have been also changing. In the case of Company A, demand for women has been weaker, and the leaders' initiatives directed towards the pay-per-performance system rather than promotion of female employees. The result is strong competition among employees.

5. Conclusion

During the twenty years from the early 1980s to 2000s, companies' management practices regarding women have changed. It is ironic that the improvement in working women's situation was brought about partly by the worsening economic situation and the weak position of companies in the employment market. Although the situation relating to working women has indeed improved, underlying factors which sustain the Japanese employment market, namely recruitment policies and practices centred on male university graduates from high profile universities, seem not to have changed. Moreover, even if women are finally provided with an opportunity in an organisation, not all working women are equipped with sufficient knowledge, skills and experience, and are able to compete with their male counterparts. There seems to be still many challenges for women to overcome including balancing work and family responsibilities and filling already produced gaps with men from past gendered employment practices.

In addition, other factors such as legislation and union activities have failed to radically improve the situation of working women over the last twenty years, although they have exerted some influence. Companies can and will operate their businesses in isolation from the societal trend in gender equality. However, it is very important to use the legal system to change people's attitudes toward gender equality: even if the impact of such measures might be limited. Also, the case of Company C allows us to be optimistic over the future development of gender equality in Japanese companies. An enforced relationship between employment policies/personnel management practices and people's perceptions, which has been continuously endorsed by leaders' initiatives, has become firmly rooted in the company over the past thirty years.

Currently, we are experiencing further economic turmoil, not only in Japan but all over the world. This new economic crisis, which started in 2007, will again influence Japanese companies' business strategies as well as employment and personnel management practices. There are serious problems in employment practices in Japan apart from gender issues. The increasing number of non-regular employees has become one of the biggest problems (Ishiguro, 2008). At the same time, as Mizumachi (2007) argues, the situation of regular employees has deteriorated – even though the workload has not decreased, companies cannot increase the number of regular employees as the cost would be prohibitive. Meanwhile, job requirements are becoming increasingly complicated and sophisticated with the speeding up of technology and markets. Under such conditions, will the situation of women in Japan improve in decades to come? Although we cannot make clear predictions on what will happen in the future, it seems that companies need to develop employment and personnel management systems that will make full use of women's potential and talents, and that a fundamental review of the systems for the benefit of all workers in Japan is also required.

6. References

Arrow, K. J. (1972). Models of Job Discrimination. In A. H. Pascal (Ed.), *Racial Discrimination in Economic Life* (pp. 83-102). Lexington, Massachusetts: D.C. Heath and Company.

Asakura, M. (2004). *Rōdōhō to jendā* (Labour laws and gender). Tokyo: Keisō Shobō.

Asami, N. (2006). *Josei jimushoku no kyaria kakudai to shokuba soshiki* (Widening of female white-collar employees' careers and workplace organisation). Tokyo: Nihon Keizai Hyōronsha.

Bank of Japan (BOJ, 2008) Gaikoku kawase sōba jyōkyō: getsuji (Foreign currency market rate, Monthly). Available at: http://www.boj.or.jp/theme/research/stat/market/forex/fx/index.htm, accessed: 10. March 2008.

Broadbent, K. (2003). *Women's Employment in Japan: The Experience of Part-time Workers*. London: RoutledgeCurzon.

Cabinet Office (2008). Danjo kyōdō sankaku hakusho heisei 20nen ban (White paper on gender equality 2008). Available at: http://www.gender.go.jp/whitepaper/h20/zentai/pdf/DKH20H01.pdf, accessed: 18. May 2009.

Goldin, C. (1990). Understanding the Gender Gap: An Economic History of *American Women*. Oxford: Oxford University Press.

Imada, S. (1996). Female Labor Force after the Enforcement of The Equal Employment Opportunity Law. *Japan Labor Bulletin, 35(8)*. Available at: http://www.jil.go.jp/bulletin/year/1996/vol35-08/05htm, accessed: 21. December 2002.

Ishiguro, K. (2008). Japanese Employment in Transformation: The Growing Number of Non-regular Workers. *Electronic Journal of Japanese Studies*. Available at: http://www.japanesestudies.org.uk/articles/2008/Ishiguro.html, accessed: 31. July 2010.

Kawaguchi, A. (1997). Danjokan chingin kakusa no keizai riron (Economic theory on the wage gap between men and women). In H. Chuma, & T. Suruga (Eds.), *Koyō kankō no henka to josei rōdō* (Changes in employment practices and woman's labour) (pp.207-241). Tokyo: Tokyo Daigaku Shuppankai.

Kimoto, K. (2003). *Josei rōdō to manejimento* (Gender and Japanese management). Tokyo: Keisō Shobō.

Kimoto, K. (2005). *Gender and Japanese Management* (T. Castelvetere, Trans.). Melbourne: Trans Pacific Press.

Kinoshita, T. (1998). "Rōdō undō feminizumu" to josei no rentai ishiki ("Labour movement feminism" and women's sense of solidarity). In A. Nakano, M. Mori, & T. Kinoshita (Eds.), *Rōdō bigguban to onna no shigoto • chingin* (The labour big bang and women's work and wages) (pp.206-226). Tokyo: Aoki Shoten.

Koike, K. (1988). Futatsu no michi (Two paths). In K. Koike, & Y. Tomita (Eds.), *Shokuba no kyaria ūman* (Career women in the workplace) (pp. 80-97). Tokyo: Tōyō Keizai Shinpōsha.

Koike, K. (1999). *Shigoto no keizaigaku: Dai ni han* (The economics of work, 2nd Edition). Tokyo: Toyo Keizai Shinpōsha.

Lam, A. C. L. (1992). *Women and Japanese Management: Discrimination and Reform.* London: Routledge.

Matsushige, H. (1998). "Rōdō chōsa kenkyū no genzai: 1995-97 no gyōseki wo tsūjite (Present status of labour research: From the achievements during 1995-97)" (A roundtable participated by Yashiro, Atsushi, Toshikazu Matsushige and Atsushi Sato). *Nihon Rōdō Kenkyū Zasshi, 453,* 2-49.

Ministry of Health, Labour and Welfare (MHLW, 2004). *Heisei 15 nenban hataraku josei no jitsujō* (FY 2003 actual condition of working women). Available at: http://www.mhlw.go.jp/houdou/2004/03/h0329-1a.html#gaiyou, accessed: 30. November 2005.

Ministry of Health, Labour and Welfare (MHLW, 2010). *Heisei 21 nen chingin kōzō kihon tōkei chōsa* (Basic survey on wage structure). FY 2009. Available at: http://www.mhlw.go.jp/toukei/list/52-21.html, accessed: 18. June 2010.

Miwa, R. (2002). *Gaisetsu nihon keizaishi: Kingendai, dai ni han* (Overview of the modern Japanese economy, 2nd Edition). Tokyo: Tokyo Daigaku Shuppankai.

Mizumachi, Y. (2007). 'Kajō rōdō' to 'kakusa' no aida (Links between 'overwork' and 'disparity'). *Sekai, March, No 762*, 71-76.

Nihon Keizai Shimbun (1984, 17. August). Raishun daisotsu saiyō 300i rankingu (The ranking of 300 Companies in recruiting new graduates in next spring). *Nihon Keizai Shimbun*, 8.

Nihon Keizai Shimbun (1990, 3. August). Josei: Hirogaru katsuyaku no bunya: 'Semaki mon' ima wa mukashini (Women: Widening their appeal: The 'strait gate' became history). *Nihon Keizai Shimbun*, 1.

Nihon Keizai Shimbun (2006, 1. January). Mitsubishi Tokyo UFJ Ginkō tanjō: Hon shiten de kanban kakekae (The birth of the Bank of Tokyo-Mitsubishi UFJ: Changing the company sign at headquarters and branches). *Nihon Keizai Shimbun*, 3.

Nihon Rōdō Kenkyū Kikō (Japan Institute of Labour, 1997). *Chōsa kenkyū hōkokusho*, No. 99: *Josei no shokugyō/kyaria ishiki to shūgyō kōdō ni kansuru kenkyū* (Research report No. 99: A study of women's work/career consciousness and their behaviour). Tokyo: Nihon Rōdō Kenkyū Kikō.

Nijūisseiki Shokugyō Zaidan (Japan Institute of Worker's Evolution, JIWE, 2002). *Kyaria keisei to shigoto to katei no ryōritsu ni kansuru ishiki chōsa kekka gaiyō* (Summary of the survey on consciousness in balancing career formation and family). Available at: http://www.jiwe.or.jp/jyoho /chosa/career.html, accessed: 09. February 2006.

Nijūisseiki Shokugyō Zaidan (Japan Institute of Worker's Evolution, JIWE, 2005). *Josei kanrishoku no ikusei to tōyō ni kansuru ankēto kekka hōkokusho* (Report of the survey on the cultivation and promotion of female managers). Available at: http://www.jiwe.or.jp/jyoho/chosa/h1706kanrisyoku.html, accessed: 09. February 2006.

Ōba, A. (1988). *Danjo koyōkikai kintōhō zenshi: Sengo fujin rōdōshi nōto* (A pre-history of the equal employment opportunity law: Note on the post-war history of women's labour). Tokyo: Miraisha.

Okutsu, M. (n.d.). Josei koyō seisaku no genjō to kadai (The present situation and issues of employment policy for women). Available at: http://www.jil.go.jp/institute/kokusai/documents/okutsu.pdf#search=%22%E5%8B%A4%E5%8A%B4%E5%A9%A6%E4%BA%BA%E7%A6%8F%E7%A5%89%E6%B3%95%22, accessed: 19. September 2006.

Osawa, M. (1993). *Keizai henka to josei rōdō* (Changes in economy and woman's labour). Tokyo: Nihon Keizai Hyōronsha.

Osawa, M. (1998). *Atarashī kazoku no tame no keizaigaku: Kawariyuku kigyō shakai no naka no josei* (Economics for new families: Women in the changing corporate cociety). Tokyo: Chūō Kōron Shinsha.

Osterman, P. (1984). Introduction: The Nature and Importance of Internal Labor Market. In P. Osterman (Ed.), *Internal Labor Market* (pp.1-23). Cambridge, Massachusetts: The M.I.T. Press.

Phelps, E. S. (1972). The Statistical Theory of Racism and Sexism. *American Economic Review, 62(4)*, 659-661.

Piore, M. (1971). The Dual Labor Market: Theory and Implications. In D.M. Gordon (Ed.), *Problems in Political Economy: An Urban Perspective* (pp.90-94). Lexington, Massachusetts: D.C.Heath and Company.

Rengō Sōgō Seikatsu Kaihatsu Kenkyūjo (1996). *Josei rōdōsha no kyariakeisei to jinji shogū no unyōjisseki ni kansuru hōkokusho* (Report on career formation of female workers and practices of personnel conditions). Tokyo: Rengō Sōgō Seikatsu Kaihatsu Kenkyūjo.

Schoppa, L. J. (2006). *Race for the Exits*. New York: Cornell University Press.

Shinotsuka, E. (1995). *Josei ga hataraku shakai* (A society where women work). Tokyo: Keisō Shobō.

Statistics Bureau (2010). *Rōdōryoku chōsa chōki jikeiretsu dēta* (Labour force survey, long time series data). Available at: http://www.stat.go.jp/data /roudou/longtime/03roudou.htm, accessed: 01. July 2010.

Tomita, Y. (1988). Joshi no koyō kanri to danjokan chingin kakusa (Employment management for women and wage gap between men and women). In K. Koike, & Y. Tomita (Eds.), *Shokuba no kyaria ūman* (Career women in the workplace) (pp. 144-165). Tokyo: Tōyō Keizai Shinpōsha.

Tomita, Y. (1991). Josei shain no ginō keisei (Female employees' skill formation). *Keizai Kenkyū (The Journal of Economic Studies), 36 (3)*, 103-114.

UNDP (United Nations Development Programme, 2009). Human Development Report: Indicators by Tables - 2007/2008 Report. Available at: http://hdrstats.undp.org/en/indicators/125.html, accessed: 1 July 2010.

Yamamoto, Y. (1987). *Joshi rōdō hōsei* (Legislation on woman's labour). Tokyo: Hitotsubusha.

Yashiro, A. (1992). Kenkyū nōto: Ōte kourigyō ni okeru josei no kanrishoku e no shōshin: Jinjibumon no kinō no jittai (Research note: Promotion of women to managers in big retail companies: Functions of the personnel management department). *Nihon Rōdō Kenkyū Zasshi*, 388, 28-41.

Yashiro, N. (1980). *Gendai nihon no byōri kaimei* (Unravelling pathology in contemporary Japan). Tokyo: Tōyō Keizai Shinpōsha.

Yatomi, K. (1997). *Jitsuryoku shugi no chingin: Seido kaizen no ōdō* (Salary system for the merit-based system: The royal road to the system improvement). Tokyo: Keiei Shoin.

Wakisaka, A. (1993). *Shokuba ruikei to josei no kyaria keisei* (Types of workplace and women's career formation). Tokyo: Ochanomizu Shobō.

Weathers, C. (2005a). *Equal Opportunity for Japanese Women: What Progress?*. Available at: http://www.zmag.org/znet/viewArticle/5264, accessed: 12. February 2008.

Weathers, C. (2005b). In Search of Strategic Partners: Japan's Campaign for Equal Opportunity. *Social Science Japan Journal, 8(1)*, 69-89.

The "Lost Decade" and Changes in the Japanese Business Environment: Consequences for Foreign Direct Investment and Human Resource Management in Foreign Subsidiaries in Japan

Harald Dolles and Yoshiaki Takahashi

1. Barriers to Japanese Market Entry in the 1980s

In the 1980s it has been pointed out in many books that lifetime employment, wage increase through years of company's services (seniority), job rotation and internal training, enterprise unions and group oriented decision making through nemawashi and ringi systems are key components of Japanese style management (see e.g. Takahashi 1984, 1987, 1990 as guiding references). In addition Japanese firms used careful screening of job candidates so that new employees' qualifications fit with the value system and corporate culture of the firm. Also frequently mentioned as a major obstacle to access the Japanese market was the Japanese industrial organization, i.e. organization of companies to large industrial groups (keiretsu) with their linkages up- and downstream the value chain, which has been described as complex, cumbersome, costly, confusing, inefficient, archaic and an invisible barrier to market entry (see e.g. Dolles 1994, 1997, 1999; Dolles & Kumar 1996; Hemmert 1993 for a comprehensive overview). For example, in 1989 the US government targeted the Japanese distribution system as the greatest barrier to market entry.

With the rise in the economic fortunes of Japanese companies in the 1980s and the high and stable growth of the Japanese economy from the 1960s to the 1980s Japanese style management received a significant degree of attention from the West and a number of authors pointed to Japanese style management as a source of competitive advantage for Japanese firms (c.f. Abegglen & Stark 1985; Aoki & Dore 1994; Clark 1979; Ouchi 1981 as examples of this stream of publications).

At the same time, it has been debated whether the Japanese keiretsu-system was in fact inefficient or to what degree it acted as a trade barrier. In any case there was an agreement that it differed greatly from the system of industrial organization of most other countries. Obviously foreign firms entering the Japanese market at that time needed to understand the nature of the Japanese keiretsu system as well as Japanese-style management, if they hoped to succeed there (Dolles 1997; Hemmert 1993).

At that time Japan offered an alluring market to foreign firms for a number of reasons. It was the world's second largest economy; incomes in Japan were considered as high and relatively evenly distributed; and the market was both sophisticated and highly competitive (Kumar, Steinmann & Dolles, 1993). However, foreign firms doing business in Japan faced extraordinary difficulties. These hardships were attributed to intangible barriers such as a lack of understanding of the Japanese industrial system (distribution and manufacturing) and market entry barriers.

To the extent that foreign companies were increasingly investing directly in their own production and sales subsidiaries in Japan, subsidiary management was becoming a crucial issue for them, too. They had to adapt subsidiary management to the local conditions of Japanese style of management. But at the same time, the attempt was made to standardize subsidiary management according to their parent company's strengths and policies. It was only on the basis of these resources that subsidiaries could hope to achieve a competitive advantage against Japanese firms who had an edge over foreign investors by being in their home market.

In this article, the now and then of management patterns of Japanese subsidiaries of German companies in the 1980s will be explored. On the basis of a local adaptation-global standardisation framework major characterizing areas will be identified in which foreign companies had to adapt to the Japanese situation during that time of high economic growth. This will lead to the development of five assumptions in regards to foreign direct investment (FDI) into Japan and the management of human resources in foreign subsidiaries in Japan. By researching the same issues in the new millennium, we will address significant changes for FDI into Japan and changes in the human resource management of foreign subsidiaries caused by the changes during the so-called "lost decade", the persistently low economic growth of the Japanese economy in the 1990s.

2. The Conceptual Framework of Local Adaptation and Global Standardisation

The two-dimensional management pattern defined by "local adaptation" and "international standardisation" in international management is conceptualized along a one-dimensional adaptation spectrum (i.e. standardisation is equivalent to no or low adaptation) in this research. The effectiveness of any management style can only be understood within the environmental perception of the managers involved. On this basis, we assume that the degree of adaptation practised in subsidiary management is dependent on how subsidiary managers perceive the difference between the parent country and the host country business culture. Accordingly we apply three modes of management on the "adaptation spectrum" (see Kumar & Steinmann 1989, 1990; Kumar, Steinmann & Dolles 1993 for details):

(1) "Mode of social obligation": The degree of adaptation practised tallies with the perceived differences between home and host country cultural influences. This is the case when the subsidiary responds to market and cultural forces in a manner that meets the imposed constraints or what is almost totally required by economic and legal necessity in the host country. In this case firms hardly have a choice other than to abide by legal and economic rules and institutions. Not adapting to these norms would mean dysfunctionality.

(2) "Mode of social acceptance": The degree of adaptation practised is greater than the perceived differences between the home and the host country. In this case subsidiary management is adapted to general local practice, although from the viewpoint of the parent company a more standardised mode might also have been feasible.

(3) "Mode of social responsiveness": The degree of adaptation practised is smaller than the perceived difference between home and host country cultural influences. In this case, foreign subsidiaries deliberately behave differently (standardise more) than what present (and changing) host country norms and management practices are perceived to dictate. By reacting differently, foreign subsidiaries strive to compensate for the handicap of foreignness or even get an edge over local enterprises. The assumption is that local stakeholders often will accommodating towards a foreign subsidiary and its non-conforming management, which in the end may even turn out to be more efficient than prevailing practice. Foreign subsidiaries thus have a change agent function in the host market.

3. Methodology and Research Samples

During the 1980s data on the management of foreign subsidiaries in Japan was gathered in four steps by a research group from Erlangen-Nuremberg University in Germany and Chuo University in Japan (see Kumar & Steinmann 1989, 1990; Kumar, Steinmann & Dolles 1993; Steinmann, Kumar & Dolles 1992 for details): First, semi-standardized questionnaires were send to expatriates working in Japanese subsidiaries of German companies operating in Japan (101 returned questionnaires) in 1985. Second, semi-structured interviews followed with 30 expatriate managers and experts working in German subsidiaries in Japan in 1986. Third, a standardized questionnaire was sent to Japanese subsidiaries of German companies operating in Japan (55 returned questionnaires, response rate 30 per cent) in 1987. Fourth, narrative interviews with 30 German expatriates working in Japanese subsidiaries of German companies operating in Japan in 1987/1988 and again in 1991/1992.

Between 2001 and 2006 semi-standardized interviews in Japan and Germany were conducted by the authors among some 60 German and Japanese executives who were involved in the activities of Japanese subsidiaries of German companies. This group included expatriates and local managing staff, bankers, consultants, lawyers, and distributors. In addition a study jointly carried out in 2003 by the German Chamber of Commerce and Industry in Japan (DIHKJ) and Roland Berger Strategy Consultants of Tokyo was used (see DIHKJ & Roland Berger Strategy Consultants 2003). The 510 German companies known by DIHKJ membership to be operating in Japan were sent a questionnaire. Ninety-seven measurable questionnaires were returned, giving a representative return rate of 19 per cent.

To explore the adaptation mode in German subsidiaries in Japan it was necessary to ascertain (1) the actual degree of adaptation practised in management functions and areas, and (2) the perceived degree of differences between German and Japanese management style. To find out the actual pattern of adaptation practised in the subsidiaries, a 5-point Likert scale was applied. In the 1987 standardized questionnaire the respondents were provided a detailed guidance on apprehension of the question posed, which had the following text:

> "Managing subsidiaries of German companies in Japan means adapting to local conditions. It also means standardising according to parent company policy. Is your management in Japan more adapted or more standardized? Please check the following items by putting a mark (X) o the scale which you think applies to you."

This question was arranged with respect to ten management areas and issues. A low score meant high adaptation, a high score less adaptation (more standardization) according to the theoretical conceptualization. To ascertain the perceived divergence between home and host country culture, respondents have been asked to evaluate statements comparing management practise in Japan and Germany on a general level in the same questionnaire. The statements pertained to the same ten management areas, e.g. "When compared with Germany, advertising is more important in Japan (e.g. more often, better quality)." A 5-point Likert scale was again used for evaluation, ranking from 1 "strongly agree" to 5 "strongly disagree". Agreement (low score) meant that the respondents perceived no divergence, and in this case no adaptation was expected.

4. Subsidiary Management in Japan in the 1980s

The findings of the surveys can be summarised as follows: The striking feature was that 92 per cent of the respondents concluded that there are differences in industry structure and management style in Japan, that require a certain level of local adaptation (see Figure 1). On the whole, management in subsidiaries of German companies in Japan followed the mode of social responsiveness. Even in the 1980s by and large, subsidiary management contained more elements of international standardisation, based on parent company skills, than elements of local adaptation.

However, a mean score of +0.14 in differences indicates that the level of standardisation and implementation of non-Japanese patterns beyond the environmentally feasible margin was not high. Rather, the subsidiaries were very cautious in introducing new patterns. And even these new styles of management were associated with a low level of innovation and changes, as indicated by the average adaptation scores.

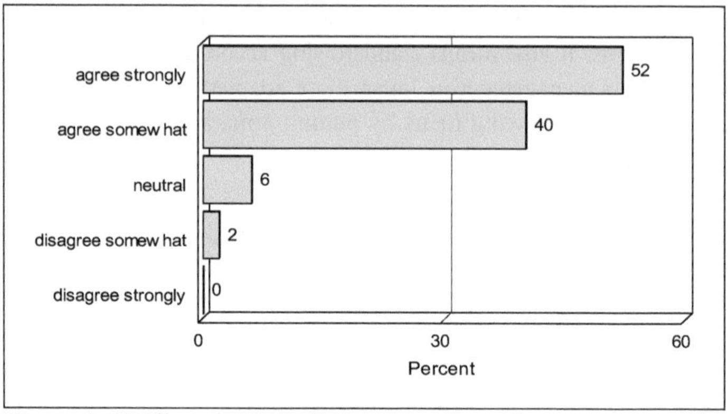

Figure 1: "Differences in industry structure and management style"

Note: n = 52 German subsidiaries in Japan

In the 1980s foreign investment in Japan was regarded rather suspiciously, not only in conservative government circles, but by the public as well. The quite unresponsive investment environment in Japan made market entry difficult for many companies (Kumar, Steinmann & Dolles 1993).

To build up a wholly owned subsidiary in Japan became only possible after a change in Japanese legislation in 1980 (Scheer 1990: 541), however this form of market-entry was chosen only by 30 per cent of the companies in the quantitative sample. Entering the Japanese market by means of Joint-ventures or other collaborating form was still the preferred choice due to high investments and the obstacles of the Japanese market. In the early 1980s 25 per cent of the companies investigated by the Chamber of Commerce even quoted that it took them more than 10 years to reach break-even of their investments (the year in which revenues exceed expenses for the first time).

The subsidiaries of German companies generally adapted their selling and distribution practice to the local system because the relationships between manufactures and distributors in Japan are considered to be very traditional and breaking them would have meant sacrificing goodwill in the market (Kumar, Steinmann & Dolles 1993).

Despite being in a highly attractive market, many companies did not have the resources to sustain their Japanese activities at that time. In the 1990s the "lost decade" was experienced by Japanese corporations as an economic crisis, due to persistently low economic growth, continuously declining asset prices and holding-up of household consumption during this period (c.f. Horioka 2006; Ishizaki 2010). This has also deterred many foreign companies from foreign direct investment (FDI) in Japan. The belief that "only a few foreign companies succeed in the Japanese market" is widely held and supported by publications of Japanese export promotion agencies.

Assumption 1: "Only a few foreign companies succeed in the Japanese market"

It is generally asserted that an investment in Japan must plan for a long period before break-even is reached. In average it was calculated that a break-even with the initial investment could be reached after 7 years at the best (Steinmann, Kumar & Dolles 1992).

In addition it was mentioned that a sustainable market share could earlier be reached by means of a collaborative market entry strategy (4 years compared to 5 years). Those figures are supported by DIJKJ and Roland Berger Survey (2003), when looking at foreign subsidiaries established in Japan before and during the 1980s (ref. to Figure 4). We therefore propose:

Assumption 2: "It takes a long time for foreign subsidiaries to reach the break-even point in Japan"

The findings of the surveys conducted in the 1980s reveal that 87 per cent of the subsidiaries investigated started as green-fields investment in Japan and only 6 firms (11%) had entered the Japanese market via acquisition (Kumar & Steinmann 1989).

Those results confirm the general observation that foreign firms only in rare cases choose M&A as their preferred entry mode. German firms also faced the problem that Japanese owners were reluctant to partner with companies, among other reasons because of a missing commitment of foreign owners to stakeholder groups, like employees, valued customers, banks, etc.). We propose:

Assumption 3: "Market entry in Japan through Mergers & Acquisitions is relatively rare due to strong keiretsu relationships"

Table 1: Perceived differences in Management between Japan and Germany

„When comparing with Germany I am aware in Japan is/are..."							
	agree strongly	**agree somewhat**	**neutral**	**disagree somewhat**	**disagree strongly**	**no answer**	**median**
Marketing more important	10	35	33	17	0	6	2,61
Differences in brand management	2	23	38	**15**	**17**	4	3,24
Product quality requirements higher	52	27	15	4	0	2	1,71
Service requirements higher	**71**	**19**	8	2	0	0	1,40
Distribution system difficult to access	**60**	**25**	12	1	0	2	1,55
Purchasing policies different	23	42	21	10	0	4	2,18
Product pricing higher	**33**	**25**	25	8	8	2	2,31
Production system different	12	17	44	10	4	13	2,73
HR Management more important	**42**	**40**	6	8	0	4	1,78
Financing policies different	12	50	23	10	4	2	2,43

Note: Figures in per cent, n = 52 German subsidiaries

There is quite some variation between the individual management functions and areas in the surveys conducted by the research group around Kumar and Steinmann. As Tables 1 and 2 show, the mode of social acceptance, i.e. conforming by the company's own choice to prevailing cultural norms and values (even though introducing new patterns would also be compatible in the perspective of having an impact of changing values), was practiced in the area of human resource management (HRM).

Table 2: Realized practices in the Management of Japanese subsidiaries

„In comparison with Germany we realize different practices in our subsidiary in Japan in…"							
	agree strongly	**agree somewhat**	**neutral**	**disagree somewhat**	**disagree strongly**	**no answer**	**median**
Marketing	21	25	13	6	8	8	2,50
Brand management	4	10	23	**29**	**25**	10	3,68
Product quality	23	29	15	13	13	6	2,63
Service	**42**	**40**	10	0	0	6	1,67
Distribution	**44**	**21**	6	10	6	13	1,98
Purchasing policies	17	25	19	13	12	13	2,73
Product pricing	**38**	**40**	13	4	2	2	1,88
Production system	15	27	15	4	10	29	2,51
HR management	**58**	**25**	13	2	0	2	1,59
Financing policies	21	31	19	12	10	8	2,54

Note: Figures in per cent, n = 52 German subsidiaries

Also as indicated by the interviews, this was necessary in terms of leadership and motivation of Japanese employees. The management style followed the documented elements of collectivism, shared responsibility and motivating subordinates meant satisfying group needs rather than individual aspirations.

When comparing the results from Tables 1 and 2 the mode of social responsiveness was practiced to highest extent in connection with product policy: Product quality and brand policy show a score of +0.89 and +0.70, respectively. The highest degree of social acceptance was demonstrated in the area of production management, followed by pricing policy and personnel management. The smallest divergence between perceived differences regarding host and home country cultural influences and actual practiced adaptation was in advertising (-0.08). This indicates that in advertising foreign subsidiaries had the least scope of choice. Conforming to perceived environmental pressure was an economic or even a legal necessity.

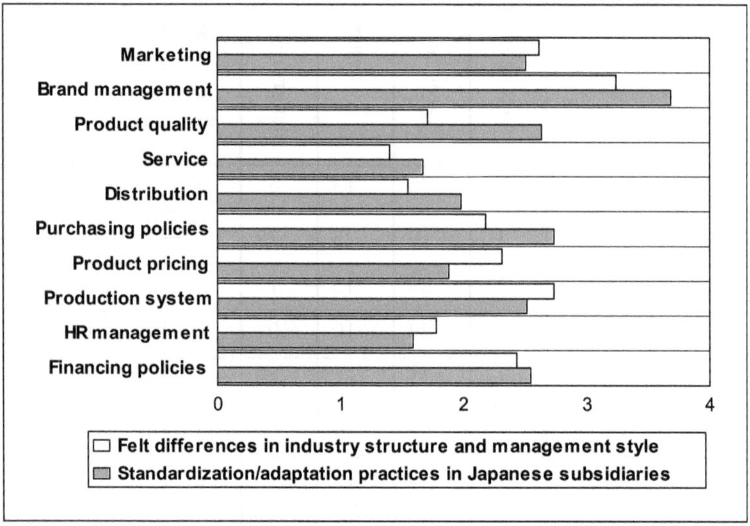

Figure 2: "Management mode in Japanese subsidiaries of German companies"

Note: median comparison, 5-point Likert scale, n = 52 German subsidiaries

There was however no case of total social obligation recognized. It seems that the Japanese environment even in the 1980s left scope for at least some choice in subsidiary management. In regards to HRM in foreign subsidiaries we propose the following two assumptions:

Assumption 4: "It is difficult for foreign subsidiaries to find capable staff in Japan."

Assumption 5: "It is necessary for foreign companies to adjust to a Japanese style of HRM in subsidiary management."

5. Subsidiary Management in Japan Today

Based on the findings from the surveys in the 1980s we attempt to analyse some typical adaptation requirements and patterns in subsidiaries of German companies in Japan again in the new millennium. The question now is, as to how far foreign companies in Japan still must, should and can adapt to the Japanese present market conditions.

Assumption 1: "Only a few foreign companies succeed in the Japanese market"

The perception of foreign companies and their long-term engagement in the Japanese market has changed in recent years. Now, the Japanese government has recognised that FDI not only brings capital to Japan, but can also exert a positive influence in numerous areas. New dynamics are expected in technology, management methods and labour market. FDI is increasingly seen as a supporting factor in Japan's efforts to reform (see e.g. Japan External Trade Organization 2011). From 1995 foreign direct investment in Japan increased, whereas Japanese FDI into Germany peaked at the end of the bubble economy and declined since then (Figure 3). Net FDI inflow into Japan reached a record high for the second consecutive year in 2008, reaching US$ 24,550 million, up to 10.7 per cent from 2007 (Yasuda 2009). It is noted, that most of the inflows came from additional investments made by financial institutions and companies seeking to increase the capital of their Japanese subsidiaries. Initial FDI accounted for only 15.7 per cent of the total FDI inflow. Apart from the FDI inflow imports to Japan have also increased more sharply than exports from Japan during the 1990s. The share of national consumption of imports varies between sectors, but is increasing overall. In manufacturing industries, the share of Japanese consumption of imports rose by approximately one quarter in the 1990s.

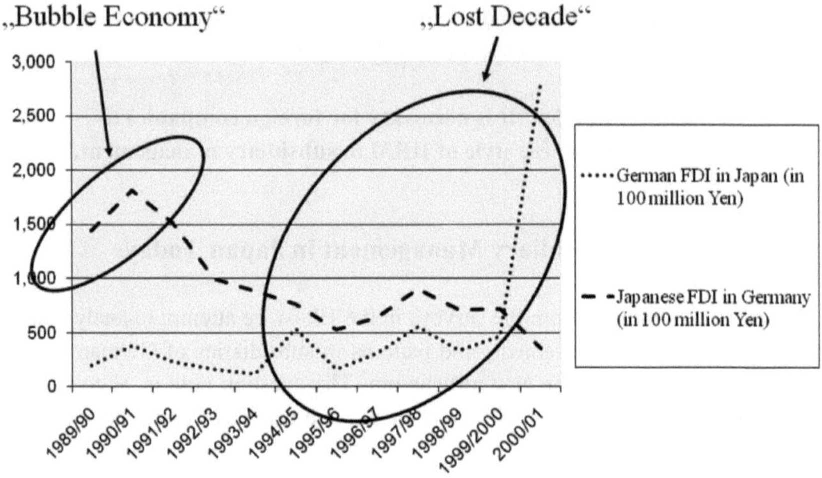

Figure 3: "Development of German FDI into Japan"

Note: Data sorted according to Japanese fiscal years
Source: Japanese Ministry of Finance

Assumption 2: "It takes a long time for foreign subsidiaries to reach the break-even point in Japan"

The majority of German companies operating in Japan today are profitable according to the results of DIJKJ and Roland Berger Survey (2003). The companies were asked about their average gross profit margin and their pre-tax profit in the early years of this millennium. 94 per cent of German companies surveyed have a positive gross profit margin. Almost one fifth of the companies surveyed achieved a gross profit margin of more than 40 per cent; only 3 per cent of the companies surveyed are operating with a serious deficit.

It is generally asserted that an investment in Japan must plan for a long period before break-even is reached (the year in which revenues exceed expenses for the first time). Across all sectors, almost half of the companies surveyed by the DIJKJ and Roland Berger took less than three years to reach break-even point (Figure 4). Only 4 per cent of the companies took, or are expected to take, more than 10 years to reach this point. This raises the question of whether, and to what extent, reaching break-even point was influenced by Japan's economic situation during the "lost decade". German firms that set up operations in Japan between 1990 and 1994, directly after the bursting of the bubble economy, tended to take longer to reach break-even. The proportion of companies that took more than six years to reach break-even grew from approximately 20 per cent (1985 to 1989) to 56 per cent (1990 to 1994). Companies that established their presence in the second half of the 1990s or later reached break-even sooner on average. In spite of the lingering crisis in Japan, they have succeeded (or expect to succeed) in reaching break-even within five years.

In about 80 per cent of the cases investigated in the interviews between 2001 and 2006 the strategic aim of the German companies was to enter the foreign market. Their Japanese collaborating partners mention that the German company possesses specific product, product technology or production process know-how which is actually not available in Japan and which offers the possibility to gain competitive advantage against local competitors.

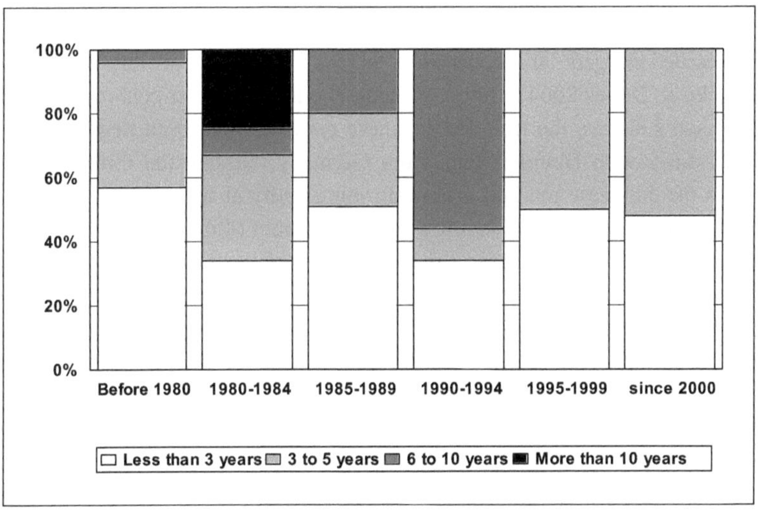

Figure 4: "Time taken to reach break-even point by German subsidiaries in Japan"

Note: On the basis of 79 German subsidiaries in Japan
Source: DIJKJ & Roland Berger Strategy Consultants (2003)

Assumption 3: "Market entry in Japan through Mergers & Acquisitions is relatively rare due to strong keiretsu relationships"

The keiretsu system worked out very well as long as the Japanese economy was growing. But the question is: how could this continue during the "lost decade" when the Japanese economy was undergoing fundamental changes. Keiretsu groups were linked through reciprocal shareholding, director dispatch, trade relations, and other schemes (Dolles 1997, Hemmert 1993, Takahashi & Dolles 1993). Cross-shareholding was established to avoid hostile take-overs, stabilise management and build up mutual beneficial relations with other companies. Cross-shareholding worked well until the 1970s, but already in the final years of the 1980s the process of unwinding the cross-shareholding of the past begun, and this accelerated in the 1990s (Moerke 1993). This development offered possibilities for foreign companies to enter the Japanese market through Merger & Acquisition (see Figure 5).

Case: Renault and Nissan Motor Co.

The case of Renault and Nissan Motor Co. is certainly a successful example of large-scale mergers & acquisitions in the beginning of this millennium (Moerke & Dolles 2004). Before Renault acquired 36.8 per cent (later 44.4%) of Nissan's shares, the troubled Japanese carmaker had been negotiating unsuccessfully with Daimler-Benz from Germany. Nissan, the former number two in the Japanese market, was performing badly at that time. It had operative losses for seven years in a row, a huge amount of debt, sluggish sales and diminishing popularity among the customers. Unlike Toyota Motor Corp. and Mitsubishi Motors, Nissan was not part of a horizontal keiretsu group, and therefore no group of companies held a major percentage of Nissan's shares (and no group of companies was trying to influence the management). Nissan's corporate governance structures were what is usually described as typically Japanese, namely a huge but ineffective board (43 directors in several positions in 1998), almost all from inside the corporation. Furthermore, Nissan showed strong bureaucratic tendencies, and the corporate culture was characterized by a lack of personal responsibility for one's own actions (Takarabe 2002). The engagement of Renault at Nissan was accompanied by the acquisition of 15 per cent of Renault's shares by Nissan through a reserved capital increase. However, there is an important difference between the two share purchase arrangements.

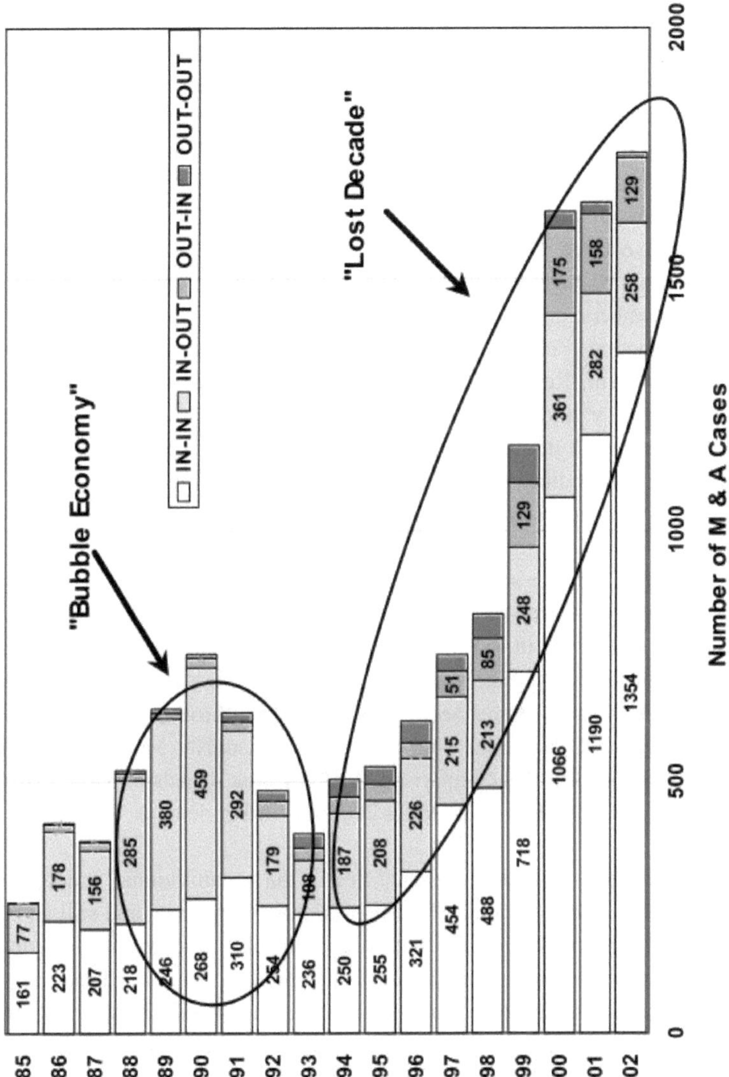

Figure 5: Merger & Acquisition in Japan during the bubble economy and the lost decade
Source: Moerke (2003)

Renault's share ownership meant voting rights and the right to dispatch personnel and make decisions, while the shares Nissan bought did not give the company any voting rights. In 2002, the jointly and equally owned Renault-Nissan bv was founded as a strategic alliance management company to define a common strategy and to manage synergies. Being the dominant shareholder, Renault exercised its right to dispatch personnel to the board of directors and restructure Nissan. Nissan adopted Renault's top management structure, with a "Group Executive Committee, CEG" led by CEO & Chairman Louis Schweitzer, a "Management Committee" that consists of the CEG and eighteen other members, and an additional group of fourteen vice presidents with corporate functions, as well as a group of four auditors. Together with this new board system, Renault started a wide-ranging restructuring of Nissan's purchasing policy and supplier relations, production structure, and model change etc. Through this merger Nissan changed from a typical Japanese corporation into a subsidiary and partner of a western-type firm. Due to this shift, the economic downturn could be stopped, and turnaround could be reached.

Case: DaimlerChrysler and Mitsubishi Motors Corp.

Mitsubishi Motors Corp. was not in very good shape when DaimlerChrysler AG offered to buy about one third of its shares. It had mounting operative losses, diminishing customer interest, and considerable delay in product development. All these features seem very much like those in the Nissan and Renault case, but DaimlerChrysler, as well as Mitsubishi Motors Corp., always refused to accept this comparison. A closer look reveals important structural differences (see Moerke & Dolles 2004 for further details).

The first and most obvious difference lies in the organisational structure of corporate governance relations. Mitsubishi Motors Corp. was, and still is, one of the core corporations of the horizontal Mitsubishi *keiretsu*. Horizontal groups are characterised by stable cross-shareholding, director dispatch and presidents' councils. And this is also the reason that Mitsubishi Motor's main shareholders came from the Mitsubishi group: Mitsubishi Heavy Industries, Mitsubishi Corp., and the Bank of Tōkyō Mitsubishi. It should be added that Mitsubishi Motors Corp. is the spin-off of Mitsubishi Heavy's automotive section in 1964, when three companies merged into Mitsubishi Heavy Industries (http://www.mhi.co.jp/en/aircon/introduction/outline/contents/index.html, last accessed 01.03.2011). Due to these structures, it comes as no surprise that the board of directors was dominated by people from the Mitsubishi group. With the investment in (and alliance with) Mitsubishi Motors Corp., DaimlerChrysler wanted to get closer to the "World AG", i.e. the strategic vision of a truly globally operating car manufacturer. The merger of Daimler-Benz and Chrysler – which can be viewed as an acquisition of Chrysler – took place in 1998 and lasted only 10 years until 2008. In 2000 the investment in Mitsubishi Motors Corp. was realized.

By buying about one third of Mitsubishi Motors Corp.'s shares DaimlerChrysler became the largest shareholder of Mitsubishi Motors Corp. However, the second-largest shareholder is Mitsubishi Heavy (14.82%), followed by Mitsubishi Corp. (5.21%). Overall, the Mitsubishi group holds about 26.21 per cent of Mitsubishi Motors Corp.'s shares – and is a powerful counterpart to DaimlerChrysler. DaimlerChrysler, of course, used the right of sending personnel to the Japanese automaker, and started to restructure the firm. Similar to Nissan, the board was reduced in size. Furthermore, the German top-management team was quite eager to obey the rules of the Mitsubishi game. It was often stated that Rolf Eckroth, as Mitsubishi Motors Corp.'s CEO, participated in the monthly Mitsubishi group presidents' council because he felt this would be necessary. Mitsubishi Motors Corp. remained a Japanese corporation – even though the major shareholder was German and the company was increasingly being integrated into DaimlerChrysler's strategy. Despite the announced dissolution of the "suppliers' council" (an association of the suppliers that used to engage in negotiations with the OEM) in order to save costs, Mitsubishi Motors Corp. continued to purchase within the Mitsubishi group, such as engines at Mitsubishi Heavy, car electronics at Mitsubishi Electric, etc. Finally, the sluggish sales in the U.S. that were responsible for a huge part of Mitsubishi Motors Corp.'s losses during the early years of the 21st century, show that DaimlerChrysler neither managed to secure proper monitoring and reporting nor risk management. With appropriate governance mechanisms, it should have been possible to track and communicate the development of the U.S. market.

The combined production of Daimler-Chrysler and Mitsubishi Motors Corp. increased their sales (Moerke & Dolles 2004). If compared with the Renault-Nissan case it becomes obvious that the performance was lower than expected. At the beginning of October 2004 Mitsubishi Motors Corp. announced the revival of their umbrella-organisation for the suppliers. This is only one indicator showing that Mitsubishi Motors Corp. – after DaimlerChrysler refused to participate in the capital increase, was therefore overtaken as number one shareholder by Phoenix Capital, a Japan-based private investment fund, and finally sold its shares to Goldman Sachs in 2005 – has returned to old organisational structures. After a few weeks the shares were sold again to Mitsubishi keiretsu companies, thus returning Mitsubishi Motors to Japanese ownership. It remains an open question as to whether this was DaimlerChrysler's strategic fault, or whether the Mitsubishi group did not allow DaimlerChrysler to act as they had wanted.

The cases show how different top management structures are executed in Japanese firms. To conclude further for both cases DaimlerChrysler-Mitsubishi Motors as well as Renault-Nissan – despite apparent changes in the Japanese keiretsu-system this form of industrial organization will most probably continue to exist in the future. They will, however, be in a weaker position to prevent foreign companies from gaining access to their members. The declining influence of these groups is also confirmed by the results of the DIHKJ and Roland Berger study. Only 7 per cent of the companies surveyed saw the Keiretsu relationships as a problem for their activities in Japan in the future. As the Japanese distribution system changes, it opens up new opportunities for foreign businesses to establish themselves in the Japanese market and build their own sales and service network based on the mode of social responsiveness. In so doing they will find it somewhat easier than their Japanese competitors to break away from traditional sales patterns and to deliver directly to retailers (consumer goods) or to end users (capital goods).

Assumption 4: "It is difficult for foreign subsidiaries to find capable staff in Japan."

Assumption 5: "It is necessary for foreign companies to adjust to a Japanese style of HRM in subsidiary management."

Change is also occurring, albeit slowly, in the Japanese labour market. A survey among the top 100 Japanese companies conducted by Asahi Newspaper in 2001 showed that 60 per cent of the companies continued with the policy of lifetime employment, while 40 per cent of the companies thought it is difficult to maintain this policy (Takahashi 2003). It is argued in favour of the lifetime commitment that the merits of growing loyalty and accumulating competences are still very important. However, when considering Japanese labour statistics it is obvious that in total the number of regular employees in Japanese companies decreased, whereas the proportion of part time workers and unemployed increased (Takahashi 2003). According to Keidanren the wage level of one third of the Japanese work force is less than half of that of regular employees and the number of part-time workers doubled during the first years of the 'lost decade' (Takahashi 2003). In 2002 Japanese companies like Matsushita and Sony changed their employment practices. The seniority-based remuneration system, consistent of a basic wage component (50 per cent), housing and family allowances and bonus payments (up to basic wage times six twice a year) and considered as one pillar of Japanese style management was replaced by a new payment system solely based on performance and merits. As an outcome the income level of regular employees gradually decreased in Japanese firms (Takahashi, 2003, 2010). Facing an – compared to the 1980s – rather unsecure employment future even within Japanese companies the attitude of university graduates and middle-age office workers changed in favour towards employment in foreign subsidiaries in Japan.

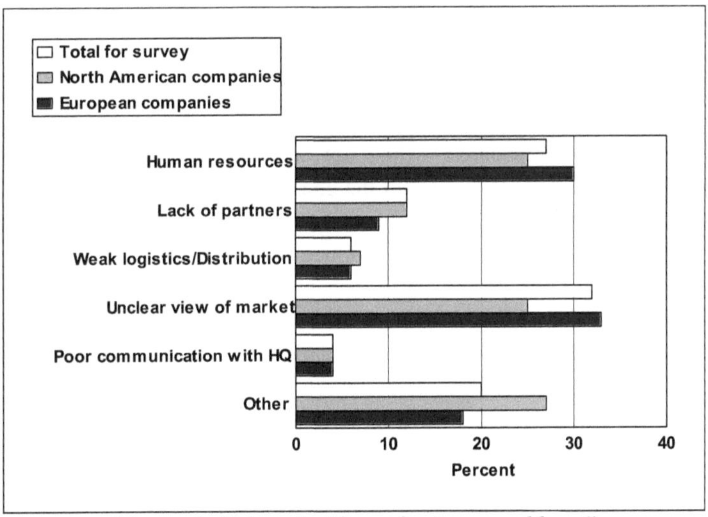

Figure 6: "Most significant business problems"

Source: Foreign Chambers in Japan Confidence Survey (2009)

In a survey of foreign companies conducted by the Foreign Chambers Information Group (FCIG) in early 2003, two thirds of companies reported that it had become easier to recruit capable staff, but in the survey conducted in

2009, finding and retention qualified personnel still remains a significant challenge to foreign companies in Japan (Figure 6 and Table 3).

Table 3: Further difficulties of foreign subsidiaries in Japan

Weak PR, market research quite poor, have not been able to proactively seek customers
Lack of marketing funds, due to budget cuts
Ongoing integration issues with domestic companies
Excessive competition whose only strategy is to discount
Demographic development, change in consumer behaviour
Eurocentric structure for the company
Intense and coordinated local competition
Unclear regulations, bureaucracy, and unclear direction of regulatory changes

Source: Foreign chambers in Japan Confidence Survey (2009)

The academic elite of Japan would not consider foreign companies in the 1990s as potential employers when the country was in the period of the "lost decade". Foreign employers are becoming gradually more popular, but still this is dependent on various factors. Once entering a foreign company, students want to assume responsibility and build their careers quickly. Career-oriented women in particular appreciate the less strongly demarcated gender-specific career obstacles in foreign companies. Asked as part of the FCIJ survey to rate employers in terms of popularity, students due to graduate in 2004 put Japanese companies in the top 23 places. Only ten foreign companies even managed to get placed in the top 100, mainly management consulting companies. The determining criteria for the selection of their future employers were visibility in Japan and company's size, associating the latter with job security.

The mode of social responsiveness in the management of foreign companies does play an important role in certain sectors, especially if there is a well-known brand associated with the foreign company. German firms generally enjoy a good reputation in Japan (Dolles & Abraham 2004). Germany is associated in the Japanese mind with attributes such as being industrious, precise and reliable. Sectors in which Germany is associated with a leading role are technology-driven such as the machinery industry, the automotive industry, medical devices, pharmaceutical products and environmental technology. This positive view is strengthened through the perceived closeness between Germany and Japan as well as the reputation of German firms as employer. However in the Japanese perception, German companies are not "fashionable" — an important criterion in the consumer sector. Here, Italy and France clearly lead the way. Foreign companies should therefore make use of the specific advantages that arise from their being different, should build on the mode of social responsiveness in their human resources management and should not abandon their management practices to fit in all respects with supposedly unchangeable Japanese customs.

6. Conclusion

Since the end of the "bubble economy" in the beginning of the 1990s negative headlines have determined the "lost decade"-picture of the Japanese economy: low economic growth, a fragile banking system, low productivity and minimal return on investment. In fact, the continuing recession during the "lost decade" has frightened foreign companies off from committing to Japan. Furthermore the Japanese market was no longer growing so strongly compared to the 1980s and therefore lost some of its attractiveness. However, this recession was also breaking down rigid structures and opening new, promising investment opportunities for foreign businesses.

Foreign investors still regard Japan as a very challenging market. Japan is continuing to be the third-largest economy in the world. Japan alone produces over 60 per cent of East Asia's gross domestic product. Even if Japan's current low rates of growth and the high growth rates of other Asian countries continue, Japan's economic output in 2011 will still be the highest in Asia. Due to the high purchasing power of private households in Japan, consumer goods manufacturers often achieve far higher prices than in Europe or the US. Japanese technology is ranked, nowadays as in the 1980s, in the premier class of numerous industries. Many innovations appear first in Japan and only then find their way into China and other Asian countries. Japan is therefore still very well placed as a starting point for a company that wishes to become active in Asia. Our interviewees confirmed that establishing a Japanese subsidiary inspires confidence among business partners throughout Asia and is advantageous in opening up business contacts.

Foreign businesses face the crucial problem of adapting strategies to local environment conditions, while at the same time attempts must be made to implement parent company policies. Too less adaptation of management style can cause dysfunctionality in subsidiary management, too much of it can distort the specific firm- and home-country advantages. This task was and still is to some extend extremely difficult in Japan, because it is culturally worlds apart from the parent country of most of the foreign firms and the Japanese environment creates the initial impression that being different from their Japanese competitors is a disadvantage. This was the case for the level of service required, distribution channels/policies, product pricing and HR management, where high levels of adaptation in subsidiary management were mentioned in our survey (Steinmann, Kumar & Dolles 1992). As our findings show the mode of social acceptance in subsidiary management was practiced in HR management. As our interviews in Japan indicate, this mode has to be seen in connection with directing and motivating Japanese employees. But in spite of such adaptation, many German firms have already decided in the 1980s to introduce their parent company HR pattern, thus following the mode of social responsiveness in HR management by providing e.g. regular vacation, performance based payment systems or career tracks for female employees.

Considering the changes in HR management in Japanese firms and how the "lost decade" has enforced changes in what were once called pillars of the Japanese style of personnel management (Takahashi 2003, 2010), the mode of social responsiveness in subsidiary management was a strategy to gain competitive advantage on today's labour market in Japan. Foreign companies also enjoy greater freedom than their Japanese competitors because they are not necessarily expected to observe all of the unwritten rules – and due to the changed economic situation even within the keiretsu system there is a positive market response, when considering market entry or growth strategies through M&A. Such possibilities also exist in the field of corporate governance as seen in the Renault-Nissan Case. It is customary in Japan for top management boards and supervisory boards to be seen as a formality, but foreign companies can transform these bodies and their meetings into an effective guidance mechanism. In the interviews conducted, German companies in Japan also mention particular advantages from their global orientation, because their Japanese competitors, especially small and medium-sized enterprises are much less oriented to the international markets. However with the increase in activity among foreign investors in Japan, the degree of globalisation and the level of international competence in Japanese small and medium-sized firms will inevitably increase.

7. References

Abegglen, J. C., & Stark, G. (1985). *Kaisha. The Japanese Corporation*. New York: Basic Books.

Aoki, M., & Dore, R. (1994). *The Japanese Firm. Sources of Competitive Strength*. Oxford: Oxford University Press.

Clark, R. (1979). *Japanese Company*. New Haven CT: Yale University Press.

DIHKJ & Roland Berger Strategy Consultants (2003). *Making Money in Japan. A Profitability Survey Among German Affiliates in Japan*. Tokyo: DIHKJ.

Dolles, H. (1994). Netzwerk mit Prinzipien (Principles of Corporate Networks in Japan). *Absatzwirtschaft. Zeitschrift für Marketing, 37(1)*, 26-29.

Dolles, H. (1997). *Keiretsu: Emergenz, Struktur, Wettbewerbsstärke und Dynamik japanischer Verbundgruppen*. (Keiretsu: Emergence, Structure, Competitive Strengths and Organizational Dynamics of Corporate Groupings in Japan). Frankfurt am Main: Peter Lang.

Dolles, H. (1999). Keiretsu: Strukturelle Merkmale und wettbewerbsstrategische Handlungen vertikaler und horizontaler Verbundgruppen in Japan. Ihre Bedeutung für die Geschäftstätigkeit ausländischer Unternehmen in Japan (Keiretsu: Organizational Structure and the Competitive Strategies of Corporate Groupings in Japan. Implications for Successful Management of Foreign Subsidiaries in Japan). In H. Eisenhofer-Halim, P. Pörtner, & H. Wohlbier (Eds.), *Facetten des modernen Japan* (pp. 379-431). Frankfurt am Main: Peter Lang.

Dolles, H., & Abraham, M. (2004). Reputation als Erfolgsfaktor im internationalen Geschäft (Reputation as Success Factor in International Business). *Japan Markt. Journal of the German Chamber of Industry and Commerce in Japan, 13(4)*, 28-30.

Dolles, H., & Kumar, B. N. (1996). Überlegungen zur strategischen Führung und Wettbewerbsstärke japanischer Untenehmen (A New Approach to Strategic Leadership and Sustained Competitive Advantages of Corporate Groupings in Japan). In J. Engelhard (Ed.), *Strategische Führung internationaler Unternehmen. Paradoxien, Strategien und Erfahrungen* (pp. 39-68). Wiesbaden: Gabler.

Foreign Chambers in Japan & Nomura Research Institute (2009). *Some Bright Spots on the Horizon? FCIJ Business Confidence Survey*. Tokyo: FCIJ & Finnish Chamber of Commerce. Available at: http://www.fcc.or.jp/fcij/bcs.html, accessed: 06. June 2009.

Hemmert, M. (1993). *Vertikale Kooperation zwischen japanischen Industrieunternehmen* (Vertical Cooperation Between Japanese Industrial Firms). Wiesbaden: Deutscher Universitätsverlag.

Horioka, C. Y. (2006). The Causes of Japan's 'Lost Decade': The Role of Household Consumption. *Japan and the World Economy, 18(4)*, 378-400.

Ishizaki, T. E (2010). *Ushinawareta jonen* (The lost decade). Tokyo: Chuo Daigaku Shuppansha.

Japan External Trade Organization (JETRO, 2011). Promoting Foreign Direct Investment into Japan. Available at: http://www.jetro.go.jp/en/jetro/activities/fdi/, accessed: 01. March 2011.

Kumar, B. N., & Steinmann, H. (1989). Managing Subsidiaries of German Companies in Japan. Some Findings of Adaptation Strategies. In K. Shibagaki, M. Trevor, & T. Abo (Eds.), *Japanese and European Management. Their International Adaptability* (pp. 244-260). Tokyo: University of Tokyo Press.

Kumar, B. N., & Steinmann, H. (1990). Managing Japanese Subsidiaries of German Companies: Some Findings for Theory-building on Foreign Subsidiary Management in Japan. In J. Stam (Ed.), *Industrial Cooperation Between Europe and Japan* (pp. 99-114). Rotterdam: ERASMUS University Press.

Kumar, B. N., Steinmann, H. & Dolles, H. (1993): Das Management in Niederlassungen deutscher Unternehmen in Japan - eine empirische Untersuchung unter besonderer Berücksichtigung von Klein- und Mittelbetrieben. Discussion Paper Lehrstuhl für Betriebswirtschaftslehre insbesondere Internationales Management, No. 2, Friedrich-Alexander-University Erlangen-Nürnberg.

Moerke, A. (2003). Quo Vadis Keiretsu? Structural Change in Japanese Inter-Firm Relations in the 1990s. In G. Foljanty-Jost (Ed.), *Japan in the 1990s. Crisis as an Impetus for Change* (pp. 11-31). Hamburg: LIT.

Moerke, A., & Dolles, H. (2004). Managing Cross-border Alliances of MNCs in Turbulent Times: A Question of National vc. Corporate Perception in Corporate Governance. In O. H. M. Yau, C. S. Tseng, & F. Cheung (Eds.), *Harmony v Conflict: Euro-Asian Management in a Turbulent Era. Proceedings of the 21th Annual Conference of the Euro-Asia Management Studies Association* (pp. 410-421). Hong Kong: City University of Hong Kong Press.

Ouchi, W. (1981). *Theory Z. How American Business Can Meet the Japanese Challenge.* Reading MA: Addison-Wesley.

Scheer, M. (1990). Das Joint-Venture in Japan (The Joint-Venture in Japan). In K. Langefeld-Wirth (Ed.), *Joint Ventures im internationalen Wirtschaftsverkehr* (pp. 536-561). Heidelberg: Recht und Wirtschaft.

Steinmann, H., Kumar, B. N., & Dolles, H. (1992). Eintritts- und Führungsstrategien deutscher Unternehmen in Japan (Market Entry Strategy and Competitive Strategies of German Companies in Japan). In B. N. Kumar, & H. Haussmann (Eds.), *Handbuch der Internationalen Unternehmenstätigkeit* (pp. 995-1011). München: C.H. Beck.

Takahashi, Y. (1984). The Character of Japanese Style Management. From the Aspect of Personnel and Labour Management. *Shogaku Ronsan, Chuo daigaku 100shunen kinen ronbunshu, 24*, 51-79.

Takahashi, Y. (1987). The Structure of the Enterprise Union and the Present Situation of Labour Participation in Japan. In W. Dorow (Ed.), *The Business Corporation in the Democratic Society* (pp. 307-326). Berlin: Walter de Gruyter.

Takahashi, Y. (1990). Human Resource Management in Japan. In R. Pieper (Ed.), *Human Resource Managment. An International Comparison* (pp. 211-234). Berlin: Walter de Gruyter.

Takahashi, Y. (2003). Formation and Changes of Japanese Employment Practice. The Disappearance of the Lifetime Employment and Seniority System. *Shogaku Ronsan, 44(3)*, 257-288.

Takahashi, Y. (2010). 'Ushinawareta jonen' to nihon kigyo no jinji jinzaikaihatsukanri no henka (The 'Lost Decade' and the changes in human resource management and human resources development of Japanese firms). In T. Ishizaki (Ed.), *Ushinawareta jonen* (pp. 281-310). Tokyo: Chuo Daigaku Shuppansha.

Takahashi, Y., & Dolles, H. (1993). Wide Human Resource Management: Structure, Practice and Strategy in Comparison Between Japan and Germany. *Shogaku Ronsan, 33(2/3)*, 389-441.

Takarabe, S. (2002). *Karurosu go-n ha nissan wo ikani shite kaetaka* (How did Charlos Ghosn change Nissan?). Tokyo: PHP Bunko.

Yasuda, A. (2009). FDI into Japan Reaches Record High for Second Straight Year in 2008. *Bulletin International Economic Research Division, Overseas Research Department, JETRO Tokyo*. Available at: http://www.jetro.go.jp/en/invest/newsroom/ other/pdf/o2009005.pdf, last accessed: 30. June 2009.

Biography

Beauducel, André is Professor at the University of Hamburg (Germany). He was awarded a PhD from the Freie Universitaet Berlin and received his Habilitation from the Dresden University of Technology (Germany). His research interests are the structure of intelligence, the development of intelligence tests, personality traits, quasi-experimental and psychophysiological research, as well as multivariate data analysis.

Dolles, Harald is Visiting Professor (full time) in International Business at the School of Business, Economics and Law at the University of Gothenburg (Gothenburg, Sweden) since 2009. He received his doctorate in international business/strategic management from the University Erlangen-Nuremberg in Germany, with a focus on East Asia. During his professional career from 2001 to 2006 he was assigned by the German Ministry of Education and Science to serve in official mission as expert on China and Japan at the economic section of the German Institute for Japanese Studies in Tokyo. He also taught in Japan before joining the German Graduate School of Management and Law as Professor of Management and International Business in 2006. Harald frequently contributes to scientific development in the fields of international business and international human resource management; entrepreneurship and innovations management; sports management and Asian studies.

Horn, Sierk is Senior Lecturer in Japanese Studies at the University of Leeds. He was awarded a PhD in Japanese Studies and Habilitation from Freie Universitaet Berlin, Germany. He has published widely in the fields of consumer behaviour in East Asia, international knowledge transfer, and strategic management of Japanese and European MNEs.

Ishiguro, Kuniko is Research Associate at the Institute of Social Science, the University of Tokyo. She received her PhD and MSc from the University of Sheffield. Before gaining her MSc, she worked in Japanese and American companies as a human resource manager. Her research interests are in the sociology of work, human resource management and gender relations in organisations.

Keizer, Arjan is Lecturer in IHRM and Comparative Industrial Relations at the

University of Manchester. His research focuses on the comparative study of employment practices and relations with a particular focus on Japan. Important themes include processes of change in national systems of employment relations; the relation between national employment practices and firms' personnel strategies, labour market segmentation, and the likelihood of institutional convergence. Recent publications include a monograph published by Routledge, entitled Changes in Japanese Employment Practices, and articles in the Asia Pacific Journal of Management, the International Journal of Human Resource Management and Work, Employment and Society.

Liepmann, Detlev is Professor at the Free University of Berlin (Germany). He holds a Diplom in Psychology and Mathematics (1968) and was award-ed a Dr. Phil. in 1975 and Habilitation in 1980. Holding a Chair in Eco-nomic and Organisational Psychology he has worked extensively in the fields of Organisation Structure, Evaluation Strategy, Aptitude Diagnostics, Marketing Analysis and Opinion Polling.

Matanle, Peter is Lecturer in Japanese Studies at the School of East Asian Studies, University of Sheffield, from where he gained his PhD in 2001. He is the author of several publications in the economic sociology and cultural geography of work in Japan and the UK. He is also the founding general editor of the electronic journal of contemporary japanese studies (www.japanesestudies.org.uk).

Matsui, Kenji is Professor in the Faculty of Education at Niigata University in Japan. His research interests are in career education and the work values of younger people. Currently he is School Principal of Niigata University Elementary School in Nagaoka City, Niigata Prefecture.

Takahashi, Yoshiaki is professor at the Faculty of Commerce and research fellow at the Institute of Business Research, Chuo University, Tokyo (Japan). He received his PhD in the Graduate School of Commerce, Chuo University. He was Chairman of Euro-Asia Management Studies Association, Senior Board Member of the Japan Society of Business Administration, and Council Member of the International Federation of Scholarly Association. He was invited by Japan International Cooperation Agency to teach on HRM and HRD at the Japan Center in Laos. He also teaches on HRM as a Guest Professor at the Foreign

University of Vietnam. Yoshiaki Takahashi is the author of many conference papers, articles and books on Japanese Management, with a particular focus on HRM and HRD. Most recently he published 'Globalization of Japanese and East Asian Enterprises: Towards an Economic Integration in East Asia', 'Management Strategies of Multinational Corporations in Asian Markets', 'Japanese Management Theory and Japanese Business Management' and 'The Impact of Globalization: Cultural Identity in Business'.

WIRTSCHAFTSPSYCHOLOGIE

HERAUSGEGEBEN VON DETLEV LIEPMANN

Band 1 Detlev Liepmann / Jörg Felfe / Elisabetta de Costanzo: Ökologischer und sozialer Wandel als Managementaufgabe. 1995.

Band 2 Claudia Marggraf (Hrsg.): Soziale Kompetenz und Innovation. 1995.

Band 3 Hans-Jürgen Resetka / Detlev Liepmann / Gerhard Frank: Qualifizierungsmaßnahmen und psychosoziale Befindlichkeit bei Arbeitslosen. 1996.

Band 4 Miriam Luckhardt: Organisationstransformation und Transformationsmanagement. 1996.

Band 5 Gisela Mohr: Erwerbslosigkeit, Arbeitsplatzunsicherheit und psychische Befindlichkeit. 1997.

Band 6 Wolfgang Battmann (Hrsg.): Stabilität und Wandel im Unternehmen. Das Management zwischen Tradition und Innovation. 1997.

Band 7 Olaf Kempfert: Arbeitsplatz Auto. 1999.

Band 8 Detlev Liepmann (Hrsg.): Motivation, Führung und Erfolg in Organisationen. 2000.

Band 9 Annette Lässig: Gestaltung der Organisationskultur. Evaluation kultureller Veränderungsprozesse. 2002.

Band 10 Ute Jatzek: Konflikte in Arbeitsgruppen. Formen, Ursachen und Folgen. 2001.

Band 11 Jörg Felfe (ed.): Organizational Development and Leadership. 2002.

Band 12 Wim Nettelnstroth: Intelligenz, Beruf und Organisationsstrukturen. 2004.

Band 13 Claudia Zuleta Luksic: Transformational Leadership and Commitment. A Study in Bolivia. 2006.

Band 14 Kathrin Heinitz (ed.): Psychology in Organizations. Issues from an Applied Area. 2008.

Band 15 Sierk A. Horn (ed.): Emerging Perspectives in Japanese Human Resource Management. 2011.

www.peterlang.de